More praise for Shannon's bl

Shannon discusses topics that are in the forefront of my thoughts and delves into subjects where other bloggers skim the surface. *TSLL* has opened my eyes to many new avenues and ways of thinking.

— Carrie from Oklahoma

The most wonderful part of *TSLL* is that it helps me see the joy in everyday actions, items, and events.

— Beth from Michigan

I am a single mom in my mid-forties, and your articles have encouraged me to be all that I can be as a person and to embrace my womanhood. Also, despite what our culture tells us, being single can be a fulfilling life!

— Kellie from New York

I've been visiting your website for a year now and absolutely love it. It's full of wonderful articles and information and has become part of my morning ritual. My day just doesn't feel "right" until I've checked out your postings.

— Gillian from Ontario

I have just discovered your blog, and I am so impressed. Thank you for writing about being a strong and independent person, especially as a woman.

— Adrienne from Atlanta

I'm writing you today to say 'thank you' for all the inspiring information you put out there. It has reminded me to hold my head up high while going through several life changes at once.

— Esta from California

I thoroughly enjoy sitting down with a cup of coffee and reading your posts each week. Such a joy! I found out about your blog through a 'simply delightful friend', who owns a big smile and a cheerful laugh. She shared that your blog inspires her to enjoy each day just a little more. I agree!

— Heather from Vancouver

Choosing the Simply Luxurious Life

A MODERN WOMAN'S GUIDE

Shannon Ables

Simply Luxurious Publishing
Oregon

Shannon Ables/Simply Luxurious Publishing
www.thesimplyluxuriouslife.com

Book Layout ©2014 BookDesignTemplates.com
Illustrations by Inslee by Design

Ordering Information:
Quantity sales. Special discounts are available on quantity purchases by corporations, associations, and others. For details, contact the "Special Sales Department" at the address above.

Choosing the Simply Luxurious Life/ Shannon Ables. —1st ed.
ISBN: 978-0692260593

Contents

For any woman who refuses to choose between femininity and independence while following a path to true contentment.

There's only one really good life, and that's the life you know you want and you make it yourself.

—Diana Vreeland

Introduction

My muse for living a simply luxurious life was born before I even knew what a muse was; in fact, she came into the world before I did. Her name was Sadie.

I can't be sure exactly when I began to adore Sadie. I doubt there ever was a moment I didn't. I was only a very small child when I realized my only sibling was hairy, had a wet nose, and walked on four feet, while I rolled around on the floor and then finally got up on my two legs. But I most certainly knew that when she passed away when I was eight or nine, a piece of our family had been lost.

Sadie, a female black Labrador, was my parents' first "child," and when she died, it was the first instance I remember of my father displaying any sign of weakness as he was visibly distraught about losing her. Then we welcomed Magadawn ("Mag") into the family, a black Lab as well, and I can still recall images of her as a puppy frolicking in the yard. I spent many an evening sitting with her, telling her my troubles and crying into her side as she lay there, perplexed by my teenage angst, which made no more sense to her than it did to me. Then there was Buddy, and he was just that, a handsome black Lab who was a pal to everyone—the cats, the kids, my mother while she puttered in the garden, and every other dog that was welcomed into the family over the years.

Don't worry, this is not a book about dogs, but what I've come to discover while reflecting upon my childhood and early adult years is the gift that my dogs gave me — they helped me understand the life I wanted to live.

As a young girl, living on twenty acres at the foothills of what residents of Wallowa County in northeastern Oregon call the mini Swiss Alps, I found myself most at ease with four-legged creatures. I came to find my most comfortable sanctuary with our animals — the family dogs, my horses, the cats, and our donkey, Festus, who was happiest when you presented your backside for him to rub his head on (I always made sure to wear my most worn-out work jeans when I obliged him). So long as you offered kindness and perhaps a treat, each of our four-legged family members would be your friend for life.

Not everyone who grows up around animals finds a refuge with them as I do. My brother, who has the biggest heart in the world, loves animals but finds his bliss on the golf course and is far more social than I am.

The gift my family's animals offered me was the ability to embrace my introversion, to revel in it and not be embarrassed by it, to lose the fear of being shunned for it or laughed at because it was odd. Any sense of discomfort about my introverted ways would come later, in my twenties, when I tried to conform to an ideal of extroversion, which I thought (wrongly) was required for success in the world, when it simply is not who I am.

But because I had the foundation of those first eighteen years — an understanding of what it felt like to be myself, the comfort I took in my own company and those of the animals in my life, the happiness with my own thoughts and my time alone — I was able to rediscover my introversion as I entered my late twenties and started to listen again to what was working for me, and what wasn't.

The gift of a muse is her ability to bring to the surface something that already resides within us but is in need of a catalyst. It's as though we need the right tool to harvest something that we can't seem to reap on our own. Some may see a muse as a crutch, but I doubt that many who have the experienced a true muse's power would dismiss it so easily.

A muse can't create what we don't already have to offer; it simply is the teasing mechanism that allows us to relax, brings us back to ourselves, and sets us free. For some it may be a particular destination—Paris, the top of a bluff way out in the country somewhere, or a favorite theater—while for others it may be a person or, as in my case, a couple of dogs.

Two events, one in March 2005 and the other in October 2009, neither planned or financially opportune, were exactly what my life needed right then, and they played an integral part in how my blog, *The Simply Luxurious Life*, which inspired this book, came to fruition.

First, in 2005, Oscar, my black English cocker spaniel, and then, in 2009, Norman, my Blenheim Cavalier King Charles spaniel, became part of my life and fanned the embers of the inner me that was begging to be reignited. How? In time, after Oscar and Norman arrived, I was able to enjoy my own company again, without feeling a sense of shame that I wasn't social enough or that I enjoyed my "me" time too much. Far too many disagreements had erupted about those issues in past failed relationships, and gradually I began to think there was something wrong with me for thoroughly enjoying doing things on my own.

Wait, how absurd is that? Absurd indeed, but the insecure person I was then had accepted these judgments, until I refused to do so any longer and created a life I loved and made no apologies for. Alongside me the entire time were my boys, my two spaniels.

Again, this is not a book about dogs or being an introvert. If you're a cat person or a plant person or a people person, that knowledge is what you want to tap into. Living a simply luxurious life doesn't just happen, and mine won't look like yours, just as yours won't look like anyone else's. And that's a very good thing, a worth celebrating kind of thing. Such a life takes conscious and sustained effort and an awareness of what puts you at ease and what fires up your creative energies — and, conversely, what is a wet blanket.

I created *The Simply Luxurious Life* blog based on my own experience as someone who wants to create a life that is fulfilling regardless of what society defines as "what should make a person happy," a life that is immune to the judgment of others. I had come to understand my basic truth — that if we live to please the world around us, we will never find joy, the ease that is our "happy place."

A simply luxurious life is something you create for yourself. While my dogs were and are my muse, I am the maestro, just as you are the maestro of your simply luxurious life. I am the responsible party who must pay attention to what matters and edit out what doesn't. I must be the person who says yes to welcoming two dogs into my life and no to items on my budget (lattes, additional channels on television, unnecessary trips in the car) that are far less important than having those four-legged companions in my life. Why? I know they will help me curate my simply luxurious life.

A simply luxurious life is not easy to create initially because it requires that we focus on quality and let go of excess. It requires us to get to know ourselves and be present. It requires us to be conscious and alert, and to have a genuine desire to live well. It requires that we keep in mind that in curating a simply luxurious life we are creating a life of continued fulfillment and joy.

Do you need an abundant bank account to create a simply luxurious life? Absolutely not. Do you need to know how to handle the money you do have? Absolutely. As the motto that appears on the blog's home page states, a simply luxurious life is refined living on an everyday income.

Do you need to have graduate degrees or an impressive résumé to make sense of this beautiful thing called life? Most definitely not.

Do you need to be knowledgeable about how the world works and how you can succeed in it? Yes, and I'll show you how.

On the blog, I often gravitate toward vocabulary associated with the art world, and this is not by accident. Your life, my life, our lives, are one-of-a-kind masterpieces that can be easily destroyed — as if burned in a fire — if we give away our responsibility for ourselves and allow others to dictate how our life will unfold. Instead, you can see your life as full of unique, innate gifts and great potential waiting to be tapped. This way of thinking about your life will yield two blessings: a life bursting with contentment while you are here on earth and a legacy that will remain in the memories of those you've influenced long after you are gone.

So you see, you are an artist. We are all artists. Whether you can paint like Picasso or barely scratch out a stick figure (include me in the latter category), you are the only artist who can create a life that will be one of a kind. And while no person's simply luxurious life will be identical to another's, we all can garner inspiration from each person or situation we have the opportunity to experience.

That is why I created the blog, and why I have written this book that tells you how you can build your very own simply luxurious life — so that whether you live in a bustling mecca like New York City or a quiet rural town of two hundred people, you can find inspiration on your own terms and apply it in a way that works for your life.

After all, life is far too short, and you have so much to offer. So let's get started. Let me show you how to build your very own simply luxurious life.

CHAPTER ONE

Fall in Love with Your Life

Everything will line up perfectly when knowing and living the truth becomes more important than looking good.
—Alan Cohen

y fondest memories of Christmas were formed in the house where I grew up, in the country nestled just below the tree line surrounding Ruby Peak in Wallowa County in northeastern Oregon. My brother and I, along with my parents, would often wake up to fresh snow on the ground, and there was plenty of time for us to lounge in our pajamas as long as we pleased, enjoying Santa's gifts.

As an adult I crave the quiet and simplicity of those childhood holidays, and so in December 2009 I made the trek from my home about 100 miles to the west to spend Christmas with my parents. I find it easy to step away from my day-to-day life there, to slow down and catch my breath. And during that point in my life, it was often during my visits to Wallowa County that I gave myself the time I needed to mull over dilemmas, contemplate ideas, and strategize as I formulated plans of action that would help me reach my goals.

My Christmas 2009 holiday getaway provided a lightbulb moment I can now only explain as serendipitous.

I love writing and reading, and I'd chosen a career as a high school English teacher, but after seven years I was feeling a deep sense of dissatisfaction. My discontent had nothing to do with my experience in education—I taught with inspiring mentors and dedicated colleagues, and worked with students who were motivated and went on to pursue amazing careers. Yet something within me was not being tapped.

I'm someone who has an insatiable curiosity for information, who seeks answers to the endless stream of questions life presents. I tend to be self-motivated and driven to always look around the next corner, and as a general rule, I refuse to take explanations or ways of living life at face value. I want to live consciously, aware of what I am doing and why I am doing it, mindfully making decisions instead of following the crowd in order to be accepted. Teaching high school, while providing a sense of positive contribution, left me feeling a bit like a robot. The creative and curious voice inside me was subtly becoming frustrated, although at the time, I wouldn't have been able to identify exactly what I was feeling beyond extremely perplexed and lost.

When I was a teenager, my first attempt at living a life I loved came as I expressed myself through fashion, a habit I continue to indulge in to this day. My sartorial choices are generally tame and subtle, but my initial efforts to mix it up ever so slightly (such as the first time I dared to wear an accessory as simple as a scarf in my small rural hometown, where T-shirts and jeans sans accessories were de rigueur) involved great gumption for the sensitive introvert that I am.

As a child, I could entertain myself endlessly without my parents' prompting or a friend's company. And as a young adult, I struggled to fit in with a social world where it was expected that everyone needed to always have people around, whether friends or a romantic flame. For a time, because I convinced myself that there must be something wrong with me, I attempted to be socially busy constantly. Looking back, I'm amazed I didn't recognize earlier that a life of intense, incessant socializing doesn't satisfy me.

I had grown up with my mother's and her father's love for preparing meals and party fare that bring people together. After a college study-abroad adventure in France, I took another major step toward a fulfilling life when I embraced my infatuation with wine, cheese, and all kinds of cooking; the Food Network was my television channel of choice for a while.

When it came to décor, I never lived in an apartment that didn't get painted (red walls in the living room—yep, that happened, and I loved it). And after I had the opportunity, in graduate school, to live alone for the first time, I fell in love with my own company again and gradually found the strength to stand up for the life I loved.

After living most of my twenties as a victim of the belief that I wasn't enough unless I fulfilled a certain formula for my life—a sheep who wanted to be married with kids, who devotedly followed a specific religion, who dressed in shapeless, acceptable clothing for my career as a teacher, who passively accepted inequalities for women—I chose to begin my thirties instead as the curator of my life, based on my own unique combination of talents, passions, values, and curiosities.

And then I began blogging.

On December 26, 2009, I was alone in my childhood home, and thrilled to be in my own company. In fact, it was by my own choosing. After spending the day doing exactly as I wished and pleased, I wrote the first post on my blog; at the time the blog was called *Simply Luxurious*, and the title of that first post was "The After-Christmas Calm."

In my effort to channel all things French this morning, I spritzed a bit of Chanel No. 5 on and watched the Barefoot Contessa while she walked through Paris talking of flower arrangements, fromage, omelets, and profiteroles, all the while walking away the holiday calories on the treadmill. I then cleaned up and headed out shopping, listening to Madeline Peyroux's *Careless Love* album, hoping to find some diamonds in the rough in the small, quaint town of Joseph, Oregon.

The day after Christmas finds shops with sale signs hanging in every window, it seems, and it was no different in this little town. Whenever I am visiting my family for the holidays, I frequent a locally owned boutique, BeeCrowBee, that specializes in making sumptuous-smelling soaps, candles, lotions, and bath scrubs and oils, as well as herbal teas. The clean, spa-like aesthetic is a rare treat compared to cluttered shops that display so many items your eyes are bombarded and aren't sure where to look. Today, as I was browsing, the owner, Will Roundy, was working away on a huge block of soap, slicing it into sellable sizes. There is just something about watching somebody at work on their craft.

Over the years I have purchased scrubs, washcloths, and towels (made of bamboo and oh, so soft, even more so after each washing), and I regularly sip Will's teas in the evening after a long day at work. My favorite blend is his lavender-scented black tea—calming and aromatic, all rolled up in one. Today I left with a bottle of lavender bath oil, giving myself another reason to pamper myself a bit more.

Au revoir!

My only intention was to share what I loved about the way I lived, which seemed so contrary to the lives of most of the people I knew at the time. With my newborn blog, I gave my life a voice in a medium that provided space for individuality and a platform to write. And even though the only person who was reading it at first was my mother (thank you, Mom!), that act of celebrating my interests rather than hushing them helped me to fully believe that I am enough exactly as I am and to revel in it.

And so I began to dance with my life, so to speak. I wrote every day for two years. I wrote about what I loved, what made me curious, how I lived, and what I've learned. On some days, multiple posts would go live. I had found my outlet. I would, and still do, lose all track of time when I sit down to write.

Somehow readers found me. With some helpful discussion and advice from a handful of bloggers I am inspired by and respect, as well as some much-appreciated mentions on their blogs, my readers increased in number each month—gradually, but steadily.

After two years and countless inquiries by readers who wanted a book to hold in their hands, I spent the summer of 2011 organizing the blog into a manuscript. At that point, I had a manuscript, but I wasn't sure what to do with it. So I kept blogging, traveling, sharing, asking questions, reading, exploring, and falling in love with my life more and more.

And then I had even more content for a book—multiple trips to France so that I could now share insights on how to travel safely and simply luxuriously to the City of Light; relationship advice, after learning valuable lessons; advice about buying a house, refinancing a mortgage, and purchasing a car; tips for maintaining a capsule wardrobe; life coaching about chasing your dreams and reveling in a full life regardless of your relationship status—you name it, I was seeking out the questions that I wanted the answers to, and the blog continued to grow, mainly by word of mouth.

And it is to the readers of the blog—those who have been reading since 2010, those who have just discovered *TSLL*, women and men of all ages—that I extend my gratitude. While I could not have predicted on that first day all that has occurred since, based on what has happened I am confident that we find the key to living the life each of us desires to live when we tap into our authentic selves, listen carefully, and then follow through, doing what we love regardless of the external chatter. Because the one thing that was present when that inaugural post was written and remains present today is that I've always been doing what I love.

We are the curators of our lives. We are able to say yes or no. We are able to take a chance and to appreciate and cultivate what is working well. Most important, we are responsible for our own contentment.

If your life doesn't sit well with you, begin seeking inspiration until you figure out the life you want and how you will live it. Give yourself the gift of a life of freedom and independence.

Living a life that you love doesn't mean the masses will applaud. It does mean you will sleep soundly at night, and that is the best gift. If at some point you hear applause, fabulous. But if not, so what?

Your heart knows when you're the curator of your life—or when someone else is. Have you ever had a strong negative reaction to an event that others are cheering and not said anything? If so, you may have been following instead of curating. On the flip side, when time passes in a flash and you lose yourself in the moment— intoxicated by life—then most likely you have found your niche.

The beautiful gift of our one and only life is that the choices we make every single day determine whether or not we're content. It is up to us to choose wisely.

What a Luxurious Life Looks Like

There are people who have money and people who are rich.
— Coco Chanel

Every woman creates a unique way of living that correlates with her values, her passions, her attitudes toward her loved ones, and many other areas that she must consciously consider as she sets out to design an ideal life.

The foundation of living a simply luxurious life is made up of substance, passion, quality, sensibility, sincerity, appreciation, and continual growth.

What a simply luxurious life is not is blindly following whatever society or the media's version of it glorifies, spending more than you make, living in a home that is not soothing or welcoming, having many "friendships" or "friends" but few relationships of real quality, creating a wardrobe driven by trends, not being mindful of your body's unique beauty, falling prey to the fears and pressures that marketers and the media push on us, or ignoring the importance of learning something new and substantial each and every day.

I'd like to begin by sharing what my simply luxurious life looks like. I hope you will see that while you and I may have similar ways of living simply luxuriously, there will also be differences, and that is perfectly fine. What we will share, however, are some fundamental convictions. Refusing to follow societal dictates that don't feel right, and finding the strength to tap into who we truly are and to share these discovered gifts with the world and those we love — that is what makes each of our lives uniquely our own.

My simply luxurious life is . . .

. . . making time to have intimate, one-on-one conversations with loved ones.

. . . nibbling on a chocolate truffle late in the evening, paired with a hot cup of lavender tea to help me unwind.

. . . walking my dogs in the early-morning hours as we greet the day (and sniff every nook and cranny — not me, the dogs).

. . . living in a home that is free of clutter.

. . . listening to old vinyl jazz records in my living room while reading a book.

. . . having the peace of mind that comes from knowing my financial house is in order.

. . . taking advantage of opportunities to continually learn new and interesting things about my passions and the world.

. . . writing letters on quality stationery.

. . . meeting fellow bloggers and readers who have similar passions.

. . . exploring locales as far away as the cobbled streets of Paris or as near as businesses in my own hometown.

. . . cooking a pot of risotto while sipping a glass of crisp white wine.

. . . staying abreast of the news enough to be an active participant in politics, but not so much that I feel unnecessary stress and angst.

. . . wandering through a museum to enjoy an interesting exhibit.

. . . taking a cooking class to channel my inner Julia Child.

. . . snapping photos on a walk or while visiting a favorite shop or boutique.

. . . watching, after a long, exhausting day at work, a favorite television show I've recorded.

. . . sipping decadent homemade hot chocolate from my favorite local shop, Colville Street Patisserie.

. . . slowly but surely decorating my home in a way that best reflects who I am but is also welcoming to guests.

. . . using all-white dishes for meals and choosing brilliantly colorful flowers, tablecloths, and napkins to accessorize.

. . . knowing when to use social media and when to turn it off.

. . . hosting a simple tapas soiree for close friends and family to celebrate an important or everyday occasion.

. . . letting go of physical things I no longer use.

. . . cutting ties to people or responsibilities that no longer support the life I'm creating and having the strength to know I am worth it.

These are a few of the many details that make up the simply luxurious life I am fortunate enough to live. As you read this book, I'll share many more, along with tips on how to make the ideas that you gravitate toward a reality in your life.

The foundation of a simply luxurious life need not be difficult to build, but it requires a clear understanding of what you value and why you value it.

I'd like to break the ice and loosen up your mind by sharing a few simple ways you can begin to define the simply luxurious life that can be yours. Start by taking out a notepad or your journal and jotting down quick answers to the following questions.

What Personal Rituals Do You Most Value & Enjoy?

Make a mental list of the things that make you smile, lose track of time, or breathe a huge sigh of relief, and then be sure to engage in these activities regularly. Perhaps it's a bubble bath on Sunday night before the work week begins. Maybe it's a weekly coffee chat with a good friend or, better yet, a monthly weekend away to change up your routine. Whatever you crave, add it to your schedule and make it a priority, one that you enjoy regularly.

What Are Your Most Valued Relationships?

One major, underlying theme in a simply luxurious life is a focus on quality rather than quantity, and that includes your relationships. If we are being true to ourselves, we cannot possibly be loved by everyone. I defer to Winston Churchill, who said, "You have enemies? Good. That means you've stood up for something, sometime in your life." And we can't possibly foster deep, loving relationships if we are friends with everyone we meet.

Choose a handful of relationships that are most valuable to you, and take the time and energy to invest in them. Yes, you will be vulnerable, but there's only one way to develop genuine, lasting relationships, and that is with time, effort, and real love. Throughout this book, we'll consider how to build and cultivate high-quality, healthy relationships.

What Types of Exercise Do You Enjoy?

It is vital that you find invigorating physical exercise that you look forward to with pleasurable anticipation, as opposed to the feeling you might have before having a tooth extracted. Regular exercise is good for the mind—it has been proven to stave off neurological decline—and it clearly is good for the body: It increases muscle mass, which speeds up your metabolism, and it also helps maintain flexibility and agility. Respect yourself and the life you want to live by prolonging the time you can enjoy it to the fullest. Maintaining a healthy lifestyle is another constant theme of this book; it is the foundation upon which we build the life of our dreams.

What Do You Like to Eat?

Make a list of the food you ate during the past week. How many items did you choose because they are not bad for you according to the diet police? Food is meant to be enjoyed, not feared; too many of us have made food an enemy. Sitting down and savoring quality, well-prepared food is a simply luxurious way of taking care of your body and overall well-being. Eating authentic (not packaged) food is a way to be respectful toward your body, and the good health that results allows you to pursue your dreams. Later chapters will discuss food and how America's definition of dieting is hurting our health.

What Simple Pleasures Do You Enjoy?

One of my everyday simple pleasures is savoring a dark chocolate truffle each night I don't indulge in dessert. This is one of my favorite rituals, and if you're choosing real chocolate from a real chocolatier, one piece will be enough, trust me. Another of my simple pleasures is purchasing a bottle of wine from my local wine shop and pairing a glass with a meal to celebrate the end of the week, unless I have plans to go out for dinner. A visit to my favorite patisserie to indulge in a croissant and *chocolat chaud* is a weekly treat. And a simple pleasure that has nothing to do with food is to carve out "play time" each day with my dogs when I come home from teaching. Seeing them romp around the house or yard in absolute delight is the perfect elixir for any frustrations or worries I might have.

What Are Your Favorite Conversation & Comfort Zones?

Whether you like to entertain or simply enjoy finding a cozy spot and getting lost in a good book, take the time to create and design areas in your home that help you cultivate what you love to do. Indoors, choose luxurious fabrics, add a beautiful, unique side table and lamp, style a lovely tray vignette, and toss a soft, beckoning throw for fall and winter. Outdoors, whether in your own yard or in a nearby park, find spots where you can indulge in sun and shade to your heart's content.

How Are Your Finances?

In order to live the life you want, you must have the funds to do so. If you don't already have a budget, create a simple way to keep track of money coming in and going out; sticking to a simple budget will help you attain your goals. Later in this book, I'll discuss in detail how to become a savvy money manager. Financial independence and security are two keys to keeping your life simple and making it luxurious.

Why Not . . . Make Your Dreams Happen?

Answering the seven questions above gives you an idea of some simple measures you can take to create your own simply luxurious life. Now let's talk about goals — the steps you'll take toward your dreams.

Ultimately, being able to live the life you desire comes down to doing some hard thinking about your dreams and staying focused on them until they are accomplished. Steven Spielberg's film *Lincoln*, starring Daniel Day Lewis as Abraham Lincoln, focuses on a few weeks in January 1865. Lincoln is resolutely determined to pass the Thirteenth Amendment to abolish slavery before the Civil War ends and the Southern states are readmitted to the Union.

Midway through the film, Lincoln has a private conversation with Representative Thaddeus Stevens, who also ardently wishes for the abolition of slavery and equality for all. In explaining to Stevens why flexibility and strategic planning are important when we try to attain goals, Lincoln speaks in metaphorical terms: "The compass points you true north but does not warn you of obstacles and swamps along the way."

Whether Lincoln actually said these words or screenwriter Tony Kushner wrote them, the explanation contains valuable, timeless wisdom.

On January 1, when you are making resolutions for the coming year, you must believe in your heart, gut, soul, and mind that you will achieve them. You will need this obstinate strength to stick to the journey you have set for yourself because there will be obstacles. There will be swamps.

Knowing this beforehand will help ensure your success. Many life coaches suggest that when you are formulating goals, you consider all the obstacles you may face and then devise advance strategies for dealing with them. I hesitate to instruct you to do this. Why? While, yes, you can predict some of the obstacles, I guarantee there will be others you can't predict. And when those unexpected moments happen after all the planning you did, you may feel that your preparation was for naught (it wasn't, but it may feel that way).

Let's get started with some thinking and a few notes that will get you on the way to making your simply luxurious life happen.

Create Your Own Unique Destiny

The woman who follows the crowd will usually get no further than the crowd. The woman who walks alone is likely to find herself in places no one has ever been.
— Albert Einstein

Trends come with each season. Socially accepted ideas of how to live our lives evolve and change with each generation. Popular culture is, at its core, a tremendous mass of people following certain products, types of music, and ways of living. The media, advertising, tradition, the zeitgeist, the people you surround yourself with — all seem to be expecting you not to stand out, because if you do, then what? It's safer to stay with the pack — so says conventional wisdom.

I love the fact that Einstein uttered the words quoted above. While this very simple concept is so full of common sense, it is an idea that many are unable to master. Sadly, many women choose to recede back into the crowd.

A woman who chooses to no longer be a follower but instead decides to lead her own life can be perceived as setting off on a lonely journey. I say "perceived" because many times people put a negative label on something they fear or don't understand.

The truth is that many people choose to wallow in their loneliness when they are alone, but this doesn't have to be the case. Taking the chance on yourself — striking out and following the beat of your own drum — is a gift to yourself.

I won't sugarcoat this idea and say that in stepping out you will experience great success immediately. But the alternative is living someone else's definition of what life should be, and that breeds discontent in a variety of forms. In order to find yourself in places you've never been, you must travel your own path, even when you don't know exactly where it will lead.

You lessen your true potential when you shrink to fit inside someone else's notion of what you *should* be, how you *should* live, and what you *should* believe. If you are willing to put forth the strength to be true to yourself, to follow where your heart, passions, and talents lead you, at times you will feel alone. But I can almost guarantee that if you choose to seek out those who are like-minded and who support your efforts instead of discounting your voice, you won't feel lonely but instead will create a life that is enriching and fulfilling beyond anything you've imagined.

In other words, instead of letting the fear of being lonely pull you back to what you know you don't want, use that fear to empower yourself to push forward until you find what you've been looking for.

You have the strength to choose your own path, and you can help that strength grow by exercising its power on a regular basis.

Discover Your Purpose

If you don't know where you are going, you might wind up someplace else.
—Yogi Berra

The key to achieving anything in life—a successful career that fulfills you, a marriage that is strong and healthy, children who are confident and grounded, a life that brings genuine contentment—is knowing what you want and acquiring the skill set that is necessary to achieve your dreams.

Sounds simple enough.

Once you know what you want, you can start the journey to achieve it; however, maybe you aren't certain about which direction to go or what exactly it is that you want. Sure, you hear from your parents, the community you live in, the media, and your friends what they think would be the best fit for you, but that is their perception, based on their understanding of who you are and what you need. How could they know more about those two things than you do?

You're an adult now. The responsibility lies on your shoulders to determine what makes your heart sing, what drives you without one glance at the hands on a clock. Until you know what that is, contentment will always be out there somewhere, waiting for you to find it.

As humans we want to be needed. We want to know that what we do — whether it is at the office, when we're with friends, at the computer, or at home — makes a positive difference. We all have innate talents. Some of us figure them out earlier than others and as young adults become very proficient at them, while others discover their talents later in life.

No matter when you come to understand your own special talents, pounce on them and turn them into a driving force in your life. When you discover your purpose, you give yourself the gift of direction — knowing what you want to do or where you want to go next. When a person realizes her purpose, she is discovering her passion, what she could spend endless hours happily involved in. Why not spend your life pursuing your passion?

Once you have discovered your purpose, the challenge becomes figuring out how you will go about pursuing it. In our modern culture, women are given so many conflicting messages, ranging from "Be a lady and be demure" to "Stand up for yourself and act like a man." My response to the latter statement is why would I want to act like a man when I am very proud to be a woman?

And in response to the former statement, being a lady doesn't mean what it used to. That is why it is very important to be proud of the fact that you are a woman in a time when so many opportunities are available that weren't there a mere thirty years ago. At the same time, you need to be willing to use your feminine charisma to convey a quiet but determined strength to accomplish your dreams.

All too often this is easier said than done, I realize. It's much simpler to take the route your parents or older siblings have traveled, but if that doesn't excite or profoundly please you, why continue down that route? Don't quit your day job just yet, but consider for a moment the possibilities of taking a chance in those hours when you are not at work to begin puttering away on the things that seem to take you out of your stressful world. Dare to dream.

Discovering your life's purpose, your passion, truly can feel as though a burden—perhaps the pressure you've been putting on yourself to succeed—has been lifted off your shoulders. Once you know what you want to succeed at, you need to discover the direction in which your energy must be spent, and that knowledge isn't always easy to come by.

When you do acquire this knowledge, it becomes easier to let go of other distractions. As you begin to create the life you have been dreaming of, you will see that the distractions are not a priority.

As you start on the process of self-discovery and discovering your dreams, celebrate the little achievements. Pat yourself on the back. Simply realizing the direction you want to go is a huge accomplishment.

Interview Yourself

Perhaps you aren't quite sure what you desire, what you are passionate about. You may know, however, that you're not passionate about what you're currently doing. Ask yourself these eight questions—actually write them down. This may take fifteen minutes or half an hour, but it is a good exercise if you are serious about narrowing down what you are passionate about.

- What am I doing when I lose track of time?
- What am I most often complimented on?

- What do others look to me for?
- What do I have the most fun doing?
- What makes me feel great about myself?
- What am I naturally good at?
- What do I most often give to others?
- What ideas, things, places, and people am I most inspired by?

As you look back on what you have written, it's very likely you will start to see a theme. For example: losing track of time shopping; receiving multiple compliments on my wardrobe choices; friends look to me for advice regarding their clothing; love flipping through fashion magazines; wearing fabulous clothes builds my confidence; having an eye for colors, textures, and patterns that work well together; giving clothing as gifts—you get the idea. A person who answers the questions above this consistently should be building a career as a stylist, a fashion consultant, or possibly a blogger on styles and trends, even if she begins just in the evening hours.

What do you have to lose by trying? Realizing your dream, spending your life involved in fashion? No dream is too silly to pursue if you have a true passion for it.

Look at What You've Accomplished So Far

This exercise is a wonderful way to remind yourself how capable you are. Take a look at where you were one, five, ten years ago (choose one, or consider all three).

Applaud your successes in life so far. Make a list of the events, moments, and successes—small or large—that have brought you to where you are today, particularly if they were memorable to you, changed your thinking, or demonstrated what you never thought you could do. Write down what these successes have taught you. Finally, based on the list of your successes, make a list of what you've discovered about yourself and what you have learned about life.

Make a Dream List

What are your dreams? What changes do you hope to make in your life moving forward? What new skills do you hope to learn? What places do you hope to visit? Keep this list short—no more than three items.

Once you have your brief, beginning dream list, take an honest look at it and choose specific goals that you want to achieve that will bring about the significant changes you want to see in yourself. Perhaps choose three areas in your life you want to improve (for example, health, style, financial security), then be clear about the goals you want to achieve within these areas.

Be specific. And make sure your goals are "smart"—specific, measurable, attainable, realistic, and timely. Why? By clarifying exactly what you want to achieve, what it will look like, and how you will attain it, you are giving yourself a map of how exactly and within what sort of time frame the change should occur if you are on task—in other words, accountability.

Call them resolutions, call them goals, call them whatever you want, but I highly recommend that you continue to improve the quality of your life, no matter how wonderful it already is. To be alive is to have an opportunity to get it right, to live up to your full potential. And if you're alive, you have more potential to discover.

Convert Your Dreams into a Plan

Think small steps. Following the "smart" goal approach, break down the various elements that need to be completed in order for your goal to materialize. Pull out a calendar and set up daily, weekly, and monthly goals based on what is necessary. A key element for the success of your goal setting is to put a positive spin on the steps you are laying out for yourself. Be willing to celebrate them. See these necessary small steps as the actions that will lead you where you want to go.

Do Something That Is Important to You Today. Repeat Tomorrow.

The only way to achieve a life in which you pursue your passions is to begin today. Small steps taken every day will eventually get you to the end of the marathon.

A funny thing will happen while you're taking these repeated baby steps. If this is indeed your passion, you'll realize that you don't mind the extra hours you're spending, say, typing away on your computer in the middle of night. You won't even be looking at the clock until someone has to nudge you and say, *"Put the computer down and go to bed."* The little steps will become a habit, and you'll begin to see glimmers of progress every once in a while. No matter how small the glimmers are, they will motivate you to take the next steps tomorrow. Have faith, take action, and watch what happens.

Rome was not built in a day, and neither will your dream come true quickly. However, it will never become a reality unless you stop contemplating and start executing your plan. Go! Write that first sentence, contact the bank about a loan, sign up for that class you've been thinking about. Start the process, whatever it may be.

If your dream truly is a passion for you, you won't be able to stop thinking about it even when you're not actively involved in it. You may become exhausted as you work toward your goal, but your mind will never shut off about what you could do tomorrow, the next day, and on and on.

Do something, no matter how minuscule, every day to further your progress. Just thinking about it won't magically plop you down at your destination. Even if you're on vacation, write your thoughts in a journal so that you can come back to them later. Do something every day that benefits the cause. These little things add up, like a puddle that becomes a pond. Eventually you will see growth, but for now, keep your nose to the grindstone and take it one day at a time.

Do something every day. It can't be said too often.

With your dreams conceived and recorded, and the steps to achieve them written down in your planner, on your idea board, or just tacked to the wall in front of your desk, you will be reminded daily what you are aiming for, what all of your hard work is meant to accomplish.

There are other helpful ways to remind yourself of your goal on a daily basis: Drive through the neighborhood where you want to buy a house, read a story based in Paris each night before you go to bed, hang a pair of the pants you want to fit into on the door of your closet. In other words, visualize what you want, and with your effort, it will materialize.

Become Unstuck

There are no prescriptive solutions, no grand designs for grand problems. Life's solutions lie in the minute particulars involving more and more individual people daring to create their own life and art, daring to listen to the voice within their deepest, original nature.
—Stephen Nachmanovitch

Some people can get this far: They know their purpose; they have a list of dreams and goals that will take them there. But they talk themselves out of going forward. They get in their own way, talking themselves into settling for their current reality and letting their dream remain a dream.

The key to becoming unstuck is to take one step at a time. How many times have you heard that advice? The reason "one step at a time" is one of the most-repeated mantras is that it is the way most of the work of the world gets done.

And with just one step, you become unstuck. As long as you are not stagnant, as long as you can take that first step, you will not get stuck again. Even when you run up against frustrations, momentary setbacks, or other obstacles, you are not stuck because—think about it—you had to do something to run up against them in the first place.

How to remain unstuck for the long haul? Stay perpetually in motion as you move toward your dream.

Dealing with Your Fears

Someone once told me not to be afraid of being afraid, because, she said, "Anxiety is a glimpse of your own daring." Isn't that great? It means part of your agitation is just excitement about what you're getting ready to accomplish. And whatever you're afraid of—that's the very thing you should try to do.
—Maria Shriver

The next time you unconsciously gravitate toward a negative thought about your abilities, the world, your relationships, or any other important matter, stop and ask yourself why you've jumped to a negative conclusion. More often than not it is because of a fear you harbor or a lack of belief in yourself. The answer? Confront the root of the problem, move past it, and refuse to allow it to affect your attitude as you work toward your dreams.

The biggest mistake any woman can make is to want something but to be too fearful to try to achieve it. For example, you might have a beautiful voice, but if you don't have the gumption to stand up and sing, no one will know. Stand up. Sing.

Facing your fears builds your confidence. When you face your fears, you learn that often the task you're contemplating isn't so daunting after all. It's the buildup in your head that makes you *believe* it will be so much more difficult than it really is.

Most of our fears come from within our own psyches. But fear can be external as well as internal. If you are thinking, for example, about relocating in order to follow your heart, your dream, and your passion, you will most likely feel at least a little fear, but you may also have fear projected onto you by others. You need to be able to hear what other people are saying but resist taking their fear onto your shoulders.

As Maria Shriver wrote, anxiety about doing something is actually your dreams wanting, aching to become your reality. This fear, this feeling, will remain unless you act on your dreams and ambitions and look them in the eye.

Dr. Barbara Rose states, "Everyone is scared in the beginning! That is just a great sign that you are moving out of the old comfort zone of your ego—that loves to cling on to the past—and you are moving in the direction of your heart and soul—which will *never* let you down!" So give in to your fear and chase your dream. Chase down that life of living your passion every day and make it your reality.

Be Willing to Grow

Change will not come if we wait for some other person or some other time. We are the ones we've been waiting for. We are the change that we seek.
—Barack Obama

Getting older doesn't necessarily mean you are growing. Each person who decides to chase her dreams and who challenges herself to turn her dream into a reality is choosing to grow. She is intentionally choosing to expand her mind, ability, talent, and opportunities. None of this happens automatically simply because a person grows older.

So make a conscious decision today to grow. Whether it is by picking up *The Atlantic* or purchasing a recommended book to learn more about what you will have to take on, take an action that promotes growth. Begin now. Decide now to grow. (While we're talking about books, here are two that can help and inspire you in your quest to find your purpose—*The Element* by Ken Robinson and Lou Aronica and *The Other 8 Hours* by Robert Pagliarini.)

Just as it's hard for parents to observe the day-to-day changes as an infant grows and becomes a toddler, it's difficult to perceive your own growth when you're in the middle of it. You may be unable to see the minute changes that are occurring, but they are adding up to what will at some moment become recognizable and abundantly obvious to yourself and everyone around you.

Everyone has moments in the middle of a journey toward a particular goal when she feels she's not making progress, when she begins to doubt she can achieve what she set out to do so many months and/or years ago.

At such moments, it is imperative to stop, gather your thoughts, toss out the negativity, and perform a reality check, reflecting back on how far you've come. What I do is pull out my journals and flip to the pages that are dated exactly a year or more ago, so that I can visualize who I was and then compare that person to who I am now. More often than not, I am reassured that I've made progress — maybe not always by leaps and bounds, but something positive and beneficial toward accomplishing my goals.

When you're experiencing a doubtful moment, stop being so hard on yourself. Don't lose the positive momentum that has built up. Make sure your focus is where it should be, and then keep striding forward a little bit each day — a slightly smaller serving size, a few more Lincolns into the savings account each month, completing each task, no matter how simple, to the best of your ability, and not wasting your time on things that don't matter.

Every positive step you take toward the life you desire and want to live today is making a difference. You may not see it now, but you will eventually. Have confidence in your small, continued efforts, which are building a solid foundation.

Let Passion Be Your Guide

Jay-Z says, "The work that you put into something is what you get out of it." I agree. Hard work is necessary for success; this is a theme I repeat throughout this book's first two chapters. But sweat, toil, and tears aren't always necessary. It may seem at first that you can't work hard without pain, but I disagree. What's required for hard work can change dramatically if the work is something you are passionate about.

Passion has an exhilarating quality to it. When you are passionate about something, it doesn't hurt to do it; the effort isn't painful, and time seems to disappear. If you love gardening, you can spend hours digging in the dirt, unaware of the time as it flies by. If you are a writer, you can sit typing away, jotting down thoughts until your eyelids decide you must get some sleep. If you are a lover of nature, you can sit and enjoy a pristine lake in the early hours of the day and pay no mind to having woken up so early. And if you are someone who loves to shop and pull a variety of outfits together, well . . . need I say more?

Just as a Boeing 747 needs an immense amount of fuel to travel safely across an ocean, if you are passionate about what you are doing, that passion will fuel you to continue to spend time and put out effort, even though your hard work won't pay off in material terms until later.

And it's not just that passion makes effort less painful. Spending time immersed in something you love is a release; it will be fulfilling in a way you've never felt before. Once you discover your passion, it is a fire that burns inside you, that pushes you to do more than you could have imagined. You're now expressing yourself because you couldn't imagine doing anything else.

You may be at a point in your life where you don't know what your passion is, or you may feel that something or someone else has been determining what you should be passionate about. If so, take the time to explore your life and your passion. Listen to your heart, and let your gut guide you as you turn to the things that are interesting to you.

As a young man, my brother could spend hours, many times an entire day, on the golf course; for him, morning turned to dusk in what seemed a blink of an eye. I couldn't be prouder of him for pursuing a life as a golf professional because it is what he is truly passionate about.

You may not know why certain ideas, events, or tasks are interesting, but for some reason they grab your attention. Paula

Abdul shared in an interview that at age four she saw *Singing in the Rain* on television and was immediately drawn to Gene Kelly and his skill as a dancer. She became mesmerized. What would cause her to be drawn to something she had never seen before at such a young age? Something spoke to her. When the Jacksons noticed her dancing as a Lakers Girl, she became their choreographer, and later she choreographed many well-known movie dance scenes, including Tom Hanks's piano dance in *Big*. The key here is that she was listening, and her parents were as well.

What speaks to you? What do you love to do, even if nobody else understands? So what if they don't understand! View your pursuit of your passion as your very own scavenger hunt. Try new things, take new classes, introduce yourself to people who are in positions that intrigue you. Don't be shy. Don't wait. This is your life, and you're in charge of it.

While the work of discovering and acting on your passion may bring toil and tears, the hours of toil will speed by and the tears will be tears of joy.

Tap into Your Gifts

There is a vitality, a life force, an energy, a quickening that is translated through you into action, and because there is only one of you in all of time, this expression is unique. And if you block it, it will never exist through any other medium and it will be lost.
— Martha Graham

It may seem at times that the thoughts you ponder, the feelings you feel are not unique. How can they be when there are billions of people on our planet? At times you may feel you are not an original; people may even try to convince you of this notion. It may seem at times that you have nothing new to give the world, but you would be very, very wrong.

The combination of your ideas, talents, place of residence, experience, education, age, gender, and physical attributes, along with so many other variables, is something that disproves the assumption that individuals are not unique. Your unique combination of gifts is your arsenal as you battle to follow your passion.

Do you have an ear for music that you can't explain and that perhaps you take for granted? Can you discern almost instantaneously the flavors in any meal you taste? Is your body able to contort in ways that others are simply befuddled by? Do you have an ability to read others' actions and intentions even when they can't explain them? Don't assume everyone has these gifts. Accept your gift, improve upon it, and offer it as a way to improve the world you live in.

You must not shy away from or stop the continual search to be the full extent of what you have been gifted to become — a combination of traits and talents that no one else will ever possess. The unique expression of the life force that Martha Graham speaks of is something that you must seek and embrace. Then you must tap into it and share it.

Often it's easier to succumb to what everyone else expects from you, what the zeitgeist seems to accept and doesn't question. But succumbing and bowing to assumptions should not sit well with you. Again, you are your own best guide. You can attain fulfillment and true contentment if you will find the courage and strength to listen to what you may know but can't explain. Then educate yourself, fine-tune your skills and abilities, and seek out coaching or mentoring from an expert in the field you desire to be a part of.

If you are to capitalize on your purpose, hard work is an absolute requirement. So are passion, love, and the belief that you have something special to offer if you are willing to follow your talents. Follow the uniqueness that resides within you, and be strong enough to say, *"Others may not understand why I believe so wholeheartedly, but right now, I need to trust myself and put forth the work that is necessary to amplify my gifts."*

Cling to this uniqueness. Grab hold of every opportunity to express it and polish it. Beef it up with the proper foundation and education.

Take a Step Outside Your Comfort Zone

> *The best protection any woman can have . . . is courage.*
> —Elizabeth Cady Stanton

Being open to meeting new people, visiting a new city you are curious about, changing up your routine a bit, or taking a taste of something you've always assumed wouldn't be to your liking—all of these gradual steps strengthen your ability to be courageous.

As Neale Donald Walsch writes in his *Little Book of Life: A User's Manual*, "Life begins at the end of your comfort zone."

Stop procrastinating and give it a try. Do your best. Learn from the results of your first attempts, and do not become discouraged.

Instead, become more comfortable taking risks. Think about Rosa Parks, Mahatma Gandhi, Martin Luther King Jr., Jackie Robinson, Alice Paul, the unknown rebel standing in front of the tanks in Tiananmen Square. Each of these individuals stepped out of their comfort zone and stood up for what they believed was the right thing to do, sometimes without even much popular support. Their work—for civil liberties and justice—demanded that they muster up courage and a willingness to place themselves in situations in which the outcome was unknown. The stance each of these courageous people took helped make the world a bit more accepting, a bit more just, and a bit more humane.

While Gandhi and King and the others performed grand and impressive acts of courage, let us not dismiss how we too can live courageously to improve our lives. After all, one must practice being courageous and be willing to step up to the plate whenever a moment presents itself (and the truth is, it's easiest when you practice on smaller matters first). If we want a life defined by our dreams, rather than one that is simply presented to us or one that we decide to settle for, we must live courageously.

Heading Off Trouble

Courage is an angel that makes the difference between a good life and a great life.
— Fairly Legal

As I mentioned previously, I'm not a big fan of trying to figure out in advance every difficulty you will face. That said, it doesn't hurt to jot down the first few obstacles you may encounter and have a strategy for dealing with them.

If you know that certain friends will not understand or support you as you pursue new goals, start to spend less time with them. If you know your parents will grill you over a decision of yours that they disagree with, bring a friend along who has your back when you stop by their house. And if your significant other feels left out or left behind, take the time to communicate clearly and honestly, providing reassurance.

Again, you can't possibly anticipate all obstacles and plan strategies for them. Plan for a few, and have faith that you will be able to deal with the rest as they come (and they will). Your confidence in yourself and your commitment to your goals will give you the energy necessary to do this when the time comes.

Eliminate Excuses. You're tired? You're too busy? You can't possibly believe the ginormous dream you thought you could accomplish will ever become a reality, so why bother? Stop making excuses. A person's own mind is often the biggest obstacle she has to conquer in order to be successful. Ask yourself: Are you getting in your own way? If the answer is yes, ask yourself another question: Is this something you really want? If you are passionate, if you will not allow that fire to be extinguished, no matter what, you'll be able to get out of your own way.

Start the Process of Being Patient. One of the consistent mantras in this book is "Be patient." I provide this counsel throughout, and even include in chapter 2 a section called "The Importance of Patience." So now, as you start to lay out your dreams and the goals that will help you achieve them, you must accept that while you may have set a deadline for reaching one of your goals and have planned diligently, the date may shift; things have a way of either happening sooner than we expected or taking way more time than we thought. While you may be ready to make your dreams a reality now, the timing may not be perfect for the other actors in your play; however, that doesn't mean they'll never be ready. Be willing to make the progress you can when opportunities come your way. Anything worth achieving or attaining takes time and an immense amount of effort.

Change Your Language. One of the simplest things you can do to change the tone of your days is to change the words you use. Force yourself to eliminate *can't* and replace it with *can*. Talk about what is working instead of what isn't. It is amazing how quickly your tone and even your outlook can shift to become positive and more hopeful—simply via the words you use when conversing with others, talking to yourself, or writing in your journal.

Find a Mantra. Consider your mantra your fuel. There will be days when you will doubt yourself, times when you will question your ability. Rest assured: You're not doubting your passion—absolutely not—but sometimes a long journey without any reassurance can result in a blow to your self-confidence. At such times, you need a boost. An easy way to provide yourself with one is to display a mantra on your wall or someplace where you can't miss it. Create a slogan that you believe in and that will lift your spirits. My mantra has always been this idea from Henry David Thoreau: "If one advances confidently in the direction of [her] dreams, and endeavors to live the life which [she] has imagined, [she] will meet with success unexpected in common hours." This quote is framed and decorates a shelf in my office so I can easily see it when I look up from my computer. It gets me revved up again every time I need it.

Accept Success. Not everything in your life is going to run smoothly. Nothing is entirely perfect and flawless. No matter what occurs, focus on what went well and allow yourself to celebrate your successes and use them as motivation to continue to have hope. The small hurdles you jump make a difference, and you must not take them for granted.

Assess Regularly. Breaking down your dreams into goals gives you a method for regular assessment of your progress. At the very least, take stock of where you are monthly; weekly is even better, and for smaller goals daily assessment can be helpful. If your to-do list says you will engage in aerobic activity four times a week and strength training twice, you want to be able to put a checkmark next to that item; that sense of accomplishment will be exhilarating as well as motivating.

Taking It to the Next Level: Be Courageous

Courage is not the absence of fear, but rather the judgment that something else is more important than fear.
—Ambrose Hollingworth Redmoon

Face what you fear. Look it in the eye and determine what exactly it is that you are afraid of. Rejection? Being laughed at? Not being accepted? Often our fears are telling us what we desire the most in our lives, and it is up to us to listen to this internal message and follow that yearning.

Gain a Sense of Control & Elevate Your Self-Confidence

I like to think of achieving a goal as sprinkling a bit of fairy dust over my life. Just as there is nothing more frightening than feeling as if you have no control as your future unfolds, there is also nothing more powerful than achieving your dreams to instill the belief within yourself that you control your destiny.

The process of setting and achieving goals is a tried-and-true approach for taking back control of everything that is within your reach. With each goal that is conquered, the feeling of control slowly returns — easing your mind, lifting a burden, elevating your spirits, and giving you an opportunity to choose where you'd like to sprinkle your fairy dust next.

Becoming a person who sets goals and successfully achieves them is like climbing a flight of stairs. With each upward progression, you are placing one success on top of another. You are building a foundation from which you are better prepared to achieve the next goal, possibly one of greater magnitude. Since with each step you are standing firm on a dream you now call a reality, the confidence you have in yourself and your abilities will rise like compound interest — gradually at first and then taking off like a mad hatter.

Feel Your Increased Energy Bolster Your Optimism

No matter how exhausting the journey toward a goal may be, when you cross the finish line, your energy is somehow amazingly replenished. A burst of adrenaline awakens your exhausted mind as you feel a new trust in yourself, the knowledge that you can achieve what once was a seemingly impossible task. As you come to trust yourself to follow through when the going gets tough, your levels of stress and self-doubt decrease.

When something wonderful occurs in your life, the burst of adrenaline, joy, and exhilaration is hard to contain. For a moment, you view the world through rose-colored glasses — and that isn't necessarily all bad. When you take a dream and make it a reality, your optimism is bound to soar. The glass becomes less half empty and a bit fuller, if you get my drift. Yes, reaching your goal most likely required large quantities of perseverance, discipline, and perhaps even tears, but you now know you can accomplish a difficult task when it is set before you — an earned peace of mind that is priceless.

With dreams, as with any goal, you must stay focused, but if you continue to believe that you will reach your dreams — that you can make them happen — and then take steps to get there, your positive attitude will help propel each step you make. As Helen Keller said, *"Optimism is the faith that leads to achievement. Nothing can be done without hope and confidence."*

Remaining optimistic takes regular work and daily reminders, but you can create a better life for yourself and a better world for everyone by seeing possibility and continuing to have hope.

Analyze Less, Act More

Perhaps you slowly make your way, inch by inch, into a cold swimming pool versus jumping in cannonball style. But the act of just doing something and not overthinking it can sometimes work in your favor. Why? To begin with, you wouldn't be considering it if it wasn't something you were interested in. Second, when we start analyzing, we welcome self-doubt, which erodes our self-confidence. Yes, I believe it is a good idea to always try to make well-considered decisions, but once our toes are on the line (which means we were quite curious in the first place), it's time to just jump in.

For example, when I was a teenager in home economics class we would design clothes to be worn on the runway. The fashion magazines I enjoyed reading of course covered New York Fashion Week, and I could only dream of one day attending. New York City was a world away from my small rural hometown of Enterprise, Oregon. Fast forward almost twenty years, and that dream opened the door to reality. After nearly two years of blogging, in 2011 I finally purchased plane tickets, reserved a hotel room in midtown Manhattan, and eagerly waited for September 2012 to arrive.

Did I know exactly how it would work when I got there? No. But I bet on myself that I would figure it out; I'd consider whatever didn't work as a lesson learned for my next trip.

I arrived on the red eye, and my first experience was receiving invitations to view the spring 2013 collections of Nicole Miller and a handful of young, up-and-coming designers. I met with fellow bloggers for rooftop drinks at Salon de Ning, brunch at Sara Beth's overlooking Central Park, and dinner at Pearl's Oyster Bar, and I took in paintings by Monet and Picasso at the Museum of Modern Art. Full disclosure: I also experienced a mini-tornado, a mix-up getting a press pass, and a blow-out at a fancy salon that was demolished by a freak rainstorm ($40 spent with no evidence of the service provided — oh, well!). However, I couldn't have asked for a more memorable trip; it helped propel my blog platform and provided me with some amazing memories.

Be Disciplined & Willing to Work Hard

In order to have self-discipline, you must be very clear about what you want and thus very clear about what you don't want. As you begin making progress toward what you desire, you will be less easily swayed to go off course. Your greater resolve will make it easier to display self-discipline and allow you to proceed forward — even if no one understands your efforts.

Nothing worth having ever miraculously occurred without hard work. There may be setbacks along the way, and you may have to readjust your sails along the journey. But the dreamer who exercises fortitude and grit doesn't stay stagnant for long.

The woman you wish to become is already within you. She's waiting for you to find the courage to reveal her to the world. Find the courage to embrace her, and you too will someday be able to empathize with Diane von Fürstenberg, who titled one of the chapters of her autobiography "The Woman I Always Wanted to Be."

Trust Yourself

With each year of life experience, as you pour over what you enjoy versus what makes you cringe, what makes your heart sing versus what tears at your heartstrings, you hone your instincts. You begin to realize what is worth taking a risk for—love, a particular career, justice, etc. And when you know what is important to you, you begin to realize that you must choose what you care about most over the fear that stands in the way.

As you begin to live more courageously, know that your actions speak volumes. Without question, you are daring to say, "The life I wish to live is worth the effort. The life I know is possible won't be easy to achieve initially, but I am willing to fight for it." You are saying, "A good life may be nice, but I know a great life is possible." With each act of courage—standing up for what you value, speaking out for those who don't have a voice, taking action when too many people are afraid to step in and help—you are creating a better life not only for yourself and those you love, but also for others you may not even know about.

CHAPTER TWO

Live Simply Luxuriously

ndré Leon Talley, who was at one time an editor on Anna Wintour's *Vogue* team, shared this definition of luxury. "Luxury is . . . to be able to take control of one's life, health, and the pursuit of happiness in a way that is joyful."

In order to live the life we desire, we need to have the freedom to seek out a course that is in tune with our inner calling. Whether we provide ourselves with financial freedom or avail ourselves of freedoms protected by law, a crucial component in living simply luxuriously is to have the means to attain freedom; only then can we spring ahead toward our dreams.

It is when we attain freedom that we can follow the mission of living simply luxuriously: choosing quality over quantity, preferring sensibility over frivolity, opting for a personal signature style over trendy fashions, and discovering a truly fulfilling life rather than being led around by the nose.

In adhering to principles like these, we follow a mandate to live consciously, to pay attention, and, as we fine-tune our signature exterior, to always back it up with an even more impressive intelligence and strong wit.

The Definition of a Modern Woman

It is interesting to consider the idea of being *modern* as we ponder the potentials and responsibilities involved in being a woman at the beginning of the twenty-first century. Women have never had so many rights and opportunities. At the same time, we face increasing responsibilities and heightened expectations.

The modern woman is truly privileged. Think about all the women who have come before us who have struggled, fought, and persevered so that we can stand on our own two feet and not need to lean against someone else for the rest of our lives. This truly is something to be celebrated.

Oscar de la Renta commented recently, "Never in the history of time has there been a woman more in control of her destiny than a woman today."

As women, we have a lot to celebrate, but our responsibilities cannot be taken lightly. Many feel it is best to try to "run with the boys," but why would we want to do that when we can be what they cannot?

Being a woman no longer means being silent and subservient. A modern woman is strong, but in a subtle, confident way that doesn't need to be abrasive. A woman's looks can be helpful, but her brains will always propel her to where she wants to go. A modern woman is well-educated; she is up on what is going on in the world around her so that no one can pull the wool over her eyes.

What can you do, as a woman, to stay true to yourself and at the same time exert a powerful impact on the modern world?

Educate Yourself

On a grand scale, you can earn a degree. On a smaller scale, you can stay apprised of the current events in the world, your country, and your community. A constant, underlying theme for the woman who wants to have a successful life is to always continue to learn. Education is without question and without exception the gateway to freedom, choice, and living the life of your dreams.

A piece of advice that's often offered to recent college grads is *"It's not what you know, but who you know."* The catch is that you do need to know quite a bit so that you can get to know the right people and make a good impression. Let's say you're at a party or a charity event. Are you informed enough to converse with anyone in the room? Your knowledge will not only give you confidence but will also expand your networking opportunities.

Nurture Kindness

It is easy to be taken in by the sensationalistic negativity that surrounds us in the popular culture, but what about kindness? The relationships and ideas we foster with kindness grow like well-cultivated plants. If we aren't willing to nurture a relationship or an idea, it can't grow.

The next time you see someone doing a good deed, extend a thank-you. Take the time to praise behavior you wish to see more of. You might just be surprised by the results.

An important component of adding kindness to your life is eliminating gossip. Few things are more contradictory than a beautiful, respectable woman who speaks poorly of others. Remember the old adage: "Small minds talk about people, average minds talk about events, and great minds talk about ideas."

Be Independent

A modern woman is, practically by definition, an independent woman, and we are all capable of living up to this expectation. A truly modern woman is someone who lives by her own means, a woman who, while she enjoys the company she finds in relationships (significant other, family, friends), isn't reliant on them for her financial survival. A modern woman is educated and disciplined; at the same time, she is passionate, which makes her an asset in the career she pursues. And while she may want to share her life with someone special, she doesn't need another person to make her life whole. She already is a whole person, all on her own.

Show Genuine Appreciation

Always respond with a simple thank-you after a dinner party or when a friend has gone out of his way to do something nice. Likewise, you can reciprocate in advance by arriving at a gathering with a bottle of wine, a beautiful candle, or another hostess gift.

Be Well-Groomed

Nothing reveals self-respect more than how you present yourself, so consider your grooming regimen — haircut, highlights, color,

manicures, pedicures, skin care, and such—as mandatory items on
your to-do list. Not only will you feel better when your hair, skin,
nails, and wardrobe are in order; knowing you look your best also
will demonstrate your high standards to the world.

Have an Air of Mystery

In our culture of reality television and tell-all books, it's rare to come
across a woman who shares just enough to keep you intrigued, but
not so much that you feel you've stepped into her boudoir. We all
must have our closest friends with whom we share our intimate
secrets; we all need to vent every once in a while, and not everyone
can afford or wants a therapist. But just because someone asks you a
question doesn't mean you are obligated to respond or post an
answer on your Facebook page. In other words, always know
something that nobody else knows; it keeps people on their toes.

Be Humble

If you are a woman who has great taste and common sense (which I
know you are), you undoubtedly have had many reasons to
celebrate. However, one characteristic of a modern woman is that
she has a healthy self-confidence that doesn't require continuous
patting on the back. An initial celebration, fantastic. Allowing your
dearest friends and loved ones to raise a glass, absolutely. But
beyond that, be reserved. Who knows? You might even create a bit
of mystery. You know something others might love to know, but
you won't be divulging it anytime soon.

Remain True to Your Word

There's nothing more welcome than a woman of her word. If you
say you'll call, follow through. If you mention you can lend a hand,
do so without prompting. On the flip side, don't offer to participate,
say, in an event that sounds great at the moment but isn't something
you'll be able to actually take part in. Initially, some people may

question why you don't say yes to everything, but with time, they'll realize that when you do promise to step up, you show up and do a lovely job.

Think Quickly, Speak Slowly

Don't open your mouth as your thoughts are still swirling about in your mind. That's the best way to insure against saying something you might regret. Before you speak, take the time to ask yourself, is a verbal reaction from me necessary?

In other words, pick your battles. Strategically employ your energies in situations that benefit you and that create more positive results for others around you. I'm reminded of the scene in *You've Got Mail* when Meg Ryan's character is in the coffee shop waiting for her anonymous chat room friend to arrive. Her tongue becomes a whip as she rapidly spouts accurate, yet hurtful comments about Tom Hanks's character, which, of course, she later regrets.

Always Leave a Tip

Do sweat the small stuff. For example, view tipping as a way of being respectful. Whether it is your hair stylist, your dog sitter, a bellboy in a hotel, or a waiter, always provide the proper percentage. Some may feel that a tip is a reward to be earned, but I politely disagree. Tipping is not in response to a service provided, but a reflection of the manners and person you are. (*Note to travelers:* Always read up on the country's customs for tipping. When in doubt, leave one.)

And the time may come when you are in desperate need of a root touch-up and are hoping against hope that your stylist will squeeze you in even when her schedule is full. In such situations, decent tippers are more likely to be accommodated.

Also, always RSVP, whether or not you are able to attend a party. When you take the time to communicate with the event host or party planner (today it's often a simple digital gesture), you enhance their ability to plan a successful event; if you can't make it, you are extending the message that you truly appreciate the invite.

Behave Well

Many things have changed when it comes to being a "lady," but some basics tend to remain the same, or at least similar. A modern lady doesn't drink too much, nor does she exhibit uncouth behavior. She minds her manners and rises above those who have none.

She keeps her own counsel, and understands that often it really is better to observe and just take things in. Thinking something doesn't mean you have to share it with the world. Our initial reactions are merely that—reactions, responses that occur perhaps without much thought. When you're faced with a decision, make certain you'll be comfortable with it in hindsight.

When you're getting to know a potential romantic partner, don't be a tease. A modern woman is confident about who she is and doesn't need to be someone she is not in order to impress. She can eliminate the games. She doesn't pretend she is interested if she isn't.

When the situation is reversed, you may need to exercise tact and courtesy so that you don't wound the feelings of someone who is more interested in romance than you are. Be true to your feelings; it is better to be honest, yet respectful, as well as up front so that no one becomes embarrassed or hurt.

Don't Apologize

A person who thinks she is in an inferior position often feels she must apologize—needlessly. I'm not saying that apologizing when you've done something wrong isn't proper—absolutely not. What I'm discouraging is apologizing for doing something that you've done with good intentions but that didn't work out. Yes, you will make mistakes. You might, and most likely will, step on someone's toes if you're continually trying to grow and improve, but why should you apologize for someone else's insecurity?

And as one of my readers commented, a modern woman doesn't apologize for her success, and I couldn't agree more. Refuse to allow yourself to be belittled; bullies try to make you feel as though they are superior because they want the control they think you have. Keep striving. Keep being you—because you are wonderful.

Be Someone You'd Admire

Who do you look up to in this world? Who do you admire, respect, and wish you could be like? Many of us can quickly come up with at least one or two people who lead lives we dream of, lives we feel would be fulfilling, gratifying, and enjoyable. Why not *be* someone you'd look up to and admire?

A modern woman takes her life into her own hands and molds it into a masterpiece. Have you started yet? Do you have a vision of what your life will look like? No matter where you are in this process, you too can be an amazing modern woman. Most likely you already are, but it all begins with becoming someone you'd admire.

Be a positive role model for younger generations. Young girls look up to their mothers, aunts, grandmothers, and other women they come into contact with. Demonstrate with your actions and the way you live your life that the life ahead of them is theirs to create.

Revel in Your Femininity

The girls who were unanimously considered beautiful often rested on their beauty alone. I felt I had to do things, to be intelligent and develop a personality in order to be seen as attractive. By the time I realized maybe I wasn't plain and might even possibly be pretty, I had already trained myself to be a little more interesting and informed.
—Diane von Fürstenberg

The gift of being a woman is that we can become whoever we wish to be. We are all more amazing than we realize. And once we realize the simple fact that we are the curators of our one and only life, we also understand that we must dive into our innate strength, all the while thinking: Who do I want to be? What life do I want to live? Whatever you wish for, you can achieve. We must continually thank and never forget the struggle of the women who came before us and paved the way for us to have the rights and freedoms to live life precisely as we desire.

Diane von Fürstenberg had her initial business success in the late 1970s as the feminist movement was gaining momentum. What I admire and appreciate about her is that she has never cast aside her femininity but rather revels in it, all the while reminding women that femininity is about equality and being able to have the freedom to live the life each of us wants, without limitation.

Women are equal to men, not inferior. It is our ability and our belief in ourselves that will dictate what we accomplish in life. You are a woman, and that in itself offers some amazing opportunities. Why not revel in this fact?

As I mentioned earlier, Diane von Fürstenberg titled a chapter in her autobiography "The Woman I Always Wanted to Be." While that phrase may sound rather simple, becoming what we've always wanted to be is no small feat. In fact, it may be the most difficult task each of us takes on as we go through life.

There are many ways we as women can revel in our womanhood. It is a balancing act, but one that I feel quite proud in trying to accomplish, as our right to do so was such a hard-won victory.

How does a woman go about becoming the person she's always wanted to be? Here's my advice:

Looks May Open Doors, but Brains & Personality Take You across the Threshold. The simplest way to become successful in a particular field is to educate yourself. Diane von Fürstenberg became savvy about marketing, Steve Jobs had an eye for design and capitalized on it to create a user-friendly computer, and Julia Child enhanced her love of cooking by taking classes in French cuisine. There isn't any secret to becoming an expert. In his book *Outliers*, Malcolm Gladwell articulates the 10,000-hour rule — that the key to success in any field is practicing a task for a total of 10,000 hours. The formula is very clear: Acquire knowledge, make a sustained effort, and exercise patience. (Looks are not part of the magic recipe.)

A Watershed Year for American Women

Did you know that it wasn't until 1974 in the United States that women legally had equal rights when it came to obtaining credit? That means getting a credit card or taking out a loan to buy a house or a car. Before that year, when the Equal Credit Opportunity Act went into effect, creditors were under no legal obligation to extend credit of any sort to a woman. A father or husband or other male had to co-sign.

Today's young women are often unaware of how recent in our history women were seen as second-class citizens who lacked the simple rights we now take for granted — like being able to financially take care of ourselves and live a life on our own. An easy way to gain appreciation for the struggles of the ground-breaking women who came before us is to watch the poignant, eye-opening HBO film Iron Jawed Angels, starring Hilary Swank, Anjelica Houston, Frances O'Connor, and Patrick Dempsey. The film follows events during the 1910s as political activists revolutionized the American feminist movement that ultimately, in 1920, gained women the right to vote.

Treat Your Body like a Temple. And do it not for your looks, but for your health. There is only so much our minds can do without a physically able body. Staying in shape is not about vanity (well, maybe sometimes). By staying in shape and being knowledgeable about what you eat and how food fuels your body, you are giving yourself more time to live life more fully and ably.

Demand Equality. Know women's history — be appreciative and never take your rights for granted. Too many women gave so much for women they would never know for us to blithely toss these rights aside. Exercise your voice — vote! (Recommended reading: *A Woman's Crusade*, by Mary Walton.)

Exercise, Develop & Engage Your Mind. Never stop learning. Whether it is taking classes at a nearby college, enrolling in an evening cooking or yoga class, checking books out of the library, or watching intriguing shows and movies, continue to absorb information voraciously. An education is something that can never be taken away from you.

Enjoy Pampering Yourself. Have fun applying your makeup, doing your hair, taking a bubble bath. Of course, it's important to keep in mind that you are more than your outer shell, but feeling beautiful sure increases a woman's confidence.

Learn to Say No. When you know what you can do and what will enhance your life, it becomes much easier to say no to things that will not be beneficial. While no one wants to hear that something they want is not going to happen, using this power is a way of respecting yourself.

Respect Your Body & Demand That Others Do the Same. If they refuse to, walk away. Depending on the culture or family environment we are raised in, women can receive mixed messages about their bodies. Do not be fooled by misguided adults and media — you, and only you, are the queen, the one and only ruler of your physique. And while we may have been trained to believe that our nose should look a certain way or our breasts should be a certain size, other people often follow a rule book that suits their needs, not our own. Care for your body — and your mind — so that they can function at their best. If something doesn't feel right, see a doctor, and if someone is invading your personal space and you don't like it, demand that your boundaries be respected.

Nurture Someone—Your Children, Your Pets, Your Dreams, Yourself. Nurturing may be engrained in most women's nature, but that doesn't mean we all are drawn to nurture in the same way. Many women want children—fabulous! I applaud responsible, loving, and devoted parents, but not every woman wants children. Some are perfectly ecstatic nurturing their own dreams as well as the dreams of those around them. Whatever or whomever you choose to care for, do it with zeal and without shame.

Break the Rules, but Follow Some Too. In the right situation it is not a bad idea to split the check. Or you might want to take the initiative to get together before you begin dating someone so the two of you can get beyond just first impressions; keep it short and show interest, but give yourself enough time to see if you have anything in common, say, outside of work. Meanwhile, it really is beneficial to let the guy ask you out. (Trust me on this one; see also "My Unorthodox Views about Asking Guys Out.") Allow a man to court you—you truly are the prize, and you should behave accordingly. And throughout the process, let him know you appreciate his thoughtfulness. Always remember: We teach others how to treat us, so respect yourself with your actions, and applaud those reactions that are respectful.

My Unorthodox Views about Asking Guys Out

In my twenties I mustered up the courage to ask a handful of guys out. And, yes, it most definitely causes the adrenaline to surge and instills a feeling of empowerment. But I have since come to realize two things. First, the adrenaline rush came primarily from the fact that I was doing something that was new, uncertain, and challenging. Second, I've learned that asking a man out implies that we are not worth being chased, that we don't have the confidence to wait to be pursued by the right guy. And when we do the asking, we lower the effort a man has to make to impress us. Waiting for a man to make the first move actually creates a kind of test of whether he is genuinely interested.

It takes great patience for women who have been raised to go after what they want to gradually and ever so subtly pique a man's interest, but not pounce. Bear in mind that, in the end, we want someone who adores us, respects us, and is willing to make the extra effort to impress us because he thinks we are worth it.

I am wholeheartedly a feminist. And when it comes to relationships, men are drawn to women with confidence as long as you are warm and approachable. You don't need to manifest your strength by asking a man out. Instead, gather your composure and simply get to know him; talk to him and be your charming self whenever you run into each other, but let him be the gentleman. We influence how others treat us by what we allow. Set the tone you want and it will be returned by a person who wants to be with you.

Note: This advice pertains to the first date. After you've gone out a few times, by all means reciprocate by planning a date. In fact, you should, to let him know you are truly interested.

Treasure Your Privacy

The human heart has hidden treasures,
In secret kept, in silence sealed;
The thoughts, the hopes, the dreams, the pleasures,
Whose charms were broken if revealed.
—Charlotte Brontë

Do you ever have internal debates about how much you should reveal and what you should leave unsaid? Whether you should reveal absolutely everything? Throughout my life I have wrestled with my answer. With much time, thought, growth, and reflection, I have found a balanced approach that works.

A reader once told me that when she received good news — something that was a great achievement for her — she would keep it to herself for an entire day and revel in the accomplishment without having to internalize anyone else's judgments (good or bad) along with it. After a day, she would share the good news with those she loved. What a lovely idea—letting your own happiness and joy be enough validation and reason to celebrate.

Whether it's celebrating about something big or just keeping track of yourself as you make progress with your small steps, learn to rely on yourself for validation. Keep some secrets, in the short term and for the long haul. That, in and of itself, is empowering.

Keep Some Things to Yourself

To him that you tell your secret you resign your liberty.
— Anonymous

In our world today, there are as many opinions as there are people, and that should be reassurance enough that we need to trust ourselves. There are so many different ways to live a fulfilling life that each person must decide what she deems important. Choosing to maintain some privacy and not share everything about our lives with the rest of the world bolsters a belief in ourselves. What you feel, what you know to be true for yourself, doesn't need to be validated by anyone else.

I am mostly speaking of our personal secrets—our thoughts, feelings, and personal situations that truly are no one else's business but our own. The trend today seems to be moving away from the idea that we should keep anything private, but I would argue adamantly for the opposite.

Knowledge is power, but so is keeping some of your business to yourself— especially your strengths and personal feelings—until you are truly ready to reveal them and are capable of handling the pushback.

Revealing all speaks volumes about one's lack of self-confidence. When I was in my teens and early twenties, I lacked self-confidence; I was unsure about what I was doing in my life and where I was going. In need of validation from others about what was going on in my life, I would divulge everything to my trusted confidantes, in effect seeking their approval. Today, as I look back, I realize why I was such a chatterbox—I needed the validation of others.

In turn, we should respect others' privacy. Identifying someone who likes to keep certain things in her life private is often easy; this is the person who doesn't ask incessant personal questions unless you offer to share. Observe the golden rule as you converse with others, whether they are close friends or passing acquaintances, and grant them the privacy you yourself desire.

Create an Air of Mystery

The mark of a chic, classy, modern woman is her ability to always be mysterious, to exhibit behavior that tends to provoke even more curiosity about her.

As one of my readers pointed out, many of us respect the *decision* to be mysterious, but it can be difficult to *actually be* mysterious and opt for discretion. After all, we are surrounded by friends, family members, and colleagues who want to know what is going on in our lives, and they become especially curious when we don't want to reveal too much voluntarily. While most of the people who want to know details about our lives do not mean to be overly inquisitive or hurtful, there are others who aren't asking because they care—they are just plain nosy.

Either way, if a question or too much inquisitiveness makes you feel uncomfortable, that is reason enough not to answer. It took quite some time for me to realize that just because a question is asked of me doesn't mean I have to answer.

This includes declining an invitation. Gracefully decline by simply saying you appreciate the invitation but have another commitment. You are under no obligation to explain the commitment, but be sure to extend your gratitude.

The question remains, how do we respectfully, tactfully, and gracefully navigate situations in which people are asking us questions? The key to the approaches laid out below is that they take practice. Choose a few that you think will work best for the situations you know you're bound to run up against and give them a shot. The more you use them, the more they will become second nature. More important, if you consistently make it known that you are not going to be gossiping, answering personal questions, or engaging in conversations that are inappropriate, in time most people won't approach you with such nonsense.

Respond to a Nosy Question with a Question

Why do you ask? Wouldn't you like to know? Can I consider you intrigued? If a questioner persists, respond with a question. In the same way, often when I'm in the middle of an impassioned political discussion, I find that the best way to calm the situation is to ask where the arguers found the information that is the basis of their opinions — in other words, from what source did you hear that? This usually stops arguers in their tracks if they have no credible source; even if they know, they have to recall the information, and that takes them off course a bit.

Redirect the Conversation (aka Change the Subject)

If a question makes you uncomfortable and the person doing the asking isn't taking your subtle hints, change the conversation altogether ("I'm going to the bar. Can I get you another drink?"), or turn the tables and give them a genuine compliment about their wardrobe, hair, etc. — anything to divert attention from yourself.

Stay on top of current events. The best way to avoid uncomfortable questions is to be preventative. Always have a conversation topic at the ready, preferably something that the other person may be aware of but that isn't gossip. Avoid gossip at all costs as it only reflects poorly on those doing the talking. Raise the bar and talk about concepts and ideas, rather than private or personal matters.

There are so many sources that can help you stay abreast of current news: NPR, *60 Minutes*, morning TV shows (*PBS Newshour*; *Today*; *Good Morning, America*; *Morning Joe*, etc.), newspapers (*Wall Street Journal, New York Times*), magazines such as *Time* and the *New Yorker* (and don't forget *Esquire* and *Men's Journal*, where you will find universal conversation starters, believe it or not), any book on the best-seller lists, and your local newspapers. The list goes on and on. And if you're ever at a loss for a topic of conversation, talk about the weather.

Ask questions of people that they'd like to discuss. People generally feel comfortable talking about themselves, as long as it's something they don't mind sharing or are proud of. Why not begin the conversation by setting an example: Pose the type of questions you wouldn't mind answering. In other words, always follow the golden rule. Whether others follow your lead is up to them, but at least you are giving them the respect you would like to receive in return.

Smile & Shake Your Head (Chuckle a Bit, if Necessary)

Words can get us into trouble, so why not say nothing at all? This may seem awkward at first, especially for the person who has asked the question that made you go silent. But had the person not asked such an uncomfortable question, they wouldn't have to be feeling awkward. Your silence is a subtle hint that this topic is not up for discussion.

Or just give vague answers. If you're not comfortable telling someone they are prying much too hard into your personal life, simply answer with a vague statement. If they ask how your love life is going, reply, "Very well, actually." And leave it at that.

When someone asks a question you'd rather not answer, busy yourself with another task or walk to another group of people — of course, excusing yourself first. If you're in a casual setting, take out your cell phone and start going through your apps or viewing your messages, or pick up a magazine or a book.

Cut to the Chase

If you are comfortable "telling it like it is" or if someone has been nagging you incessantly, just tell them the truth: "I'm not one to share such personal information." Better yet, if someone is pestering you with questions about why you are still single or when you and your husband are going to have a baby, you can state very bluntly, "My private life is none of your business" or "Your questions are getting a bit too personal." Something I've always wanted to offer in this scenario is a question of my own: "And would you like to share with me the secrets of your sex life, or is it so boring that you have to inquire about mine?" Okay, that's probably a bit over the top, but truly, it wouldn't be that out of line.

Always remember: The only reason you need to not answer a question is that it makes you uncomfortable (and this is always easier to discern if you haven't been drinking or have had just a few sips). A modern woman is always aware of her environment, knows her boundaries, and respects herself first.

Insist on Self-Confidence

When a woman becomes her own best friend, life is easier.
—Diane von Fürstenberg

A young girl unaware of the manipulations of the media and the world around her is a refreshing and hopeful sight. She embodies so much promise, so much potential, and she lives in a world where so much is available to be achieved—truly a world that is hers for the taking. But then puberty and the teenage years begin, and the world, her peers, and sometimes her family members begin to expect certain things, often influencing her according to their wishes and not her own talents and desires.

Even when a girl comes from a loving and supporting home, the real world is not for the faint of heart. But if you are a young woman who will take the time to turn down outside pressures and ignore the zeitgeist, and instead become disciplined and resolute, you can learn about yourself and come to genuinely like yourself. At the same time, you will challenge and become your best self. If you can do these things, the world will be yours to do with as you wish.

I'm so thankful that my mother has never asked me once when I was going to get married or pressured me to start thinking about grandchildren, but I realize there is much pressure out there for women to do both—and sooner rather than later. It seems that the longer most women wait, the more pressure comes their way.

Some may succumb to these pressures, but more and more women are bravely standing up and living life on their own terms. Never before in history have women waited longer to get married, held more master's degrees than men, held more of the jobs in the US economy than men, or as single women been more likely to own a home than their male counterparts. (This is not at all an attack against men. I love men. Life wouldn't be complete without them, but what they achieve women should be able to achieve as well.) Women clearly are realizing their potential, taking life and molding it according to what works for them—not to suit what society, family, or friends may expect.

Whether or not you want to have kids, get married, or be the owner of your own company, I encourage you to first understand how to stand on your own two feet financially, arm yourself with an education, and then set out boldly along your desired path. You can live an amazing life. I guarantee it will involve struggle—anything worth achieving does. But a beautiful and fulfilling life awaits the woman who will work for it.

Put Yourself First

You have to leave the city of your comfort and go into the wilderness of your intuition. What you'll discover will be wonderful. What you'll discover is yourself.
—Alan Alda

I have always loved this quote by Alan Alda. I first came across it when I was in my early twenties, and I have kept it either in my idea journal or on my idea board ever since. It is a necessary reminder that when doubt rises within, we must look deeply into ourselves rather than run back to what is comfortable.

The journey at times may be difficult, frustrating, or uncomfortable. There are moments when you will think it absolutely makes no sense, but the result of facing all these obstacles is a beautiful prize — the discovery of who you are. Each person does it in her own time, in her own way, and at her own pace. Whenever you choose to discover who you really are is the right time; the point is that you must do it.

Most people find making the decision to put themselves first quite a bit easier than the actual process, but one of the best pieces of advice I can give is to allow yourself to gradually become comfortable with your own company.

When you are able to be by yourself, you then are able to listen to what your gut or heart or soul is saying — in other words, the message that is waiting to be heard. As Littlefoot's mother in *The Land Before Time* says, so simply and perfectly, "Let your heart guide you. It whispers, so listen carefully."

Wherever in the world you might be, society will always rush and whirl around you, pulling and tugging at you to stay in the fray. But keep this in mind: Society wants you to stay consumed with its insanity for its benefit, not yours. It is adult peer pressure.

You will need strength if you are to step out of the hustle and bustle and make time for yourself. Don't worry: Society will be there when you're ready to get back into it again. After all, it needs you.

If you are in a quandary or have never considered getting to know your wants, your desires, and your talents, think about how you can increase your quality of life based on the contentment, self-satisfaction, and peace of mind you will have found.

It will take strength, but aren't you worth it? After all, as Aristotle reminds us, "Knowing yourself is the beginning of all wisdom."

Set Your Sights

When one door closes, another door opens; but we so often look so long and so regretfully upon the closed door, that we do not see the ones which open for us.
—Alexander Graham Bell

Why do people gaze so longingly on their past? While most of us accept that life is perpetually changing and that nothing can be considered routine for long, we generally find comfort in what we know or have known, even if it isn't all roses and fairy dust. Based on our lives so far, we all know how to behave, interact, and respond to others, and we go to bed at night comforted in that knowledge. Until things change.

Liz Tuccillo's novel *How to Be Single* concludes with a message any woman can heed, regardless of her marital status. Often the life one has planned takes a detour and begins to follow an unexpected course, but instead of trying to conquer the new course, we fight it like a child who has been transferred to a new school. Instead of embracing the new opportunities that lie ahead, we stubbornly waste energy cursing the need to change.

Shedding the desires of the life you thought you wanted—in essence letting go of a dream that will never be—isn't easy. It's like trying to wriggle out of a dress that fits you like a glove, compared with unbelting a robe that simply falls to the floor. It takes work and conscious, careful effort.

Changing course while in the middle of adulthood or really at any point after you've spent time, emotions, and energy pursuing a goal—realizing you cannot travel it anymore and must choose a different path—is daunting, even frightening at times. Sometimes the decision to pursue a different life is made for you, and sometimes it is a decision you make for yourself in order to realize an even better dream.

Let's say you thought Joe was the person you were going to spend the rest of your life with, but when it came down to it, your dreams were at completely different ends of the spectrum. Or what if you find that the career you began to study for in college is not the one your heart is engaged in? You must recognize that if you have to go against your principles in order to make your dream happen, it is not a dream you should continue to pursue. And is it really a dream if you would dread each day you were living it?

Changing the game plan can feel at times as though you are starting from scratch. However, if you take into consideration all the experience you have gained, all the people you have met, and the education you have absorbed, you actually are ahead of someone who is just starting out. Take advantage of your lost dream and use it as proof that you are that much closer to finding the path you were intended to travel. Instead of defeat, see it as an evolution for yourself and for your growth. As Oprah Winfrey puts it, "The whole point of being alive is to evolve into the complete person you were intended to be."

Stop looking behind you, and instead start striding forward. The future is waiting. Christopher Columbus said it best, "You can never cross the ocean unless you have the courage to lose sight of the shore."

If You're Single . . .

Being single used to mean nobody wanted you. Now it means you're pretty sexy, and you're taking your time deciding how you want your life to be and who you want to spend it with.
—Sarah Jessica Parker

It wasn't until I reached my thirties that I realized that the constant quest I conducted when I was in my twenties to find a mate was provoked largely by the outside world—media, parents, friends, etc. — rather than an internal desire on my part to couple up. Sure, I enjoyed the companionship, but I didn't enjoy being seen as a puzzle piece rather than the unique individual that I am.

Finally, I decided to be honest with myself about what I needed in order to live a fulfilling life, and one that didn't require me to compromise my values. At that point I realized that my life became richer — far more amazing and fulfilling — than I ever imagined it could be.

Why? Because I began pursuing a life based on what was a priority to me — self-respect; leaving a lasting, positive legacy; working toward equality for all; living a life of balance that fosters inspiration and enjoyment, independence, and compassion. When I began focusing on my priorities, it didn't matter whether I was involved with someone or not — I was happy either way. And when I realized that I was solely responsible for my happiness, the relationships that I did become involved in were even more fulfilling.

Too often I subconsciously sought out relationships to complete the picture, to rid myself of the nagging coworkers, relatives, and ignorant Nosy Nellies in my life, to be free of their judgments. But even when I would enter into a relationship, there was always another expectation and another, and I quickly realized the world would always have an opinion. I had to decide if I was living to appease the world and waste my life or instead could become strong enough to live the life that truly fulfilled me. Well, I think you know my choice.

Currently I am single, and I've never been happier. It's not because I'm single that I'm happy, I just happen to be single, but I now know how to make myself happy regardless of my relationship status.

But because there is so much societal pressure on those who are single — to lose the label and latch on to someone, whether they are ready or willing to do so or are not — let me share with you some tips on how to revel in an amazing way of living.

Being single should be one of the most enjoyable times in your life. The freedom, the choices, and the options are endless. As long as you have the confidence to claim the single life and celebrate it, you'll live the life you want.

Follow this checklist and you'll be exuding confidence that will knock everyone's socks off and leave you enjoying every single minute.

Own It. Yes, you're single, and thank goodness! Make a conscious choice every day to revel in the benefits of being on your own. Don't allow your married friends or family members to define you for yourself. If they offer solace or pity, have a ready comeback that expresses your confidence and sense of humor and that immediately demonstrates that being single is as much a choice as being married. For example, in response to the annual holiday question "So, are you seeing anyone?" I have actually responded, "I see lots of people. In fact, just this past summer I had the opportunity to see a good friend in Paris, then hop the channel and watch the Olympics in a pub with a few fun blokes." Whatever it is you use as a comeback, include examples of the life you love living to spark a different conversation. Let people see that there is more to living well than simply having a significant other. After all, the possibilities are truly endless, and who knows what intriguing person you might meet tomorrow.

Accept All Invitations. The beauty of being single is that you don't have to coordinate schedules. With that in mind, accept all invitations, even if they are to an art exhibit you haven't the foggiest idea about. By keeping an open mind and stepping into new and different situations, you are exposing yourself to new avenues for inspiration and for networking with all types of people. These connections could lead to a new job, a new travel destination, a new friend, maybe even a new love. Consider it a broadening of your

education, and welcome it. Who knows when your knowledge of
Andy Warhol paintings may come in handy?

Pursue Your Passions. Feel fortunate that you now have the
opportunity to explore what makes you lose all track of time.
Perhaps you receive a job offer that requires a move to another state
or another country; the good news is you can leap at the opportunity
without straining a relationship. So often people choose a profession
at an age when they don't even know what makes their heart sing
simply to answer the demands of a relationship that is in its infant
stages. While you may already have a career that is well on track,
don't be afraid to start a blog, open a small business, or explore your
hobbies more deeply; as a single woman you have time you can
devote to such a pursuit without worrying about balancing your
professional and personal lives.

Be Well-Read. If you want to feel confident enough to strike up a
conversation with almost anyone, know what to talk about.
Knowledge comes from reading as well as doing. So pick up that
best-seller if it indeed piques your interest, or gather your girlfriends
and start a monthly book club. If nothing else, it will be a great
excuse to catch up and enjoy a glass of wine or a cocktail. And when
we are left to our own devices to seek out the information that
interests us, we begin to become more in tune with ourselves.

Know Your Style. Nothing exudes more confidence than a woman
who walks into a room holding her head high and wearing
fabulously tailored clothes. Regardless of your shape — tall, short,
pear, apple, whatever — rock what your mother gave you. If you
have amazing hair, take it up a notch by asking your stylist to add
just enough highlights and layering to make even Jennifer Aniston
envious. If you have curves to challenge Brigitte Bardot, feel free to
flaunt them — a little less in the day and a touch more at night.

Either way, take the time to explore what best accentuates your body and your style.

Ten Ways to Strengthen Your Self-Worth

Ordinary riches can be stolen, real riches cannot. In your soul are
infinitely precious things that cannot be taken from you.
—Oscar Wilde

Self-worth. What is it exactly? And how does one find it?

When I searched for a clear answer to that question, my "ah-ha" realization was that we all have self-worth; it's a matter of finding it—and not by validation from other people, but within ourselves. Self-worth is different from self-esteem. Self-worth is something all of us possess on the day we are born, whereas self-esteem is something that develops as we grow. But due to circumstances— some beyond our control and some well within it—we lose sight of our self-worth and forget our own unique value. Once you accept, acknowledge, and truly know that you are intrinsically worthy, the amazing journey of finding your purpose, discovering your passions, and living your most fulfilling life can really begin.

Love & Value Yourself. Your dreams, your boundaries, and your needs come first. This is not selfishness, it is self-preservation. It is being responsible for yourself.

Cut Out the Negativity. Be positive. Your attitude is the most powerful determiner of your possibilities and your future. Be the energy you need to propel yourself forward. If you have people in your life who never lift you up but instead are always reminding you of your faults, pull the plug on those relationships. They deflate your self-worth. While I genuinely believe all people want to be successful (and each of us has our own definition of success), sometimes we get in our own way. While we may work to achieve success, often we sabotage ourselves without even knowing it, or we head in the wrong direction. Success is determined by each decision we make on a daily basis — to work harder or just get by, to save a little each month or frivolously spend our money on entertainment and shopping, to open our mouth in anger or bite our tongue and walk away until our emotions are intact. All of these decisions are our choices to make, and each one of them can build us up or tear us down.

Spend Time with People Who Love You. I'm talking about people who love you for who you are, who support you, and who aren't jealous of your aspirations and success. In other words, you need to be around people who have their own lives and dreams to chase and who desire to create a more fulfilling life for themselves as well.

Identify Your Strengths & Build upon Them. Writers are constantly told to write about what they know. In the same way, we all need to focus on what we do well and further develop those muscles, building upon what is working for us already.

Set Goals for Yourself and Make Plans to Achieve Them. Then follow through.

Reward Yourself for Making Progress toward Your Goals. Celebrate your accomplishments. And don't feel guilty about it.

Don't Compromise Your Integrity or Your Values. Stick to what you feel is right.

Raise the Bar Higher. Always do your best, and never hold back because you're worried about someone else. In other words, don't pretend you can't do something that exceeds expectations and perhaps surpasses the achievements of others simply to spare their feelings. If they are of mature character and are secure in themselves, they will appreciate being pushed to do their best as well.

Trust What You Feel. Have confidence that what you are feeling is valid. Even if no one else understands why you are uncomfortable, hopeful, happy, or cautious, respect your feeling and try to understand it. Don't allow others to discredit how you feel or make you believe that what you're feeling isn't important. You are feeling this way for a reason; take the time to figure it out.

Take Responsibility for Your Life. Your success rides solely on your shoulders; be thankful for the opportunities you have and refuse to see them as a burden. Success is possible, contentment is attainable, as long you grasp the reins of responsibility and are determined to lean forward and do the work, standing up for yourself along the way.

The dictionary definition of self-worth is *one's worth as a person, as perceived by oneself.* Some of us are blessed to grow up in a family that instilled a strong work ethic but also validated everyone's feelings, value, and potential. Sadly, though, some people did not have this type of childhood.

The truth is, you can have the self-worth you seek because it resides within you. It resides in taking your life back, making sound decisions about whom you surround yourself with, standing strong in what you know, and always choosing to learn and grow.

The Importance of Patience

He that can have patience can have what he will.
—Benjamin Franklin

Good wine, sun-ripened tomatoes, the appreciation of a home's value, and vintage clothing all have one essential element in common—time. In other words, someone recognized the potential value in each of those things and decided to wait, to hold back . . . to have patience.

Let's continue this game. What do these concepts have in common: weight loss, earning a degree, becoming the CEO of a company, training for a marathon, and becoming a *New York Times* best-selling author? The theme is most definitely perseverance coupled with . . . you've got it—patience.

Patience is a hard quality for the ambitious to master. So many people seem to want everything now. Impatient people may assume that patience is asking you to waste your time or, worse, to be lazy. But it is quite the contrary.

Patience involves staying focused, continuing to hone one's skill, talent, or craft, waiting for the perfect opportunity when your skills will be at their best and opportunity will exist at its highest potential. In order to allow your patience to pay off, you must, while you are waiting, persevere. Use the time in limbo to improve, grow, and learn—with your mouth shut (unless to ask questions) and your ears open.

Professional wrestler Brian Adams puts it this way: "Impatience breeds anxiety, fear, discouragement, and failure. Patience creates confidence, decisiveness, and a rational outlook, which eventually leads to success." The high school diploma or bachelor's degree you now mindlessly include on your résumé most likely took four years—*four years*, not just a few days—to attain. But success can't come if you are remaining idle in one spot and not furthering yourself. You must also persevere.

Your first day on the job or your first attempt at any new venture will not be pretty, but if you're willing to put your nose to the grindstone and stop looking up so often, you'll accomplish everything you've hoped for and, most likely, more than you ever imagined. After all, as Ralph Waldo Emerson reminds us, "Patience and fortitude conquer all things."

Patience must be married to perseverance. While you are being patient, you must continue to strive forward, to work toward your dreams and allow yourself to learn, make mistakes, and learn some more. It is through this dynamic process of patience and perseverance that you will grow and come closer to your definition of success.

As Jean-Jacques Rousseau reminds us, "Patience is bitter, but its fruit is sweet." Cheers to that.

After years of having a hard time seeing the value of patience, I am now well aware of the treasure such a virtue is. Think about it in reverse for a second. How would you describe an impatient person? A few things come to mind: feeling overwhelmed, rushed, unappreciative, dissatisfied, lacking motivation or perseverance, being quick to anger, and premature in ending something before it's had time to blossom and bear its fruit.

In order to persuade and motivate you to welcome even more patience into your life, I offer below five benefits of acquiring it.

You Gain Clarity

How much time are we really saving if we have to go back and correct mistakes that have resulted from our impatience? When we slow down and decide to not rush, things and people move at their natural pace. As we begin to see things as they are, we are able to see the grand picture and to gain perspective. Opportunities we might have missed had we been speeding through life are now much easier to see.

You Enjoy the Pleasures of Anticipation

When I set a goal or look forward to something I've planned for the future, the anticipation is often just as pleasurable as the event itself. The run-up to an event is something that shouldn't be erased or condensed. It is all right to require children (and adults) to wait until Christmas Eve or morning to open presents. It's quite exciting, really, to make plans a month or two, maybe even six months, in advance and to eagerly wait for what will occur while you're doing the planning and prepping.

And who doesn't love the prepping? Planning for the wedding, getting ready for a first date, shopping for the getaway vacation you've planned for more than a year—these are part of the fun and the memories you will never forget, so don't rush them. The journey truly is part of the joy. Why not savor it?

You Learn Lessons

Whenever a challenge in life has knocked us backward or caught us by surprise, the immediate reaction is a feeling of failure, a loss of faith, or a dip in our self-confidence. But if we will allow some time to pass and let our bruises heal, the lessons of such experiences will eventually come to light. So the next time you hear "no" when you were sure you'd hear "yes," give yourself time, and you'll soon come to realize an opportunity for growth.

You Discover the Truth

When we make ourselves wait until some time has passed before making a final decision, we allow the truth to present itself. The funny thing about the truth is that it's always there; we just need to be able to see it. If we rush, we can skip over important information that might have changed our minds entirely. Should you sign that contract, go out on that date, spend half your paycheck? When you allow yourself time to mull it over—sleep on it, if you will—usually an answer will emerge that will sit well with you and your consciousness for a long time to come.

You Achieve Contentment

Often when we achieve something, we leave little or no time to savor it, and immediately rush on to the next goal or the next thing to acquire. Slowing down allows us to truly appreciate what we've accomplished and not take it for granted. Having patience allows us to be submerged in the awareness of being contented and satisfied. Why would you want to quickly toss that away?

All in all, patience is something that calms things down, allows life to take a breath. Instead of constantly seeking what's in the future, let's savor the present moment we are fortunate enough to be in right now. After all, true contentment is the simple state of having peace of mind, and peace of mind comes with quieting our lives rather than quickening their pace.

Often our initial goal in wanting something is to attain what we think we don't already have, but ironically, by slowing down we come to realize how rich we are and that what we seek is already in our grasp.

As a woman, your destiny is up to you. If you will seek out like-minded individuals and stand together with other women and those who respect the rights and equalities of all, anything is possible. Do not place limits on yourself. And don't allow others to do so, whether knowingly, to fit their agenda, or out of ignorance.

Choosing Quality over Quantity, Style over Trends: Why It Works

Quality is never an accident; it is always the result of high intention, sincere effort, intelligent direction, and skillful execution; it represents the wise choice of many alternatives.
—William A. Foster

One of the main components of living a simply luxurious life is choosing quality over quantity in all areas—your friendships and relationships, your clothing and food, your entertainment and travel experiences, your living space, and many more.

But often many choices are presented to us, and we become unsure or uncertain about identifying quality. How do we determine what is of high quality versus what is only posing as such but is actually not the real deal?

By setting standards.

When you set standards for your life—how you allow others to treat you, how fabric should feel on your skin, how a garment should look on your body, how the food you eat makes you feel, how you should react to an experience, the maximum you will spend on your rent or mortgage—you are deciding on what is high quality (meets or exceeds your standards) and what is low quality (doesn't meet your standards).

If we aren't paying attention, events can take the reins, and we can find ourselves just following along. That is not a healthy way to live, and I guarantee you that allowing this to happen will not result in a simply luxurious life. When we allow others' choices and behaviors and society's preferences to dictate our decisions, we are not setting standards for living that will result in a high-quality life. We need to flip that situation on its head and allow life to respond to our expectations.

When we do that, when we set the bar of excellence where we want it to be and remain consistent in our standards, we discover what we desire and automatically brush aside what we don't value. For example, if you are clear about your values and what you will and will not tolerate, you will avoid people who challenge you for being who you are and instead discover people with similar expectations.

Be prepared for some pushback. Initially setting standards may be difficult. While always expecting the best is a lifelong endeavor, it will get much easier as you hone your ability to say no and at the same time become better able to determine what meets your standards and what doesn't.

Let's look at an example from the world of business: Apple has consistently set high standards and created an environment of excellence. As a result, customers know that the Apple logo on an electronic device means it is a quality product, and Apple can maintain high prices because of its adherence to a high standard. In other words, the company chose not to follow the crowd simply to get along. It set the bar high, and guess what? Customers continue to flock to Apple. Setting the highest standards worked.

W. Somerset Maugham had a nice way of putting it: "It is a funny thing about life; if you refuse to accept anything but the best, you very often get it."

It will take time. First, you will need to set your standards, which will be based on what you value. Then you must remain unapologetically consistent.

Here are some ways to set high standards and demand quality in your everyday life — small gestures that, taken together, can help you create a simply luxurious life. Add specifics from your own situation for a wonderful life that is tailor-made for you and what you value.

- Fuel your body with food from the earth. Eliminate processed foods and refined sugars.
- Surround yourself with people who are positive, hopeful, honest, and inspiring.
- Buy clothing that is made well, that will last more than one season, and that fits your signature style.
- Keep fewer items in your closet. Hold onto high-quality items that you wear consistently and that give you stylish options.
- Live in a home that suits you in terms of its style and square footage. Don't worry about impressing your family, friends, or neighbors.
- Save up for one quality vacation every year (or every two years) that widens your perspective on life.
- Find downtime to relax and recharge so that, when you do socialize for fun and at work, you are your best self.
- Forget about following the crowd — not because you want to be different, but because something else is

more interesting, more comfortable, or sits better with your conscience, interests, or tastes.

- Say less, but when you do speak, be clear and sincere about what you say.
- Cherish a handful of dear friends. You may not see them every day or even every week, but you know they will be there for you in good times and bad, just as you will be there for them.

You may have a vision of a life that you want but that you feel isn't attainable. The truth is that such a life actually can be yours. Your actions and your decisions not to act will dictate where you set your standards. The life you create will be based on the actions you repeatedly take.

Setting the standards for your life is completely within your control. Take a moment and assess what you value in each area of your life (personal, professional, financial, etc.), then determine whether you're meeting your own standards. You can do it. You simply need to live consciously each and every day. As Aristotle said, "Quality is not an act, it is a habit."

CHAPTER THREE

Becoming Financially Savvy & Independent

The saying goes, "Money can't buy you happiness." But the reality is that money is the currency by which we achieve our dreams, build a sound foundation we can rely on when challenges and emergencies confront us, and take control of our lives.

Forty years ago, women in the United States couldn't buy a home in their own name or have their own credit cards; instead laws required their fathers or husbands to sign for them. Since that time, women's advocates have fought for and won basic financial rights that many of us, especially younger women, now take for granted.

Having your own money means you are able to live your life on your own terms, to determine its course and be responsible for the decisions you make along the way. While having your own money and the ability to spend it as you choose is liberating, it involves taking responsibility for your life, saying "My life matters." That, in turn, means not wasting your life by following someone else's idea of what you should do.

Instead, you need to take the time to discover your passions, your talents, the world, and what you can offer it. In order to offer up your talents, you must create a solid financial foundation so that you are independent and able to withstand opposing opinions and criticism, as in some parts of the country and world traditionalists adhere to the notion that a woman's role in society is an inferior one.

Becoming a strong and independent woman does not mean acting like a man. Being a woman is an empowering identity of its own, one that should not be cast aside. Being a woman has many benefits and can lead to great success if you can be strong and sure in your direction and focus, while at the same time remaining feminine, refined, and a bit mysterious.

True Wealth: What It Is & How to Attain It

A simply luxurious life is based on the concept that less is more, but it revels in the deliciousness of high quality, complementary style, and an appreciation for the beauty that surrounds us in décor, fashion, nature, and people. One does not need to maintain a stratospheric bank account. However, it would be a mistake for me not to emphasize that being secure financially leads to a priceless peace of mind that contributes greatly to a well-balanced and simply luxurious life.

Wealth, as expressed in monetary terms, will be different for each of us. However, I'll bet that 99.9 percent of us could agree that being wealthy comes down to a state of mind.

In one of the daily e-mails I receive from the website *DailyWorth*, the writers raised a question that is beneficial for all of us to ponder: What does wealth feel like? What does it allow us to do? What does it provide?

As you think about your answer, start by relating it not to material wealth, but instead to the emotions wealth would evoke within you. The reality is that material items — the clothes, the house with the extra bathrooms and bedrooms, the vacations — are secondary manifestations of a truly wealthy life. The more important point is that we are wealthy when we can enjoy these luxuries without guilt and without accruing debt.

To be truly wealthy, a woman should be financially secure, be a good manager, and, as a result, have peace of mind about her money.

The definition of financial security can vary from one financial adviser to another, but the bottom line is this: When the unexpected lean times occur, do you have enough to last until you can get back on your feet? Some say you should have a cash reserve of three months. Suze Orman takes the toughest stance and strongly suggests eight months. However, we all must start somewhere and then be steadfast in adding to a rainy-day fund each month.

A money market or other account that is separate from your daily checking account is the best way to eliminate self-destruction, which is what I call unnecessary, spontaneous withdrawals. (Money market accounts typically yield a slightly higher interest rate than standard savings accounts.) However, you should be able access the money in such an account within a few days.

Financial security also includes the future and making sure that each month you contribute to a retirement savings account to the fullest of your capabilities—preferably 15 percent of your take-home pay, but at least 10 percent.

In order to have wealth, we must be able to trust ourselves with the money we've worked so hard to earn. Once we become disciplined, have clear goals, and know when we can have fun with our money, we are that much closer to allowing ourselves to reach true wealth and our full financial potential.

Creating a sound financial cushion for today's unexpected moments, for tomorrow's adventures, and for our retirement results in peace of mind. The financial security we create for ourselves and our families is priceless, and ultimately, isn't peace of mind what wealth boils down to? If you haven't done so already, choose today to take control of your finances and become the captain of your destiny.

The Benefits of Being Financially Independent

One of the cornerstones of a healthy, stable, independent life is being financial independent.

Money is not always fun to talk about, especially when you don't have much of it or are in debt, but ignoring it will never solve the problem or create successful habits that will better support your dreams.

Whether you are single or married, you need financial independence. Once you have it, you can make big and small decisions because you want to rather than because you have to. There are many benefits of becoming financially independent, including:

Freedom to Pursue What Makes You Happy

Once you have a financially sound foundation, you can pursue your passions, spend your free time as you wish, travel the world if you choose, treat your children or save for their education, pamper yourself, take that cooking class you've had your eye on, or learn a new language or two—in other words, you are able to live in a manner that fits who you are. You come to better understand the direction your life should take in order to arrive at your desired destination.

When you have enough money to pay the bills without asking for help, when you have the funds to buy those tickets to Paris without asking for a handout, or when you have enough cash to live the life you desire without putting it on a credit card, you become free. Free from owing anybody anything. Free from guilt. Free from obligation. Free to help those you love and care about because now you can. Free to be single if you choose and to marry because you want to, not because you have to. Simply free—and what better state of being is there?

Elevated Confidence

It can take time to become financially independent. For some it will take longer than others. No matter how long it takes, when you reach a point where you have enough to live on comfortably, you will realize how capable and disciplined you are. A sense of accomplishment will wash over you, and if you are like most people, you will see an increase in your confidence—and that is a very magnetic and beneficial characteristic.

Healthy Relationships

Financial difficulty can be a major stressor in a relationship. When you get your financial situation in order and know that you aren't dating someone because of how much money they make but because you love being with them (and vice versa), you are on a much more stable foundation, one that will support a lasting relationship. Do yourself and your partner or future partner a favor: Respect yourself enough to take care of yourself financially. Being needy isn't attractive. Confidence is. One way to gain it? Become financially independent.

Peace of Mind

One of the simplest, most effective, and sound aids to living a healthy life is consistently getting a good night's sleep. And one way to ensure you sleep well is to have your finances in order—knowing you don't have impossible debts, knowing you're able to pay your bills each month, knowing you have extra money in the bank. Nothing is more sleep-inducing than knowing you can take care of yourself financially.

Know Where Your Money Goes

I think the nicest thing you can say about a woman is that she lives well, and she lives below her means.
—Suze Orman

We all know how much money we bring in. What very few people know is how they spend that money.

And while I have seen some very complicated programs for staying on top of one's spending, it really is as simple as basic math. Take out a calculator, along with a piece of paper and pencil, and add your income and subtract your expenditures, or allow Excel to do the calculations for you. Either way, eliminate unnecessary stress by doing the math each month. No matter how little you bring in on a monthly basis, you can put yourself on the path to financial success simply by being mindful of how much money you can spend and staying within these boundaries.

Whether you are writing a check, using a debit card or cash, or a credit card, be sure to record each transaction. At the end of each day, sit down at a notebook or your computer and enter each expense. I use a simple Excel spreadsheet program that sorts my expenditures into categories and keeps running tallies. Visit the blog www.thesimplyluxuriouslife.com/money/ to see the "Basic Monthly Budget" illustration, which shows the monthly system I use to keep track of my expenditures. You can download a version of the chart on this page as well.

At the end of the month, compare your paycheck and/or other incoming amounts with the outgoing expense tallies. This simple exercise will give you a solid grasp on exactly how much you are bringing in and how much you are spending.

Have a Monthly Date with Your Finances

On the first of the month or the day you receive your paycheck, make yourself a cup of tea, turn on your favorite music, sit down, and pay all your bills. Make this a monthly ritual. Write down all your expected expenditures, even ones that haven't arrived in your mailbox yet, so that you can see exactly where you stand financially as you approach the new month. Doing this at the beginning of every month lets you know exactly how much you have to spend on discretionary items and events.

Once a check or automated withdrawal clears the bank, go back to your notebook or into your program and check it off. Doing this lets you know exactly where you are with your monthly finances. Doing a little bit every day means you won't have to sit down once a month for hours trying to match everything up.

Be sure to include the money you are saving. David Bach, author of *Smart Women Finish Rich*, suggests a saving strategy that each month puts money into three baskets:

Retirement. Save approximately 10 to 15 percent of each paycheck.

Emergency Savings. If you're able to start with only $20 to $50 a month, that's okay. Gradually begin adding more as you are able. But make a promise to not touch this money unless it truly is an emergency—a necessary vet surgery, a car accident, etc. The exquisite Diane von Fürstenberg dress that would be perfect for your interview? That's not really an emergency.

Dreaming Money. Place regular monthly deposits into an account that is not attached to your checking account so that you aren't tempted to dip into it when your checking money is running low. Choose a money market account with a higher interest rate than what you would receive with a regular savings account.

Simple Ways to Trim Your Budget

The film *Confessions of a Shopaholic* prompted me to contemplate ideas for how each of us can take control of those moments when it seems a pair of shoes is far too fabulous to pass up or when a pair of jeans fits much too well to not take it home this instant.

In chapter 4, I encourage you to stock your closet with quality basics, classics, and other pieces of fabulous clothing. But when your budget is tight, how can you be the responsible adult you know you are and just walk away?

Below are ways to trim the excess from your life so that you are creating more quality and putting your hard-earned money toward those dreams, goals, and responsibilities that are at the top of your priority list. The first time I sat down to make a list like this was several years ago after I'd purchased my first house. It was important to me to become a homeowner. However, I knew I'd have to tighten my belt a bit, and that meant I had to become creative. Below is the list of ideas I came up with:

- ✓ Assess all your utility bills and determine what you can live without — reduce the cable package, bundle your phone and Internet, etc. Pay for what you need and use regularly; eliminate the rest.
- ✓ Call your credit card company, and if you are a cardholder in good standing, negotiate a better rate.
- ✓ Transfer high credit card balances to a new "no interest for a year" card or to a card that doesn't have an annual fee.
- ✓ Buy magazine subscriptions for more than a year at a time. The savings is usually quite astonishing. And create a magazine swap with friends.
- ✓ Check out books from the library rather than buying them.
- ✓ Clip or print coupons and take them to the supermarket with your grocery list.
- ✓ Pay bills online (save the stamps).
- ✓ Lower the temperature on your hot-water heater.
- ✓ Use warm water when washing your clothes instead of hot.
- ✓ Turn off the lights when you leave the room.
- ✓ If you frequent a particular coffee shop, purchase a gift card at the beginning of the month and place a budgeted amount of money on it. As you use the card, hold yourself to this amount.
- ✓ Cook at home.
- ✓ Eat out only on special occasions or at restaurants likely to serve food you couldn't make yourself.
- ✓ Have the oil in your car changed and the tires rotated every three months or 3,000 miles. (The mileage between oil

changes is greater with newer cars; get the dealer's recommendation.)

✓ Become creative with leftovers.

✓ Hold a book swap.

✓ Use a credit card that gives reward points for places you frequent (hotels, coffee shops, movie rentals, etc.).

✓ Make water your drink of choice.

✓ Forgo the gym membership. Instead, schedule a one-time session with a personal trainer and ask for exercises you can do at home to achieve the results you desire.

✓ Play board games, a tradition that has lasted because they are socially entertaining — and free.

✓ In the winter, lower the heat by a few degrees; in the summer, increase the air temperature ever so slightly.

✓ Discover chores and tasks that you are paying someone to do that you or someone in your household can easily do instead.

✓ Observe the speed limit to become a better driver and save on gas.

Ask yourself, What power am I gaining from my money? At the end of your life, be the person who can say: I took advantage of the power of the money I earned and put it to great use for myself and my family, which ultimately created peace of mind for me now and in the future. Use the power of your money to purchase peace of mind, not more stuff.

Creative Ways to Save Money but Keep the Quality

Money can be our master, or we can be the master of our money. I have a feeling we all would prefer the latter. There is no reason we should allow money to get the better of us.

In order to harness the power money can give us, we need to be conscious of how we live and how we spend the money we have worked so hard to earn. Let me share with you some ways to spend wisely, refrain from spending when it is not necessary, and, as in the first suggestion below, spend more in order to save in the long run.

Cost per Wear

People sometimes ask me how I justify and can afford some of the more expensive items in my wardrobe. While I have a very limited clothing allowance, when I choose to purchase an item for a price that may seem a bit astronomical, I make my calculations based on "cost per wear."

What does that mean? Let's take designer jeans. My favorites are Citizens for Humanity and J.Brand. As a teenager, I was continually frustrated with jeans that weren't long enough and didn't fit me correctly, which at the time made me feel there was something wrong with me. But then I discovered longer lengths available in brands that cost a bit more, and I was more than ready to put down the few additional bucks.

The rationalization behind cost per wear goes like this: If I wear a pair of $150 jeans 75 times, they are actually $2 jeans. And while some may say, but your checking account is still missing $150, my argument is that the quality of the jeans allowed them to be able to be worn 75 times, saving me from buying a similar, cheaper pair that wouldn't have gone the distance.

I know not everyone will agree with this approach, and, of course, if the money isn't available, the jeans must stay on the rack. On the flip side, however, if the funds are there, and you know the item will fit beautifully into your lifestyle, then don't feel guilty for choosing quality. Another benefit: One fabulously tailored quality item tends to bring other items in your wardrobe up to its level.

Why Not . . . Buy in Season?

When farmers markets open up in early spring, I am reminded of the opportunities to save money that come with warmer weather and fresh, local produce.

Mireille Guiliano, author of *French Women for All Seasons,* emphasizes that one should eat produce that is in season. Not only is this a healthy choice; it is also a frugal choice. Seasonal produce is cheaper because often it has been grown locally and consumers aren't paying transport costs.

To help determine what to look for when you head out grocery shopping, check out the Epicurious website; go to their "seasonal ingredient map," which makes it easy to determine what is in season where you live.

Choose to Live Below Your Means

As we make mindful decisions about spending our money more wisely, we should also, as mentioned previously, place between 10 and 15 percent of each month's income into savings (retirement, emergency, dreams). We must look honestly at what we will need to live on in the future and then get real about how we handle money today in order to have those funds when we need them.

In today's culture of instant gratification, that may feel like a slap in the face, but think about it this way: When most people retire, they will live on approximately 75 percent of what they lived on earlier—and that's if they were diligent about their retirement savings. Becoming used to living below our means will mean less shock down the road and allow us to save now for a grand future when we do retire.

How do we do this? How does one live below her means? Here are a few suggestions:

Spend No More than 35 Percent of Your Income on Your Mortgage Payment or Rent. In years past, it was suggested that a mortgage or rent payment should be a third of your income or less, but today many people are paying 50 percent or more. If you are exceeding 35 percent, get creative and come up with ways to downsize. It may take some time and result in some limitations today, but you will be saving for tomorrow.

If You Have a Car, Be Smart about It. Leasing a new car every two years simply to keep up with your neighbors will not bring true contentment, but it *will* strap your monthly budget. Find inner contentment by pursuing a life that is truly fulfilling, one that does not need validation from others (there's more on discovering your purpose and finding fulfillment in chapter 1). By simply taking your current vehicle in for the recommended overall servicing, including oil changes and tire rotations, every three months, you can have a car that runs efficiently and save considerable amounts on repairs. Recently, I traded in my car of eleven years to buy a new one. It was not something I wanted to do as I did not want the payments, but I am on the road constantly, and those of us who depend on our car for employment need a vehicle that is safe and will last if cared for properly. After taking the time to seek out the best loan rate and to educate myself about the car I wanted and how much my trade-in was worth, I went to the dealership by myself—but with knowledge on my side—and was able to negotiate a price I knew I could afford for a vehicle I knew was worth the price. The key is to know the priorities in your life. If a car is necessary, take care of it by investing in the proper maintenance so that it will perform well for a good long while.

Eat Out Less. There are many benefits to eating meals at home, beginning with keeping more of your hard-earned cash in your pocket. Not only are you saving money, but you are aware of what you are eating and promoting a nurturing environment within your home. Make eating out a special occasion, and make cooking meals an opportunity for sharing time with those you love.

Eliminate the Excess. If you're serious about getting your financial house in order, you're now looking more critically at where your money is going. Perhaps you've become aware of how much money you are wasting on the "latte factor." When you realize that making your own coffee at home could save the money you've been trying to raise for that summer beach vacation, you might find a way to make the necessary changes.

Four Tricks for Cutting Spending

Sometimes we're stuck in old habits of spending and can't seem to shake them off and make a spending breakthrough. Try one or more of these tricks to get out of your rut and into a more conscious way of spending.

Spend Cash Only. Put the credit and debit cards away. Handing cash to the grocery or boutique sales clerk often makes it easier to comprehend how much money you are spending (or wasting).

Spend Less than You Earn. This sounds simple, but many of us have become accustomed to buying things even when we don't have the actual funds. This is where we get into trouble with credit cards. Simply put, *If you don't have it, don't spend it.* You will thank yourself later. The Suze Orman quote that appears earlier in this chapter is pinned to the idea wall in my office, and I find myself looking at it whenever I am tempted to make a purchase I may not be able to afford. It tends to immediately put into perspective what matters when it comes to financial security and peace of mind. After all, just a few decades ago women weren't expected to know how to handle their finances without help. The truth is, being financially savvy is empowering and truly sets you free to be the person you want to be and to live the life you have dreamed for yourself. Do the math, keep it simple, and spend less than you earn.

Use Only One Credit Card. Keeping only one credit and canceling all other cards is tremendously freeing. If you don't have multiple cards, the likelihood that you will run up monthly debt is drastically reduced. And if you have only one card, you are more likely to make savvier decisions. Some might argue, why have credit cards at all except for emergencies and travel? But it's always a good idea to have one on hand. Have a look at Suze Orman's best-selling book *The 9 Steps to Financial Freedom* for more detailed advice and ideas.

For One Week, No Spending. Each month, challenge yourself to choose one week during which you won't spend a dime. This will take some organization and planning ahead, but it is possible. Think of all the unnecessary spending you will have saved yourself.

Becoming the Master of Your Credit Cards

Credit cards can be a blessing or a curse, depending upon how you use them. The key is to not view them as free money because as we all know (though it's easy to forget) they aren't. In fact, if you don't pay the full balance every month, you should look at them as a crafty scheme for sucking money out of your checking account.

When it comes to credit cards, we truly are in control. We can choose to dip our toes into the waters of self-inflicted debt, or we can, with great gumption and strength, walk away from those gorgeous peep-toe pumps. When we exercise the option not to charge, we will later be grateful and stress-free, and we won't have to worry about an exorbitant bill landing in our mailbox.

It's important to become educated about how to successfully use a credit card because the reality is that it is actually okay to have one. In fact, if you are going to need to have your credit score checked for anything, you will need to have at least one line of credit.

Once you are aware of the power of credit cards, the most important thing is to remain responsible and financially savvy about your financial situation. Here is a list of things to keep in mind in order to successfully carry a credit card.

Shop Around before Choosing the Best Card for You. Regardless of which bank your checking account is associated with or which offers arrive in your mailbox, make the effort to shop around on the Internet for the best credit card for your spending habits and lifestyle. There are many websites that provide advice, including Consumer Reports, BankRate.com, and other top financial blogs and magazines. If you travel often and would like to earn miles, compare all available options and see if the black-out dates work for your schedule. If you don't want perks but are simply interested in a low rate, be sure to look at the introductory APR (annual percentage rate) as well as the fixed APR. Whatever your needs, take the initiative and choose a card that best suits them. Whatever you decide, I strongly suggest you open only one personal credit-card account (see "Use Only One Credit Card," earlier in this chapter).

Don't Choose a Card for the Perks. Again, your lifestyle and needs will help you decide on a card, but if you don't fly regularly or routinely shop at particular stores, you most likely need only a basic card. The good news is that the rate will often be lower with a basic, no-frills card, and you generally won't have to pay an annual fee. Other perks may include cash back or bonus gifts, but I'd rather take a lower rate and spend the extra money when I want to rather than use my credit card to earn money. A credit card is not a savings account! There are far better ways to earn and save money.

Know the Terms of Your Card. Interest rate, penalty charges, credit limit—reading the fine print is crucial in order to protect yourself against late-payment fees or exceeding your credit limit and to understand what will happen if you do miss your payment, etc. The interest rate should be one of the most important determining factors when you are considering a card, but be sure to look at the introductory rate (which usually lasts only a few months) as well as the fixed APR, which is always a little bit higher.

Don't Buy Things You Can't Afford. The likelihood that you'll be able to pay it off later is rare if you can't afford it now. Remember: Financial security is the foundation of a better life and the beginning of peace of mind. View your credit card as an extension of your checking account. If you can't pay it off by the end of the month or within two or three months, don't use it.

Review Your Statement Each Month. Check each of the charges to make sure they are yours. If you see a questionable charge, contact your credit card provider immediately and dispute it.

Make Payments on Time. Paying online is simple and secure. Set up alerts to remind you when your statement becomes available.

Always Pay More than the Minimum Payment. Do so unless you are in the process of paying off a higher-rate credit card; in that case, pay the minimum until the higher-rate card is paid off; then increase your monthly amount.

Maintain a Good Credit Rating. How? Pay your card in full each month. If this isn't possible, keep your amount owed to 30 percent of your credit limit. Credit-rating agencies take this number into account when determining your score. Understand that the mishandling of your credit card can result in the inability to take out a loan to buy a house or a car, start a business, etc. Good money management takes disciplined decision making, and if you will remain disciplined, your life is yours to create. Take control of your money; refuse to allow it to control you.

Never Use Cash Advances. And when you receive such offers in the mail, shred them immediately.

Negotiate for a Better Rate. If you are a cardholder in good standing, make it a yearly habit to negotiate a better rate, based on your status as a reliable customer who pays her bills on time. If the customer representative on the line can't help you, ask nicely to speak to a manager or supervisor.

Protect Your Cards and Account Numbers. To prevent unauthorized use, draw a line through blank spaces above the total when you sign receipts so that the waiter or vendor can't add a tip or other amount you didn't intend. Keep a list of your credit-card numbers and the telephone numbers of each card issuer in a safe place in case your cards are lost or stolen.

Before Closing a Credit Card Account, Know the Effect on Your Credit Score. It is best to have one credit card and maintain it properly so that lenders realize you can handle the responsibility, as reflected positively in your credit score. Having no lines of credit often has a negative effect on your score.

How to Get Out of Credit Card Debt

If you have credit card debt that you aren't able to pay off in full monthly, sit down and create a plan to eliminate it.

I can comfortably admit that the knowledge I am going to share about credit card debt comes from personal experience. This is not something I am proud of, but I am not ashamed of it either. After all, as long as we take the lessons we've learned and improve as we move forward, they are not wasted opportunities. Little did I know that my increased knowledge of money would allow me to buy a house, sell it, and buy another, as well as begin a blog that would allow me to live a life I only once imagined. In other words, wonderful lessons and opportunities can bloom from our mistakes, if we are willing to learn.

I've never been someone who disrespects money. I've always balanced my checkbook at the end of each month and paid my bills on time (often early), but at one or two points in the past I have racked up a credit card balance beyond what I could pay down in full each month, and it is not a comfortable feeling.

Now I am out of debt, and my peaceful sleep at night is priceless compared to anxiety that would have resulted if I'd succumbed to the lure of the fabulous designer clothes I could have bought — along with a looming balance that would still be waiting to be paid off. I've read more than a handful of books on money management by Suze Orman, Jean Chatzky, and David Bach, and this is what worked as I freed myself from those looming balances:

Assess the Reality of Your Situation. How much debt do you have? Consider all your credit accounts (cards, home loans, car loans, student loans, etc.). The student loans can be handled slightly differently, but credit card debt and anything other than your mortgage should be included as "bad" debt.

Set a Goal. What is your deadline for being debt-free? One year from now? Three years?

Look at Your Income & Expenses. No guessing is allowed. Take the time to look at all your expenses (mandatory and discretionary). Then look at what you earn.

Determine How Much. Based on how much you earn, how much can you pay each month to complete your goal by the set date? In her book *The Difference: How Anyone Can Prosper in Even the Toughest Times*, Jean Chatzky presents a plan to rid yourself of debt on $10 a day (a minimum of $310 paid down on debt each month).

Trim Your Budget. Now take a look at where your money goes each month. Do you really need two pedicures at your favorite spa, or can you spend $9 on OPI nail polish and do your toenails at home, saving $50 to $100 a month? Do you love books but are spending more than you realized on Amazon? Start visiting your local library. (For more ideas like these, see "Simple Ways to Trim Your Budget," earlier in this chapter.)

Know Your Credit Score. Each year you can check your credit score for free. Visit one of the big-three credit reporters — Experian, Equifax, or TransUnion — to see exactly where you stand. Jean Chatzky breaks down in detail exactly how your score is tabulated and what scores are preferred.

Pay Down the Highest APR First. There are many philosophies about how to pay down multiple cards, but to me it makes the most sense to pay down the card with the highest APR first, making only the minimal payments on the lower APRs until the more expensive card is completely paid off.

Negotiate a Lower Rate. Don't be afraid to call your credit card company and negotiate for a lower rate. Bring up all your positives as a customer — the length of time you've held the card, the fact that you always pay on time, etc. Then, if you're getting nowhere and you have the ability to transfer your balance to another card, threaten to cancel the card.

Consolidate, if Possible. If you already have a card that offers interest-free balance transfers and a 0 percent APR for a year or two, transfer your other card balances onto that card. Why? *Interest free.* This will give you time to pay down your balance without incurring interest on what you owe, which, in turn, saves you money. Just keep in mind the regulations — how long the grace period lasts, etc. If none of your current cards offers this option, look for a card that does (they are out there). There are three key things to look for—the rate, the fine print, and the fees (annual, late payment, etc.).

How to Stay Out of Credit Card Debt

Once you have followed these steps and wiped your balance sheets clean of debt, become very disciplined and continue to remain debt-free.

Don't Carry Your Credit Card with You. If you have to have it with you for some reason, write FOR EMERGENCIES ONLY on a piece of paper, fold it around the card, and wrap it with a rubber band. At least you will have to think twice before using it.

Shop with a List. *Real Simple* did a study that revealed women who think they are successful are women who make lists. Avoid unnecessary purchases, and don't leave home without your list.

Shop for Groceries Once a Week. Take time to plan your meals for the week. Then on the same day each week, gather up your coupons, your list, and your cloth grocery bags and head to your local market.

Withdraw Cash for Your Monthly Grocery Budget at the Beginning of the Month. I'm capable of letting my cravings increase my grocery budget unnecessarily, but when I know I have only so much cash each week for grocery shopping, I shop more wisely and keep my cravings in check. As a result, I am forced to be more creative in the kitchen and use what I have.

Don't Be Afraid to Put Something on Hold. If you're shopping and come across a dress that catches your eye but you're not sure it's worth the strain on your budget, put it on hold. If you ask, most boutiques and shops will hold an item for at least a few hours, if not a full day, at no extra charge. If you still want it the next day and can afford it, go back and get it; if not, you've saved yourself some money.

It's Okay to Return Items. Don't feel guilty or ashamed about changing your mind. It's your money, and if you bring a purchase home and find you don't want it as badly as you initially thought, return it.

Refuse to Follow the Crowd. While your friend, neighbor, or parents may have fabulous furniture, clothing, or outdoor equipment, you do not know the state of their finances. However, you do know yours, and you know what it takes to keep yourself financially secure — paying your bills on time, staying out of debt, and saving for retirement. The *New York Times* reported that in 2010, about 75 percent of Americans approaching retirement had on average saved only $30,000. That's absurd! Hopefully they enjoyed their third car because their retirement may not be all that enjoyable. Don't get sucked into doing something because other people make you feel inadequate.

The best feeling in the world is financial security, and one of the biggest contributors to stress in life and in relationships is money, so make sure to handle the money you earn wisely.

CHAPTER FOUR

Building a Signature Style: Dress for the Life You Want

I don't understand how a woman can leave the house without fixing herself up a little—if only out of politeness. And then, you never know, maybe that's the day she has a date with destiny. And it's best to be as pretty as possible for destiny.
—Coco Chanel

The way you present yourself to the world is a statement of how you feel about yourself, your hopes for the future, and your general perception of life. While there is no one correct way to adorn yourself, there are a few wrong ways.

The key is to *care*. Whether or not you are able to afford designer duds from Net-a-Porter or tend toward Nordstrom Rack fabulousness, wear your clothes well, and be your most confident self. Secondhand stores, consignment stores, chain stores, and local boutiques regularly offer many fantastic deals, as do online retailers (be sure to sign up for their regular sale alerts). Being able to balance high and low price points is all a matter of knowing what looks best on your figure, understanding your skin tone, and focusing on the message you want to convey with your clothing.

As you become more confident in who you are, your style will evolve, but always be true to quality over quantity (though don't be afraid to mix high and low), to your physical assets (trends are not advised if they don't flatter you), and to your budget.

Throughout this chapter you will find specific tips on how to identify and create your unique signature style; an explanation of the benefits of creating a capsule wardrobe and how to do it (I will even take you into my closet and reveal my capsule wardrobe); and a list of the essentials to shop for, from top to bottom and everything underneath.

As an online stylist, I have had the opportunity to work with clients from around the world as they begin to create capsule wardrobes—clothing that lets them present themselves, apparently effortlessly, with confidence and style, and that frees them to focus on the parts of their lives they deem most important.

I am confident that after reading this chapter you will have the tools to be your own stylist. In fact, my blog contains a frequently updated page of essential wardrobe items for fall and spring to help you shop for the foundation pieces each wardrobe needs; visit www.thesimplyluxuriouslife.com/shop-tsll/. However, if you would like assistance, stop by the blog's "Stylist Services" page — www.thesimplyluxuriouslife.com/stylist-services/ — and learn how to hire me as your personal stylist.

How to Create a Signature Style

Simplicity, good taste and grooming are the three fundamentals of good dressing, and these do not cost money.
— Christian Dior

You most likely know a few people who have their own unique, consciously chosen "signature style" that they confidently express to the world without saying a word about it unless they are complimented. After reading Rebecca Moses's gorgeously illustrated and eloquently written book *A Life of Style*, in which she discusses the various ways style can be cultivated and shared, I began to ponder even more seriously how the idea of possessing a signature style ties in to living a simply luxurious life.

I concluded that creating a signature style, which can be done and expressed in so many different ways, is a mandatory ingredient if you are to create the life you desire to live. After all, a signature style requires you to know who you are so that you can not only express yourself honestly, but also create the life that fits most comfortably with your authentic self.

The first step in creating a wardrobe that is quintessentially you is to understand the various elements of your signature style. Creating it is a very personal thing. By definition, no two signature styles are alike. Where you live, your body type, your eye color, your bone structure, your personality — these and many more factors come into play as each woman sets out to distinguish her very own style.

The most important piece of advice I can offer is this: Embody a style that is true to who you are and what you believe, and that penetrates beyond the surface. After all, the clothes you wear are meant to accessorize and complement the life you wish to live, not dominate or become the only focal point.

What You Wear

Style is different from fashion. As Coco Chanel so timelessly reminds us, "Fashion fades. Only style remains." Having style means knowing what clothes flatter your body best, which colors complement your skin tone, and which cuts will never look stunning on you no matter how sensational they look on the runway.

There's peace of mind in knowing that no matter what walks down the catwalk each season, only certain cuts warrant your attention. Knowing which skirts to gravitate toward and which dresses to stay away from will become innate, but it can take time to gain this knowledge, which, for better or worse, is unique to each and every one of us.

With all of that said, what you choose to wear on a daily basis, out to dinner, to parent/teacher conferences, or on a first interview reveals to onlookers how you feel about yourself and whether you really know who you are and what strengths you possess. Without uttering one word, you can have an entire conversation with someone, again for better or for worse, based on your signature style.

Body Language

First impressions are a very funny thing. The trick is to accept that they exist and embrace them—and, more important, to understand what you want your first impression to be on whomever you meet on any given day.

Stand up tall; walk confidently but in a feminine manner; sit with good posture and be aware of your body; face each person you are speaking to; extend a welcoming hand or kiss on the cheek; be warm, but be aware of your personal space bubble; set your boundaries (everyone's will be different); refrain from tugging at your clothing in public or touching your hair or face too often (such gestures hint at insecurity); and when you smile, do so with sincerity.

Scent

Choose a scent you love, one that is of good quality, and remain loyal to it. You can choose one for day and one for evening, and one for summer and one for the more frigid months. Whatever scent you choose, make it your own and wear it every day.

Accessories

Mireille Guiliano describes her signature style as always looking pulled together with the help of two key accessories: scarves and necklaces. For someone else, it may be beautiful earrings and fantastic heels. Ines de la Fressange always looks well dressed, and her footwear of choice is a pair of flats.

Creating a Capsule Wardrobe: Why & How

When we feel confident about how we look, our mood is elevated, and when our mood improves, so does the environment around us. Many people assume that one must have endless cash on hand to build a spectacular, classically chic wardrobe, but they are wrong.

The key to creating a chic capsule wardrobe on a budget is to have a plan, and a little bit of patience. Yes, I know, having patience isn't all that much fun in the short term, but trust me, over time, if you are patient, your wardrobe will contain exactly what you want and need to wear, no matter what the occasion, and it will last for more than one season, which in the long run saves you money.

I don't know what everyone's budget looks like, so I'll use myself as an example. During my first half dozen years of taking home a teacher's salary, I was lucky to have $50 to spend on clothing each month. While my budget has increased a bit, those early years taught me to spend my money wisely, and I am forever thankful for the lesson, even though it wasn't fun at the time. (See, things do happen for a reason!)

Here are some key tips to follow to create a quality capsule wardrobe on a budget.

Mind Shift: What Does a Great Closet Look Like?

Carrie Bradshaw's well-stocked celebrity walk-in closets brimming with clothing and shoes unfortunately create an image in our minds of what we mistakenly believe good style requires. Pop the champagne now, because you can celebrate: You do not need such extravagance or endless options to have a quality wardrobe!

More does not mean better when it comes to living simply luxuriously, and that includes your closet. And as researchers have demonstrated, when we have too many choices, we become nearly numb and our decision-making skills are decreased. What does that mean? That we must become clear about the wardrobe and style we want to exhibit; we must create a plan and be resolute in sticking to it, so that the clothes we wear regularly look outstanding and will last.

Make a List

Now that we've cleansed our minds of the unnecessary hype of the overstuffed closet, it's time to get busy making a list. In this section, I lay out and discuss my capsule wardrobe (and later, in the section titled "Keep It Simple," I break it down for the seasons of fall/winter and spring/summer). When I made these lists, I needed to be honest about the lifestyle I lived (job, responsibilities, etc.), the image I wanted to project to the world, and my personality.

It is also imperative to understand what looks best on your body. Remember to choose styles that flatter your physical assets, but always keep three essential style basics in mind:

- Revel in your feminine figure—whether it is full, slender, boyish, etc.
- Know your skin tone and choose colors that flatter it.
- Dress in thirds, not halves. Determine the vertical halfway point on your body, then avoid creating a visual line there with belts or hems. Instead, go for a division into thirds, which lengthens the body and slims the silhouette.

Once you are clear on what makes your body and life unique, choose items that can easily be mixed and matched—skirts, blouses, bottoms, sweaters, dresses, etc. Choose a handful of colors that work for your skin tone and stick to them. For example, I am a navy lover, so I own a handful of navy items (skirts, dresses, scarves, sweaters, blouses), and that makes it easy to mix and match bottoms and tops throughout the week. Keep it simple. Always include neutral colors that work well with others (black, white, ivory, camel, gray, brown, navy), then selectively add one or two "pop" colors that work for you.

A capsule wardrobe does not include accessories, coats, evening/special occasion dresses, camisoles, lingerie, shoes, workout clothes, etc. It does include day-to-day uniform pieces—tops, bottoms, daytime/work dresses.

Do your best to keep your capsule wardrobe list to ten to fifteen items per season. And always keep a second list of accessories to complete your look—scarves, sunglasses, handbags, sophisticated special-occasion dresses, lingerie, sleepwear, jewelry, belts, hats, jackets/coats, etc.

One at a Time

A fundamental lesson — one that took me a while to learn on my limited budget — was that buying more doesn't mean I'm creating a better wardrobe. I may be able to purchase three tops with $100 and have three different options for a month, but usually the quality doesn't hold up; the tops don't make it through the wash/dry cycle successfully, and my $100 is gone.

What you purchase with the extra money you spend on a quality item is the assurance that it will look good each time you wear it — not just the first time.

The goal in creating a capsule wardrobe is to create a closet from which you can grab any item at any given time and feel confident that it will spotlight you and allow you to project the confident and beautiful woman that you are. When you purchase quality, this is the extra you are buying.

Begin by creating a list of the essential items you need (for my ten essential items, see below). Once you have your list in hand, slowly start shopping through it. Most likely, if you're shopping for quality items — which is what you should be doing if you want your wardrobe to last — you'll be able to buy only one item with $100, so investigate the item carefully, try it on, feel the fabric, and then take extra care of it at home. In a year's time (excluding fantastic end-of-season sales), you'll have twelve quality items. It doesn't sound like a lot, but you'll be thankful you were patient.

Purchase Quality Basics: Ten Essential Wardrobe Items

Very few times have the quality basics I've splurged on disappointed me or caused me to regret spending the money I handed over. I have been very well pleased with, for example, DVF's Maja Two dress in periwinkle, J.Crew's telegraph pencil skirt (I like them 27 inches long instead of the standard 23 inches), Laundry's white eyelet dress for summer, J.Brand jeans, and Eric Bompard's classic navy cashmere V-neck sweater. If you are willing to wait and save so that you can purchase items that are not trendy but timeless, you'll be excited to open your closet for each new season. You'll own pieces that you love to wear and that you don't have to purchase again and again and again.

By now you probably already have noticed that I am a "list" girl. I have created many wardrobe lists for myself based on books and magazine articles I have read, and I continue to edit and tweak as I gather new ideas. The first few authors that come to mind are Tim Gunn, Stacy London, and Nina Garcia, but there have been many more.

Below are my top ten wardrobe essentials, the fundamental pieces I have found to be the most versatile and most functional. They all allow the beautiful woman who is wearing them to shine. These are items you should invest in (that is, spend money on). For each, buy the best quality your budget allows.

Quality Jeans

A quality pair of designer jeans is more than worth the price. Not only will good jeans hug your body in the most flattering way, but you'll be wearing them for many years to come.

I am five-eleven, and as I mentioned earlier in the book, as a young girl I had a horrible time finding jeans that were long enough. Then I learned that what I needed was available but was going to cost a bit more. I soon realized that the things I would be paying for — garments of unquestionable quality that would last longer and give me a beautiful silhouette — were more than worth the price, and I saved up to be able to afford the more expensive jeans. I've never looked back. Some of my favorite brands for my figure are Citizens for Humanity, J. Brand, Rock & Republic, MiH, and Notify.

The versatility of jeans makes them a must-have as a wardrobe foundation piece. Expand your possibilities by including different styles. In my closet I have straight-leg and skinny jeans, including a pair to wear with flats and one with heels. And don't forget boyfriend, boot-cut, trouser jeans, and cropped or ankle jeans for spring and summer.

Trench Coat

Begin by purchasing a classic khaki trench that you can wear with jeans, dresses, and skirts for either day or evening. The flattering classic belt tie is a wonderful feminine component as it cinches your waist and displays your figure.

Once you own a khaki trench, you can branch out into colors (red, yellow, green, prints) or other classic tones (black, white, or navy). One of my go-to outfits is my dark denim straight-leg jeans, ballet flats, a blouse or classic T-shirt, and a trench. *Voilà!* I'm ready for just about anything.

Cashmere Sweaters

Whether you wear it with a dress, skirts, jeans, or dress pants, you can dress a cardigan or pullover cashmere sweater up or down, depending on the situation. A cardigan can be paired with a beautiful camisole or sleeveless blouse that shimmers; a luxurious cashmere V-neck sweater can be layered and accessorized with a beautiful scarf.

Let a cardigan fall open, or wrap a belt around it for a more cohesive look, and remember that lightweight cashmere sweaters can be worn in the spring and summer as well. Quality cashmere sweaters are worth the investment; they will last for many seasons, become even softer with each wash, and continue to hold their shape.

To ensure lasting quality, purchase at least two-ply cashmere (four- to six-ply for more warmth). Make sure it passes the touch test (in other words, is nice and soft); test it to see if it bounces back from your touch, and be sure it drapes beautifully but isn't so thin that you can see your hand beneath it. The majority of my cashmere sweaters are from France's Eric Bompard; they come in endless color options and classic necklines and are always available (be sure to note the French sizes and order accordingly). However, Ralph Lauren, Joie, Equipment, and other designers offer top-quality sweaters as well.

Dress Pants & Skirts

A pair of well-made dress pants in camel, black, gray, or tweed is a wonderful way to enhance the mixing and matching of the pieces in your wardrobe. There are many different styles to choose from depending on where you want the waistband to hit and how you want your legs to look. Wide trousers elongate your legs when paired with a slim-fitting blouse and belted waist. Slimmer legs allow you to pull off a very professional look when you pair the pants with a cardigan and blouse. Heels look wonderful with dress pants, very feminine.

Choose a style of skirt that flatters your figure. I am a tremendous fan of pencil skirts. Not only do they drape beautifully on many different body types (as long as you are willing to wear heels); they are also easy to find in department stores and boutiques in all lengths, colors, and prints.

Other popular skirt styles include A-line, pleated, wrap, trumpet, and tulip. When purchasing a skirt as a staple item, begin by choosing classic colors that can be worn with a multitude of different tops; camel, black, navy, and gray are all great for mixing and matching with the tops in your wardrobe. Or choose a print skirt to pair with a solid silk blouse.

Leather Jacket

You can include many different types of jackets in your wardrobe, but a short leather jacket is a versatile piece to have on hand. It allows you quite a bit of freedom as you pull together casual, yet stylish outfits; for example, pair a leather jacket with jeans for a weekend outing or use it as part of a casual dress ensemble.

Consider black, brown, camel, or even jewel-tone leather jackets. Always make sure that the jacket fits well through the shoulders and that the sleeves hit just below your wrist bone. And if you would rather not wear leather, there are many beautifully made faux leather jackets available.

White Shirt

Diane Keaton is a perpetual reminder of the seemingly endless ways you can wear a white collared shirt. Worn with skirts (knee-length or full), jeans, or dress pants, this is one of the ultimate versatile wardrobe items.

Not to worry if you don't wear the classic long-sleeved, buttoned-up design; there are many other styles—for example, a beautiful asymmetrical neckline, three-quarter-length sleeves, or capped sleeves.

Pair a white shirt with a skirt, accessorize it with a belt, and wear it to work. Or combine it with jeans, beautiful earrings, and heels; roll the sleeves up, leave the shirt untucked (if it is tailored), and appear effortlessly casual, yet chic. When you have this foundational piece in your wardrobe, you will be able to layer with ease and accessorize as necessary to create a long list of outfits.

Blouses

Your taste and lifestyle will propel you toward different styles of blouses—long-sleeved, short-sleeved, or sleeveless. You will want to have a few blouses in your closet. Again, pair them with jeans and skirts, layer them with cardigans or jackets, and enjoy the peace of mind that comes from knowing you can wear them to work or out on a date.

When you choose a silk blouse, you are choosing quality and versatility. Silk is exquisite to wear against the skin during the warm summer months, but it also keeps you warm when layered with suits and cardigans in the winter.

Nautical Top

Many essential wardrobe lists don't include a nautical top or sweater, but if you tend to choose casual over dressed up, you will want to include this item. When it's worn simply with a pair of ankle jeans and flats, it immediately elevates a woman's style rating because it looks so effortless but at the same time creative.

A nautical top is an absolute classic. One of my favorite summer outfits is my white ankle skinny jeans, a long-sleeved boat-neck nautical top, and nude flats — simple, yet guaranteed stylish and comfortable at the same time. And just because winter and fall come around doesn't mean you have to pack the stripes away. Beautiful nautical sweaters look and feel absolutely luxurious on the skin, and they keep you warm as well.

History of the Nautical Tee

An 1858 French law introduced the navy-and-white-striped knitted shirt called the *marinière* or *matelot* as the uniform for all French navy seamen. The original design featured 21 stripes, one for each of Napoleon's victories, in a distinctive block pattern that made sailors who went overboard easier to spot in the waves. It is typically made with a boatneck neckline. Later it became a favorite of workers in Brittany (Bretons) and thus is often called a Breton tee. When Coco Chanel introduced the design to the fashion world with her nautical collection in 1917, it became popular with the masses.

Versatile Black Dress

While the term "little black dress" (LBD) is more often used, I have chosen to refrain from including the adjective "little." Too many people take wearing a black dress as an opportunity to show lots of skin, which in my opinion detracts from the purpose of the black dress, which is to create a flattering silhouette of a woman's figure.

Always be on the alert for a black dress that calls your name. You never know when you'll come across something you can't imagine not having in your closet for those unplanned, last-minute occasions.

A sheath dress is a wonderful staple for either work or play. (A sheath is often confused with a shift dress. A shift is less fitted, while a sheath is more tailored to your figure; both hang to just above the knee.)

Choose classic black to fulfill the black dress mandate, or purchase that often overlooked classic color — navy. Any neutral, classic solid color is wonderful for the foundational dresses in your closet. You can belt the waist, add a jacket, or accessorize simply with a beautiful scarf or statement necklace.

Whether you purchase a black sheath dress, a black wrap dress, or a beautifully short cocktail dress with long sleeves, you are set to look amazing as long as the dress is tailored for your body and projects an air of mystery.

Wrap Dress

Diane von Fürstenberg has me hooked, and for a very good reason. The wrap dress again is an item with legs — in other words, mileage — when it comes to getting your cost per wear. A wrap dress can be worn in so many different settings and can be accessorized in so many different ways to meet your needs. Be sure to include one or two in your closet.

To purchase a quality garment at a fabulous price, watch for DVF end-of-season sales (December/January and June), and always choose one size larger than you would normally. Depending upon your body type, keep similar-colored camisoles on hand to wear beneath a wrap dress to avoid showing too much cleavage.

One of the wonderful side benefits of creating a quality, but simplified capsule wardrobe is that you won't feel you have to be out shopping every weekend. Instead, you can waltz into your closet, knowing that you have something perfect for whatever your day may bring and that you can enjoy any occasion without fretting about your outfit.

The Necessary Details: Shoes & Accessories

The right pair of shoes can make all the difference when it comes to completing a look. Candace Bergen has said that no matter what one's wardrobe costs, if the clothes are paired with good shoes, everything looks high quality. She makes a very sound point. As long as your clothes fit well and your hair and makeup are in place, the shoes can take the entire look to the next level.

Ten Essential Shoes

Here are the ten essential shoes I recommend every woman have in order to be stylishly pulled together, no matter what the occasion.

Ballet Flats or Loafers/Slippers. Once I realized how versatile ballet flats were for my lifestyle (work, play, errands, weekend, casual, travel), I quickly convinced myself to buy a few quality pairs—in nude, black, a bright color, or a print. I live in a few styles from Tory Burch (Reva and Eddie ballet flats) and Vera Wang, and I dream of wearing Lanvin. The price is worth it because they will last. (Remember cost per wear.) Ecco also makes incredibly comfortable flats for a reasonable price. The feminine and slim-fitting slipper (often called a loafer without the tassels) is also a wonderful flat style that is available in many styles, colors, and textures. I currently have Sam Edelman's Alvin in leopard, and I love pairing it with dark denim and black jeans as well as black trouser shorts in the summer.

Brown-hue Thong Sandal. When these have a few details or embellishments, they are perfect to wear in summer with ankle jeans, a skirt, or a dress. The past few summers I've been wearing a pair of Tory Burch's Miller sandals.

Classic Black Pump. A black pump is perfect for work with a wrap dress, sheath, suit, or trousers. Pointed toes tend to elongate your leg, and they work ideally with cropped pants, but either pointed or rounded will do, depending on your outfit. Nine West offers classic styles at very reasonable prices, but if you can invest in a pair of Christian Louboutins or Manolo Blahniks, you must add them to your wardrobe. One of my favorite pairs of black pumps is a pointed-toe Manolo pair I found at a consignment shop. I re-heeled them once ($10), and they look great and function fabulously.

Nude Heels. A treasure to be had. Whether with jeans or a dress or outfit of any color, this is *the* pump you want to have in your closet. Choose a round toe, pointed toe or a peep-toe; either way, I have a feeling you will fall in love. My most recent pair is from Stuart Weitzman — Nouveau nude, patent-leather, 4-inch, pointed-toe pumps. What I love most about them is that I can wear them with nearly everything. My dream pair is one from Jimmy Choo.

Tall Boot. Boots for fall and winter are a style must; we want to stay warm but still look stylish and pulled together. Ideally, have a pair of stiletto or wedge boots as well as flat bottoms, and have both a black and a brown or tan pair. There are many ways to wear a pair of stiletto or wedge boots — with a dress/skirt, wrapped around a pair of skinny jeans (perfect for day or evening), or with a pair of boot-cut jeans. And, as mentioned, it doesn't hurt to have a pair or two of flat boots for traveling and for those days when wearing heels doesn't suit your mood. And if you're wary of height, opt for a wedge, which is easier to wear and much sturdier than a stiletto but still offers a bit of height that helps elongate your legs.

Espadrilles. Another shoe that is fun for summer, can add height without the wobble if you opt for a wedge, and can be paired with capris, shorts, or a dress is the espadrille. Tory Burch has a pair, and Michael Kors's classic espadrille wedge works well with just about any wardrobe choice, but there are many other options available. Stop by Zappos to take a look at their seemingly endless inventory. Flat espadrilles are also an option with summer casual-chic attire.

Kitten Heels. The height these shoes provide is perfect for those days when you know and want to look feminine, yet have tired feet from wearing sky-high heels all week. A brand I've tried on and been impressed with while shopping at Nordstrom is Ivanka Trump's; she makes a very well-priced line of kitten heels in classic colors and leopard print as well. A dream pair would be Valentino's Rockstud patent leather sandals.

Evening Heels. Going out is the opportunity to be exactly who you are without any rules, so let your shoes begin the fun. Choose a designer classic black sandal or a more conversational sandal or pump with a peep-toe.

Wellies and/or Uggs All-Weather Boots. I tend to live in my Hunter wellies during the spring, when I'm out in the garden or visiting local nurseries to select annual plants for my yard. The choices that are available make it all the more fun. Currently, I love my yellow boots, and I just added a packable navy pair to keep in my car for trips to the Oregon coast.

Booties, Ankle Boots, or Shoe Boots. A few years ago I fell in love with the bootie. In black or nude (and so many other options — think leopard!), it is a fun alternative for the fall and winter when you want to cover more of your foot but have the feel of a fabulous heel. Sticking to a budget? Choose Sam Edelman's or Calvin Klein's. The sky's the limit? Have a look at Lanvin's.

Accessories and Handbags to Always Have on Hand

The power of the right accessories is amazing. For me, shopping for accessories has been a learned skill, but as I gradually became aware of what items each of my pieces of clothing could use and what would balance and complete my wardrobe, I became much more adept at accessorizing. I've become a tremendous fan of the creative challenge of searching for an ideal and true-to-my-signature-style accessory with every shopping outing.

A few of the ways to learn what works best for you when it comes to the accessories you'll purchase are to *first*, experiment — try it on in the store and imagine it with pieces you have in your closet at home. *Second*, let fashion magazines be your guide. Notice how stylists have put together ensembles. Not only are they skilled professionals, but they are working with items that are available in stores at the current moment. *Third*, ask a store salesperson how they might accessorize a particular outfit. This doesn't mean you have to buy what they suggest. I've worked in a retail store, and since I was a lover of fashion myself, I just assumed most customers knew how to accessorize or organize a particular look for themselves. What I learned was that even if they did, I knew the store and its merchandise and could offer suggestions and ideas. I was better equipped to direct them quickly to something that would be flattering and thus eliminate frustration. Don't be afraid to ask for guidance.

Think of these accessories as you strive to complete an outfit:

- *Belts* — Own a variety: skinny, large, corset, etc.
- *Scarves* — Buy large silk scarves in prints or solids depending on your dress, blouse, or coat, and cashmere and/or other wool scarves for winter.
- *Earrings* — Have fun with chandeliers and teardrops, but also own simple earrings and stylish hoops.
- *Watches* — Ideally, own two styles and/or colors so that, regardless of your outfit, the watch completes the look. Options to consider — *type of band*: leather or metal; *size of band*: skinny, thick, etc.; *color*: black, brown, white, gold, or silver; *fit*: traditional or bracelet (often you can size them at the boutique for free).

- *Broaches* — They are perfect for changing the neckline of a blouse or dress (Oprah and Sarah Jessica Parker have mastered this technique), or for arranging a scarf, or just placed as an accent on a jacket or coat.
- *Necklaces* — Think proportions and statement pieces. A simple black sheath dress can look different each day if you pair it each time with a necklace that makes a different statement.
- *Hats* — Fedoras, straw sun hats, newspaper boy caps, berets. Have fun trying them on, and notice which ones make your facial structure pop.
- *Cuffs or bangles* — Adding a gorgeous, oversized cuff to your wrist is a simple way to make a classic solid dress or look rise to the next level.
- *Handbags* — With each year of my life and after donating or tossing too many cheap handbags to count, I am more convinced than ever that quality is the key to the handbags we bring into our lives. If you are purchasing a classic, stylish piece, do yourself a favor: Investigate the design and color you want and save up for it. The three stylish handbags you will need to always have at the ready are a tote for work, a clutch for evening, and a top-handle handbag for day to day. Another quality item to keep your eye out for is a luggage tote for your weekend getaways (more about this in chapter 9).

How to Pull Off a Sense of Effortless Style

The way the world reacts to how you wear an ensemble can open doors, create opportunities, and help make life a dazzling adventure. Never let yourself down, or let the world down, by not living up to your style standards.
— Nina Garcia

Kate Moss, Lauren Hutton, Alexa Chung, that woman you saw at the café on your trip to Paris—they all seem to have pulled together their look without batting an eye, as though they did it by instinct. How do you achieve this appearance of effortless style? When it's something you see in a magazine, a stylist has done the work. But you've seen them just as I have when you're out shopping, dining, vacationing—women who look spectacular (in, for the most part, classic styles), yet have pulled themselves together in a way that looks effortless and exhibits their unique beauty. Here are a few ways to hone and refine your very own effortless style.

Use Fashion as a Tool, not a Remedy

With each new season, new fashions are displayed in stores and boutiques, and it is imperative that a woman understand that fashion cannot fill a void. Putting together a wardrobe of depth takes a passion that only you can truly find within yourself. If you've had a terrible day at work and feel that going on a shopping binge will make you feel better, if only for a moment, you really aren't doing yourself any favors. In this instance, you are allowing shopping to suppress your feelings of frustration at work. When you go shopping, make sure you are doing it with the sole intention of loving the process. Don't allow it to become stressful or emotional because that is when you will make decisions you will regret.

Know Your Body

Each season trends emerge, but a woman who is able to see through the trends and instead can see what will work in her wardrobe for the long term is heads and tails above the majority of the shopping population. If you have a curvy figure, you will recognize immediately that a full skirt won't show off the true beauty of your body like a sheath dress would. Every woman has her assets that she needs to focus on. Make sure your purchases reflect your uniquely beautiful physique.

Choose Classy over Trendy

Speaking of trends, think of them as you would a simple summer T-shirt. Most likely it will last only one season, and while it will make a statement immediately, it will date you next year. Don't spend too much money on superficial trends, because these are perpetually changing. Instead invest in classics that will add depth to your wardrobe.

Invest (and Save)

As long as you have the funds, purchase quality. This is always the best idea as long you are certain you will wear it again and again. I always look at it this way (keeping in mind my finances): A Diane von Fürstenberg wrap dress I've had my eye on is $400, but I know I'll be able to wear it four to six times a year, so the price in my mind automatically drops. (This is the cost per wear idea, as mentioned in chapter 3). If in the dress's lifetime I wear it ten times, it is a $40 dress. What a deal! And most likely, I'll wear it much more than that, which makes it a steal. Quality items are worth the investment because they stand the test of time and continue to look fabulous.

Can't Stop Thinking about It?

This last piece of advice has no scientific backup whatsoever. But here goes: If, twenty-four hours after you've tried on a piece of clothing you are still thinking, dreaming, and imagining yourself wearing it to certain events, go back and purchase it. This relates to a very important point in deciding what to wear—you really need to love what you are wearing.

If you combine all of these approaches, you'll project increased confidence in how you look, and when you feel confident, it shows. Confidence cannot be faked—well, at least not very well.

But I think that is why those women you so admire with the camel coats, suede booties, boyfriend watches, ankle pants, and

classic clutches are so mesmerizing—they make it look easy. And
the reason it appears this way is because once they've decided what
they're going to wear, they know they look great because of how
they shop and approach the idea of style. Once you've put the outfit
on, you should be able to relax and do whatever your day demands
of you without having to worry about your clothes.

So here's to *being* that woman you once only admired. Before
you know it (and many of you have already reached this point),
people will be impressed with your effortless style.

Keep It Simple: Focus on Fifteen

Many women become overwhelmed by the choices fashion offers
and become frozen into not shopping at all, instead wearing the
same clothes until they are threadbare. Others purchase far too
much; in their effort to always look perfectly styled, they break their
budget.

The simply luxurious approach to building your wardrobe
centers on the ten wardrobe essentials discussed above, divides
them into two seasons, and for each season focuses on just fifteen
pieces of clothing (including multiples of skirts, pants, tops, etc.).

Why, you might be wondering, would someone want to limit
their fashion purchases?

- It forces you to be very clear about what does and
  doesn't work with your figure, signature style, and
  lifestyle.
- It allows you to purchase and create a high-quality
  wardrobe that lasts for more than one season.
- It saves you money. You aren't being persuaded by the
  stunning blouse in the window that you had no intention
  of buying when you walked out the door.

Inspired by Jennifer L. Scott's book *Lessons from Madame Chic*, I downsized my closet for the peace of mind and the relief to my budget, and as a way to create an even simpler way of living well.

Before you begin creating your seasonal capsule wardrobe, answer the following questions (my answers immediately follow):

- What roles do I play on any given day? High school English teacher, lifestyle/fashion blogger, doggie mama, aunt, friend, significant other.
- What celebrity style do you most want to emulate, and how would you best describe that style? Sarah Jessica Parker, Ines de la Fressange, Charlize Theron, Jennifer Aniston—chic, classic casual.
- In the past, what was I wearing when I was at my most confident? Pencil skirts, heels, dresses, well-tailored jeans/trousers, simple, classic color choices that flatter my skin tone.

As you move through the process of creating your seasonal capsule wardrobes, keep in mind your signature style, but now refine it further based on your answers to these three questions.

Once you have identified the style that makes you feel your best and the clothes and shoes that work with your daily demands (for example, if at work you are expected to be involved with a lot of movement, perhaps you don't want to wear as many skirts or dresses, but rather look for quality trousers and jeans), start thinking about your ten wardrobe essentials. Determine the seasons each would fall into (some will be versatile), and focus on adding these pieces to your wardrobe and discarding the rest (hold a yard sale, take the garments to a consignment shop, or exchange with friends).

You may be wondering whether shoes count in the fifteen or less rule. What about workout clothes, lingerie, coats, special occasions, etc.? The simply luxurious wardrobe that keeps the number of clothing items per person to fifteen or less does not include coats, blazers, dresses for special occasions, lingerie, camisoles, accessories, shoes, or workout clothes.

Here are examples of my seasonal capsule wardrobes:

Spring/Summer

Cotton pencil skirts (1 beige, 1 navy)
White cropped jeans
Navy cropped trousers
Ivory lightweight cashmere sweater
Nautical top
Silk blouses (1 striped, 1 print, 1 solid)
Shorts (cotton and linen)
Jeans (boyfriend and cropped)
Summer dresses (2)

Fall/Winter

Wool and lined-cotton pencil skirts (1 black, 1 camel, 1 navy)
Cashmere sweaters (1 navy, 1 ivory, 1 color or gray)
Silk blouses (1 long-sleeve, 1 capped-sleeve)
Straight-leg jeans (dark denim)
Black skinny jeans
DVF wrap dresses (2)
Sheath dresses (1 black, 1 navy, 1 gray)

As you can see, it's simple. The focus is on items that will last, paying no mind to trends. It's very easy to mix and match these items, and don't forget that accessories can help change the entire feel of an outfit.

Our lives are already overwhelmed, and while I have a great passion for fashion and am enthralled with each New York Fashion Week, knowing I don't have to find the money to purchase every obscenely priced item that catches my eye lets me breathe a sigh of relief. It is possible to love fashion and not be a slave to it, as well as to not love fashion but still respect the power that comes with being well-dressed.

Become a Savvy Shopper

Those who can indulge exclusively in top designer duds are few and far between — and, in my opinion, they are missing out. A savvy shopper, no matter what her budget, mixes and matches and often doesn't buy many, if any, top designer items because of their lofty prices.

But the fashion magazines and blogs do have a purpose: They preview the styles that will be in the stores, and they demonstrate how to bring items together to create stunning and inventive outfits.

On a different note, a savvy shopper is also someone who makes a list, sticks to her monthly budget, and waits until end-of-season sales (December/January and June/July) to find a bargain on those black leather knee-high boots she's had her eye on since August.

Once you know the styles that look best on your body and how to pull together outfits, take the time to shop your local consignment, vintage, or secondhand store. A savvy shopper can mix and match the high and the low. No one needs to know that paired with a chic $100 silk blouse is a skirt that was only $15.

Why Not . . . Shop Consignment?

Designer labels. Exquisite fabric. Beautifully tailored garments. You might think such clothing will be out of your reach if you stick to your budget; however, the luxury of owning top-quality clothing is possible when you shop at consignment clothing stores.

The struggle (and the pleasure) of shopping consignment is that it takes time to find items that work well in your closet, but finding that perfect pair of J.Brand jeans at $69 instead of $189 is a lovely reward for the fiscally smart woman, as well as the fashion lover.

It Saves Money. While it would be wonderful to be able to hang designer items in our closets regularly, paying for them without reaching for our credit cards is impossible for most of us. However, when you shop consignment, you can purchase designer clothing at greatly reduced prices, and staying within your clothing budget each month promotes sound sleep at night.

It's Eco-Friendly. When I purchased my first pair of black Manolo Blahnik pumps from a consignment boutique in Seattle, I tweeted about it to my followers. The first comment was not an ecstatic one about finding the shoes; instead it congratulated me on being environmentally friendly. Since then I've read about the book *Overdressed: The Shockingly High Cost of Cheap Fashion*, and I'm now convinced that if I can wear something that has been previously owned but is in good condition, I am helping the environment in a small, albeit somewhat selfish, way.

You'll Find Top Designer Items. Shopping consignment is a fantastic way to add value to your wardrobe. Here are a few of the treasures I've found — a Carolina Herrera khaki summer dress reduced to $299, Christian Dior black knee-high boots marked $210, Chanel handbags for $500, a Vince sweater for $30, and a Stella McCartney cashmere sweater for $199. Not all of these items made their way into my closet, but they were available in the consignment shops I frequent. My point is that you don't have to pay full price for designer clothing if you're willing to go hunting and be patient.

The Selection Is Fantastic. Finding many labels in one location instead of having to pop into boutique after boutique for each individual designer saves you time and headaches.

It Helps You Create a Signature Style. At a traditional department store or boutique, you are able to purchase only the current season's styles. In a consignment shop you may have multiple years to choose from. You can create a unique wardrobe that is unlikely to be duplicated as the items aren't as widely available as they once were.

You'll Be Seasonal and On Trend. Whenever I stop in at my favorite consignment shops, whether in spring, summer, fall, or winter, I know that the clothing on the rack will coordinate with that season. And since the owners and staff stay on top of current trends, I'll be more likely to find items that work in the current fashion environment (aside from classics). Consignment shops offer choices that will work in most women's wardrobes.

When to Splurge, When to Save

You've gotta have style. It helps you get up in the morning. It's a way of life. Without it you are nobody. I'm not talking about a lot of clothes.
—Diane Vreeland

Whenever I receive sample-sale reminders in my e-mail in-box, my shopping instinct kicks in, and I get excited. Who wouldn't, when the top design houses offer an opportunity to purchase potential investment pieces at shockingly reduced prices.

However—and this of course applies to all of your shopping—you must decide what is worth spending still a very pretty penny on and what is not.

The key to keep in mind is that your foundation pieces, the skeletal system of your wardrobe, should consist of quality fabrics and tailoring. These items, if you want them to go the distance and always look fabulous, are going to be pieces that will cost more but that will be worth it in the long run. (Remember cost per wear.)

On the flip side, it's okay to scrimp on items that you'll wear for just one season and never pull from the closet again, or faux pieces that look just as striking as the original but don't break the bank.

Below is a list of items to save up for and items to not break the bank over. As always, though, there are exceptions, so I have made a list of limbo items that might go either way, depending on the situation.

Splurge/Investment Pieces

> Jeans
> Dresses/skirts
> Suits
> Sweaters (cashmere)
> Coats/jackets — winter and all season
> Shoes (work, flats, boots)
> Dress pants
> Couture
> Bras
> Handbags

Limbo

> Panties
> Sneakers
> Exercise clothes
> Classic button-up shirts
> Pajamas
> Vintage
> Scarves
> Jewelry
> Swimsuit
> Shoes (occasional)

Save/Trends

> T-shirts
> Belts
> Hosiery/socks
> Shorts

Lingerie: A Perfect Opportunity for Luxury

As a teenage girl growing up in America, the message I received regarding lingerie was much more focused on wearing it for others than on wearing it for one's own pleasure and enjoyment. However, reading Jamie Cat Callan's book *Bonjour, Happiness!* gave me an entirely new perspective on why women should wear luxurious lingerie every day of the week, specifically for themselves (the French approach), and not feel guilty about it.

With my shift in perspective, a few years ago I stopped in to a lingerie boutique in Portland, Oregon, and immediately noticed a difference in the fabrics, the subtle details in design, and the fit of the garments. It was not cheap, but the lingerie I purchased that day is still with me and in wonderful condition. As a Valentine's Day present to myself each year, I try to invest in a couple of additions to my lingerie wardrobe. I love knowing I am wearing beautiful lingerie, even if no one else sees it. Keeping a few wonderful secrets to ourselves is always a good idea.

Why Not . . . Wear Luxury Lingerie?

Below are a few specific reasons you too should consider wearing luxurious lingerie every day of the week.

Feel Beautiful. The value of lingerie should be first and foremost to the woman who wears the garments. If along the way there are fabulous side effects, all the better. When you wear lingerie that is beautiful, fits properly, and feels comfortable, you begin to feel beautiful no matter where your daily routine takes you.

Help Your Wardrobe Shine. When you choose the right pieces, you help your clothing hang properly. Good lingerie optimizes your beautiful figure, smoothing, lifting, and narrowing where needed.

Boost Your Confidence. When you feel beautiful, your confidence gets a boost. When you wear lovely lingerie to work, to do errands, and for other everyday business, as well as out on dates and wherever your life takes you, you possess a quiet self-confidence that can't be taken away.

Keep the Romance. When a woman feels confident, takes care of herself, and loves her body, that attitude carries over into her personal life. Having a healthy feminine side is quite attractive; it helps keep the romance alive, no matter how long you've been with your partner.

Every Day, Not Just for Special Occasions. Again, I want to reiterate the importance of wearing quality lingerie every single day. Choose to care for yourself, revel in the body you've been given, and treat it well.

It may take time to build up your lingerie wardrobe. Think about purchasing a bra and briefs pair every Valentine's Day, birthday, or half-birthday, regardless of your relationship status. Consider this a gift to yourself that is richly deserved.

Remember: When you purchase quality lingerie and care for it properly, it can last for quite some time. And always know that you are worth this splurge as you save up for your next purchase.

When Shopping for Lingerie . . .

. . . keep these things in mind.

Know Your Correct Size. Bra sizings at department stores and boutiques are usually free, so if you aren't sure if the bra you're wearing fits properly, ask for help in determining your correct size.

Choose the Color Wisely. Match bras and briefs. You will always want to have nudes and blacks on hand for everyday clothing, but have fun with color too, depending upon the mood or the energy you want to convey. Think about color as a way to boost your mood.

When You're Wearing White. For some reason, this rule is sometimes forgotten, but if you are wearing white blouses, T-shirts, jeans, skirts, dresses, etc., always make sure you wear bras and briefs that match your skin tone for a flawless look.

Make It Your Style. Choose what works for you, flatters your figure, and makes you feel beautiful.

Choose Quality over Quantity. As you begin to build your wardrobe, the only way to ensure pieces will last and always feel comfortable is to purchase quality lingerie. While garments may look good in ad photos, pay careful attention to the finish, edges, and seams. Feel the item, and see how it feels against your skin. I can say from experience that there is a tremendous difference between wearing Victoria's Secret lingerie and quality French lingerie made of silk. The latter is going to last and feel wonderful each time it is worn.

Caring for Your Lingerie

Once you have selected the perfect lingerie for your lifestyle and wardrobe, keep your investments in tip-top condition by caring for them properly.

- ✓ Wash by hand in cold water.
- ✓ Use Woolite or an equally gentle laundry detergent.
- ✓ Dry flat.

Pulling It All Together

The key to creating a successful wardrobe is having a plan and not being intimidated by the latest fashions strutting down the runway. One essential element is gathering information on each season's fashions and deciding what will work best for you.

As an avid list maker, I keep notes on items I am looking for (capsule items to be replaced, accessories that would be perfect with a particular outfit) and carry it with me in my planner. This way, when I am shopping I can look for pieces that will add real value to my closet and increase my outfit-building options.

Remember, finding your style and expressing who you are to the world on a daily basis should be something you look forward to.

Why not do it with a conscious approach, a respect for yourself (your body, your lifestyle, your needs), and an understanding that shopping is not something to feel guilty about if you do it in moderation and within your budget.

Street-style bloggers are the new darlings of the fashion media, and the latest trends become available hours after they walk down the runway. Thanks to sites like Moda Operandi, seasonal trends are old before they are even new. But what about the shopper who is simply trying to purchase pieces that flatter her figure and who wants to build a lasting signature-style wardrobe?

The *Wall Street Journal* recently commented on the "overexposed" state of fashion and noted that, in response, the concept of wearing an item that is a few seasons past its birth date is actually becoming more feasible and welcome. Why? Nobody wants to be wearing the same thing as the next stylish person walking down the street. We all—especially those of us who want to live in simple luxury—want to look our best at all times, whether that means wearing the latest trend or not.

How can we do that? How can we ensure we are looking our best regardless of what we catch a glimpse of in the March or September fashion issue? Here is what I've discovered.

Remember What Really Matters

While looking as chic and stylish as one of Rachel Zoe's muses every time we leave the house may be desirable, the reality is that even the people whose fashion style we admire don't look head-to-toe fabulous 24/7. The key is keeping straight in our minds what matters most—our behavior, attitude, and rapport with other people. After all, if our clothing rocks but our attitude leaves something to be desired, the clothes we wear don't really matter.

Find a Cobbler

Carrie Bradshaw may have had more than 100 pairs of Manolos, but we don't all need to have shelves of shoes to exude exquisite style. However, when it comes to shoes, do purchase the best quality you can afford. Initially it may be hard to spend $200 on a pair of leather ballet flats, but you will be able to wear them for years with them still looking like new and your feet won't hurt at the end of the day. Acquire the items on my "Ten Essential Shoes" list earlier in the chapter, then take care of them. Leather boots? Polish them seasonally. Worn-out heel? Take them to your local cobbler, who can re-sole them for pennies (my go-to guy resoled a consignment pair of Manolos for less than $15).

Keep a List

For any type of shopping, lists are a wonderful resource. They keep us focused and reduce unnecessary purchases. Keep a list of your capsule wardrobe items and the ones you need to add or replace, as well as accessories that would beautifully complement what's already in your closet. Take best advantage of sample and seasonal sales and their wonderful price reductions by knowing exactly what you want.

Ignore Trends, Unless . . .

. . . they work for you. Each season I do my best to help the subscribers to my newsletter navigate the trends and decide which to splurge on and which they can fantasize about but save their money. Why? Because so many trends (think peplum, cut-outs) date a wardrobe as soon as the following season rolls around and will not be worth the exorbitant price. On the other hand, leather and stripes can carry over from season to season if chosen properly.

Have a Tailor You Can Depend On

Not too long ago I ripped a seam in one my favorite trench coats. It was an investment piece, and I was not about to toss it aside, but I couldn't fix it myself. My local tailor repaired it in less than an hour; for less than $20, I had my trench coat back looking as if nothing had happened. Knowing you have a tailor you can depend on will give you the confidence to buy a piece that is perfect, except perhaps for a little fixable detail—pants that are too long, dress hems that should be nipped, or a top that needs an additional dart.

Shop Regularly Just Because

Especially if you shop consignment, but even for regular boutiques, department stores, and online sites, regularly shop the racks. You never know when an item you have your eye on will be discounted (often for a limited time or until it sells out) or when new items have arrived that will sell out quickly.

The Power of Quality

Over the past few years I have come not only to believe the mantra "Quality over quantity" when it comes to clothing, but also to live by it. I now have fewer clothes than I had before, but they are higher-quality items that I can wear season after season. I am still building my magnum opus, but I finally feel that for once I am actually making progress as opposed to taking one step forward and two steps back, as I did when I purchased cheaper items that didn't last. Be willing to save up and purchase quality items, even if it means purchasing just one or two items a month.

The Small Details

Shoes transform your body language and attitude. They lift you physically and emotionally.
—Christian Louboutin

When *Vogue*'s contributing editor Lauren Santo Domingo shared her best advice on clothes shopping, she placed high importance on the details—that is, on accessories. Shoes, belts, scarves, jewelry, handbags: All can change and elevate an outfit immediately. As long as your capsule wardrobe consists of classics that are easy to mix and match and that are of high quality, the accessories will make the entire look shine. Always be on the lookout for stunning shoes, quality bags, chic scarves, and statement-making belts or jewelry. It's a simple way to change an outfit you've worn for years.

Go through your closet and assess what you really need in order to enhance your capsule wardrobe, and decide what you can toss, what simply needs to be tended to, and what type of accessories to shop for. Then keep the list with you at all times. Before you know it, your very own magnum opus will begin to materialize.

CHAPTER FIVE

Creating a Sanctuary No Matter What the Size

Simplicity does not mean want or poverty. It does not mean the absence of any décor, or absolute nudity. It only means that the décor should belong intimately to the design proper, and that anything foreign to it should be taken away.
— Paul Jacques

Y our well-being begins at home. If you are not certain of anything else, you must at least be comforted by the knowledge that your home will welcome you, inspire you, and rejuvenate you for the next time you step outside. A comfortable, beautiful, and secure home is a key component of a simply luxurious life.

Make It Your Space

In every apartment, townhouse, or stand-alone home I have rented or owned, I have immediately set out to create a space that became mine. I was given the standard advice that I shouldn't paint my rented apartments, yet each time I signed a new lease I boldly painted every wall in every room before moving in my furniture.

My graduate school apartment had one red wall; I painted a dining room wall in the first house I purchased a deep chocolate, and my mother and I playfully applied a gold texturing technique to the living room and dining room walls of my apartment in the beloved Nob Hill neighborhood of Portland. I was required to either pay for the walls to be repainted back to their blah, off-white color when I vacated or paint them myself, but each time I harbored not one regret. Making the space I live in truly my own home has always played a significant part in my ability to relax there, and that was well worth the time and money I put forth.

Anytime you step outside your home, you are endeavoring to do something, to be something, to present yourself to the world. I strongly believe that you should always put your best self out there, whether as a professional, a friend, or someone involved in the community. We all know it can be exhausting to always be on your "A" game, and so your home should be the hug you return to at night — clean, secure rooms furnished and decorated to remind you about what and who you love and why you are trying to live the life you have chosen; a comfortable, clean bed for a sound night's sleep; and in the morning, once you are rested and ready, windows that let in the natural light that beckons you back out into the world.

Few of us have the budget to hire an interior designer, but that's not necessary. In this chapter, I'll share with you some easy-to-accomplish ways to create a welcoming sanctuary that is unique to you and what you value — simple approaches to creating a luxurious effect that will enhance your quality of living.

Why Not . . . Create a Sanctuary?

There is nothing I appreciate or look forward to more after a long day at work or when I come home from a vacation than crossing the threshold of my home and knowing that I will find tranquillity, peace, and comfort within my four walls.

No matter how many square feet we inhabit, living in an environment that comforts, soothes, and nourishes us is crucial to a balanced and energized life. So often the lives we live out in the world are busy, overscheduled, and demanding. We need a soft, safe, and soothing place to return to, a place that is truly our own.

Each person's best environment — the place that meets this need — will be different, but no matter what your aesthetic, you'll get very beneficial results from paying attention to a few basics.

Grab a Paintbrush

Study after study has proved that our brains respond to color, so be sure to choose colors for your living space that evoke a peaceful, calm feeling. You can always add splashes of color with the furniture or accessories you choose, but if you are going for rooms that will restore balance and peace of mind, your significantly large spaces (such as the walls and ceiling in the living room) should be fairly natural or at least neutral in color. (Yes, I realize I just mentioned I once painted my living room red; that was when I learned that too much color works against the idea of a calm refuge.)

There is a reason for choosing natural tones over bright, electric hues. While an intoxicating magenta may strike your fancy for a moment, in the long run it will be emotionally exhausting.

It takes just a trip to your local paint store, minimal talent with a paintbrush, and some patience to promote the tranquillity you seek in your home and life. If choosing the perfect color is somewhat intimidating, another option to keep in mind is to remain true to the "historical colors" that every paint line offers. Visit any paint store for information on what colors would look best in your space.

Use Natural Fibers

The five-star hotel bed and the picture-perfect room in *Elle Decor* magazine—what do these two scenarios have in common? Among others you could list, three that contribute greatly to creating a home that is a sanctuary are natural-fiber sheet sets, linen slipcovers, and cashmere throws. The soft and luxurious textures of Egyptian cotton and other natural fabrics help create a room that is appealing to the eye, and they are addictive upon first touch.

If you're on a limited budget, start with 100 percent Egyptian cotton bed linens. Overstock.com carries quality sheet sets in a wide range of colors for less than $50 (and shipping is less than $3); Amazon also offers reasonably priced sheet sets. Then move gradually to bamboo towels, and add a cashmere throw to snuggle in when you can treat yourself.

Natural Light

The more natural lighting, the better. If you're like most people, watching the changes of the seasons and Mother Nature's shifting moods is a reliable way to boost your mood. What better way to begin the day than with the morning sun streaming through a window? Natural lighting can have a tremendously positive effect on your outlook, so let in the light!

One reason I fell in love with my 1930s Normandy-style house, where I've lived for more than eight years, is the floor-to-ceiling picture window in my great room. Granted, the amount of fabric I needed to buy to make curtains wasn't cheap, but when I'm in that room, watching the day pass by or the rain spatter against the windows, the expansive view makes me feel less enclosed and secluded from the external world.

Do yourself and your well-being a tremendous favor, and do your best to rent an apartment or buy a house that has windows on at least two of the four walls in the rooms where you sleep, relax, and eat.

Tend to It

Cleaning the house or apartment is a chore we often do begrudgingly, but ultimately we feel rewarded and satisfied when we're done. To make it easier on yourself, try to schedule a time each week when you will do a quick run-through of your house or apartment, cleaning as you go. If you do it each week, you'll able to reduce the amount of work you do overall (in other words, don't let things get out of control or too dirty), and you will have a home that is always clean and welcoming. Visit the "Décor" page on my blog www.thesimplyluxuriouslife.com/decor/ for a specific and simple printable plan for keeping your sanctuary pristine without hiring a cleaning service.

If your time and energy are limited, block out ten or fifteen minutes a day for cleaning one room of your house or apartment. At the end of the week (sooner if your place is small), your entire home will be clean; plus, you will have gotten a bit of extra exercise every day.

Think about it: After a long day at work, when all you want to do is walk through the front door and relax, wouldn't it be nice to know you can look around your home and see a clean space? It's one less thing to worry about, and most certainly soothing for the weary soul.

Remove the Unnecessary

After the Great Recession hit in 2008, many people were forced to live with less, and what many have discovered is that simplicity is actually very liberating. After all, when you have fewer things to worry about, you are able to project your time and energy into more constructive and rewarding pursuits. While memories may be tugging at you if you've had to rid yourself of certain memorabilia, remind yourself that the memory will always remain, but the thing, the object, is just that — a thing.

Whether or not you're motivated by finances, the simple act of de-cluttering your home will allow you to take a deep breath, followed, if my experience is typical, by a sigh of appreciation. Once a year I make a list of all of the closets, pantry shelves, and drawers that I want to go through and "edit." Then I tackle one space at a time so the overall task of weeding out doesn't become overwhelming. After a couple of weekends, I have stayed on top of potential clutter and at the same time become aware of all that I do have. Sometimes after a cleaning blitz, I realize I have enough "treasures" for a yard sale.

Be Selective

Your home is your sanctuary, just as your body is your temple, so guard it, protect it, and be selective about whom you invite into it. You are probably shrewd about who you invite into your inner social circle; if you're smart, you gravitate toward uplifting, positive people. It's just as important to take great care in choosing the people you will allow into your home.

Americans tend to be easygoing about welcoming people into their private residences. In other countries — France, for example — it's a privilege to be allowed to enter someone's home and even more so to be permitted to wander beyond the living room.

Just because most people allow their guests to roam freely doesn't mean you have to if it makes you feel uncomfortable. After all, this is your sanctuary, your place to find peace, comfort, and reassurance after your time out in the world.

The Luxury of Living Alone

Did you know that more than 50 percent of American adults are single and 31 million (approximately one out of seven) live alone? In *Going Solo: The Extraordinary Rise and Surprising Appeal of Living Alone*, sociologist Eric Klinenberg hones in on this cultural shift, which is occurring not only in America but in most industrialized countries around the globe.

Those of you who are living alone and loving it probably aren't surprised by the numbers cited above. If you are living with someone and thinking about getting a place of your own, I'd like to encourage you by sharing the benefits I've experienced from living alone—by choice—for the past thirteen years. And if you're on your own and not yet at peace with the arrangement, perhaps my take on it will help you appreciate the pleasures it offers.

The first time I lived alone was when I was a sophomore in college; my roommate had moved back home for the summer, and I stayed to work. At first, not having someone around was daunting and threw off my sense of balance, but what I came to discover was that once I approached living alone with a welcoming mind-set and realized how much freedom I had to design my own life, I was giddy about the lack of constraints.

My roommate returned in the fall. The rest of my undergrad experience went quite well, and I enjoyed sharing my apartment with someone. But I had had a taste of the solo way of living, and I was a convert. I began to live alone in earnest in grad school, and I haven't looked back.

Here are ten benefits of living alone—why, at least at some point, you should give it a try.

You Become More in Tune with Who You Are

The security of your own four walls allows you to do as you please without being judged, and you are more likely to indulge in interests, activities, behaviors, and reading material you genuinely are drawn to, without editing. When your activities aren't being observed—everything from the music you find soothing and restorative to the magazines you subscribe to and the food you prefer—you relax more thoroughly and your true self eventually emerges.

Living Alone Can Strengthen Your Creativity

Choosing to live on your own encourages you to think about how you will design the life you want. If you love to cook, you can plan a festive dinner party; if you love wine, you might map out wineries and invite friends to join you for a weekend wine-tasting tour. You learn to look to yourself for ideas for entertainment and pleasure; you're no longer relying on someone else to provide these ideas.

Creativity also comes into play in how you decorate. I have had so much fun seeking out treasures at consignment shops and yard sales, following my own instincts and impulses and decorating my home according to my own vision. I have felt an enormous sense of satisfaction in seeing it come together just as I've envisioned it.

You Grow in Self-Sufficiency

In choosing to live alone, you are saying to yourself, I can do this. Over my years of living on my own, I have learned about taking care of my pipes, how to work with an old radiator system, how to decrease my electricity and water bills to stay within my budget, and much more. It's kind of like knowing how to change a tire. When you know you can take care of yourself, you stamp out a fear that may have existed, and your confidence gets a boost.

You Learn Fiscal Responsibility

Choosing to live alone is a sign of financial independence. Most elderly men and women prefer to live on their own and not with their children if they can afford it. Why? For one thing, they have more control to design a life that is conducive to their needs and desires.

Not only is living alone a sign of financial independence; it also teaches responsibility. You are the only one making sure your bills are paid on time and tending to the upkeep of your home. Stepping up and taking on these responsibilities brings a rewarding sense of satisfaction.

You Can Truly Relax

One of my favorite things to do after a long day at work, or when coming home after a few days or weeks away, is to fill my claw-foot tub with soothing verbena bubble bath, turn on soft French music, and melt. When you live alone, there is a peace of mind in knowing that your schedule within your home is your own. You don't have to wait for someone to get out of the bathroom, you don't have to shut out the blare of the television, and you can rest assured that if the kitchen was clean when you left, it will be clean when you return.

Living Alone Can Sharpen Your Focus

Whether it's a morning workout routine, the diet you are following, or the work you are trying to get done in your home office, living alone allows you the flexibility and solitude to be uninterrupted, reduce temptations, and erase most distractions so you can accomplish what you are trying to achieve.

You'll Strengthen Your Social Life

What Eric Klinenberg has discovered about people who live alone, versus those who live with a family, partner, or roommate, is that the former actually have stronger social lives. Why? Living alone prompts you to step outside to seek entertainment and activities outside the home and thereby meet more people. On a related note, social media makes it easier for us to stay in contact with friends and family without having to live with them.

A Solo Lifestyle Improves Your Emotional Well-Being

Having a place to lower all our defenses, let our hair down, and occasionally perhaps sing at the top of our lungs without fear of judgment is something we all need in order to keep our balance emotionally.

Living alone also allows us to stay in tune with what is truly going through our minds without distraction. As Twyla Tharp points out in her book *The Creative Habit*, it is when we are alone that we can hear our passions and respond to what they are calling us to do. It is when we have a sanctuary that is absolutely our own that living can be truly blissful and most fulfilling.

Living alone does not equate to being lonely. Any one of us could be in a room with a sea of people and still feel lonely. Ultimately, we control our thoughts and our attitudes, and that is what dictates whether we feel lonely or content with our own company.

You Can Create a Serene Sanctuary

We all need a safe and welcoming place to be when it seems nothing is going right, or when we need a place to just shut out the noise, the gossip, and the demands of the world, family, and friends. While it is possible to feel this sense of sanctuary while living with others, it can sometimes be more difficult. So when you live alone, at the end of a week of presentations, planning, and lengthy to-do lists, knowing you can come home to a place that will ask nothing of you except paying the rent/mortgage is quite comforting.

It's a Healthy Way to Set Boundaries

The decision to live alone saddles you with more financial responsibility, but socially and emotionally it makes it much easier to set boundaries. Whether it is your family, your friends, or even the person you are dating, having your own home draws a very clear line in the sand. The homeowner/renter dictates who is welcome and for how long.

In March 2012, Kate Bolick contributed an article titled "Divide and Conquer: Married but Separate" to *Elle* magazine (US) that explores the idea of living separately from your spouse in order to cultivate a stronger relationship. While I doubt that this is the domestic structure I will want if I choose to get married, Bolick's article contains some interesting ideas about why so many couples (mind you, they don't have children) are choosing an approach that might initially seem odd but that might actually, depending upon the couple, be quite beneficial and attractive.

Choosing to live alone is an exhilarating experience that I highly recommend. Some people may not be able to understand why someone would want to live alone or may even try to stigmatize those who choose this lifestyle, but it has real benefits. It takes strength to want to get to know yourself. It takes respect for yourself to desire to know what it is that truly makes you giddy and rejuvenated. Living alone gives you the opportunity to answer such questions.

Whether you choose to live alone for a year or thirty years, do it for the adventure and see what you discover. You might just come to find that there is a part of you that is waiting to shine and that you just needed some breathing room for it to burst forth.

Room by Room

Much like each pair of shoes in a woman's closet, each room in a home serves a specific purpose. The bedroom provides rest and privacy. The living room offers warmth, indulges an impulse to gather friends and family, and promotes natural conversation. The kitchen sets the stage for nourishment and good health. Decorating and furnishing each room in your home so that you can use it to its fullest potential takes time and attention, but when it comes to design and décor, more definitely doesn't mean better. Let me show you — room by room — how to create a sanctuary that is luxurious, but one in which you can simply and easily find comfort without unnecessary stress.

The Boudoir: The First Step to Creating a Beautiful Sanctuary

We spend approximately a third of our lives sleeping, so it is important that your bedroom (your most private sanctuary) invite peace and a restful night's sleep. Why not turn your bedroom into a welcoming escape, a personal sanctuary that luxuriously beckons you to dive into bed?

Materials for a Beautifully Made Bed. The first step in creating such a bedroom is to design and construct a beautiful bed. Here are my suggestions for the basics of a beautiful bed.

2 Euro pillows
4 standard pillows
2 accent pillows
A duvet
A beautiful silk or cashmere blanket
A favorite set of sheets made from Egyptian cotton (minimum 400 thread count)

Steps for Making Your Bed. Some mornings, making your bed, no matter how easy this is most days, is an accomplishment. But when you have five minutes, take the time to make your bed neat and beautiful so that you can smile when you come home at the end of your day.

1. Place your fitted sheet on the mattress as usual. Then lay the flat sheet over the fitted sheet. Tuck in each of the two long sides, but not the bottom, and execute the double foot fold (designed so that you can easily slide your feet in): Bring 6–12 inches of the bottom end of the sheet up toward the head of the bed, then fold it back over itself toward the end of the mattress, leaving "wiggle room" for the feet. There will be no sheet to fold under the end of the mattress because it has been folded on top of itself.

2. Fold the duvet and place it at the end of the bed.

3. Prop two Euro pillows up against the headboard.

4. Stack two standard pillows on top of each other (four total, two on each side of the bed), and place them in front of the Euro pillows.

5. Place two accent pillows in the front of the stacked pillows.

Other Ideas for a Tranquil Space. The bed is the essential piece of furniture in your bedroom, so design the room with the bed as the focal point. Choose a bed that will fit comfortably while allowing room for at least a small chest of drawers; if you have a large room, consider an armoire to supplement your closet space. Paint the walls a calming color (white, beige, soft blues or greens), and hang a few pieces of soothing wall décor. Use bedside lamps rather than ceiling lamps (unless you want a chandelier). A night table should hold just reading material and a clock; eliminate other clutter, and greatly reduce or completely eliminate the pieces of technology you keep in your bedroom. If space permits, it's nice to include a bench or an upholstered chair.

An Inviting Foyer: The First Impression of Your Home

The entrance is the first impression others will have of your home, so take time to create a clutter-free, functional space that also reveals a touch of your personality. Here are a few essentials that can help create an aesthetic that says who you are and welcomes your guests in comfort and style.

Rug or Runner. An additional layer over the flooring warms up the space and adds a personal, welcoming touch. It also protects the floor beneath.

Table or Small Console. A piece of furniture that fits into a small space, allowing for traffic, provides a place for incoming mail, keys, and essentials that need to be handy when you're heading out the door.

Unique Dish or Tray. On the table or console, place a catchall for anything you need as you dash out the door. Combine décor and function by choosing a bowl, dish, or tray that catches your eye and is large enough for keys, change, and other items that you use regularly but can lose if they're not put in a reliable place. Yard sales are a great place to look for a unique bowl; it probably won't cost much, and no one else will have one exactly like it.

Overhead Light or Table Lamp. You will be opening your door to people—sometimes ones you don't know well—so make sure you have ample illumination for safety, but not too much light, which could make your guests uncomfortable. Since you will typically need only one light source, invest in a lamp or fixture that is as beautiful as it is functional.

Mirror. Your foyer should be welcoming to guests, but most important, it should be functional for you. Hang a mirror on the wall so you can check your makeup and/or wardrobe one last time before going out the door. I have a four-foot vertical mirror made from beautiful old windows the landlord had ordered removed from my Nob Hill apartment in Portland. When I asked the contractor if I could have one of the pair of windows he was removing, he obliged, admitting he was keeping the other for himself. (Great minds think alike!) From there, my mother gave me the idea of removing the glass and placing a mirror inside the frame. My dad drilled two holes on either side so that it could be attached to the wall, and it has been with me, and hanging in my foyer, for eleven years. It's unique, functional, and a reminder of a period in my life that I thoroughly enjoyed.

Coat Rack, Hooks, or Coat Closet. You need a simple way to keep outerwear and other items of everyday clutter (dog leashes, umbrellas, shoes) out of the middle of the floor and off the backs of chairs. Everything has a place when you have something as simple as an easy-to-reach set of hooks.

Painting, Sculpture, or Hanging (optional). If you have ample wall space in your foyer, add a beautiful framed piece of art, or place on the table or sideboard a piece of sculpture that complements your décor. Another fun idea is to use a wall map of the world and place pins where you've traveled; you can make your guests feel welcome by inviting them to place a pin on a location they've visited.

Chair or Bench (optional). If you have space, a foyer greatly benefits from a bench or chair, which eases the removal of shoes, wellies, and winter boots.

A foyer is the perfect place to meld style with function. You can introduce yourself to guests without saying a word, ensure that they feel welcome, and most important, leave the house feeling organized and prepared for whatever the day may bring.

Your Own Private Spa

Real estate appraisers and brokers agree that a remodeled full bathroom will earn back approximately 60–70 percent of its cost when you sell your house or apartment. The only other major remodel that consistently gets these results is the kitchen. So why not turn your average, everyday bathroom into a spa-like retreat?

Whether you have a small or large space, and even if you are renting, making your bathroom a tranquil and inviting space promotes a calmer state of mind. After all, most people spend a significant amount of time there each morning and each evening.

Five years ago, I took on this challenge. I gutted my master bath down to the studs and remodeled it, and I couldn't be happier with the results. I had just seven feet by five feet to work with, but I was able to create a serene environment for putting on my makeup each morning and for pampering my skin before a restful night's slumber.

No matter how much space you have or what your situation is (I've painted many a rental bathroom in my past), we all are capable of sprucing up our bathrooms, whether by hiring a contractor or by picking up a paintbrush and making a few simple changes.

Here are fourteen simple steps you can take toward a luxurious and welcoming spa-like bathroom:

Paint or Wallpaper Walls in a Calming Color. Choose white with a soft undertone, or blue, yellow, green, or earth tones. If you'd prefer wallpaper, small rooms such as the bathroom are a great place to choose bold prints, but in a neutral color.

Keep It Clean. Each time you exit your bathroom, leave it as neat as possible. Wipe down the countertop and leave as little on it as you can.

Keep the Essentials in Organized Baskets or Shelves. Organize your lotions, beauty supplies, bubble bath, oils, scrubs, and loofahs so you always know where to find them. When you organize these items in pretty baskets, they serve as décor as well.

Eliminate Clutter. Create a home in drawers, baskets, canisters, and cabinets for as many items as possible. The less you place on the counter, the more tranquil the space will feel.

Add a Dimmer. When you want to soak in a soothing bubble bath, a simple way to soften the mood is to dim the lights. If you don't already have a dimmer in your bathroom, you don't need an electrician; it's an easy fix. Simply purchase a dimmer switch, turn off the electric current to that room, and follow the instructions carefully. Most likely you're handier than you thought!

Incorporate a Beautiful Scent. Not everyone likes candles or aromatherapy—after all, they become one more thing that sits on the counter—but you can bring in scents with the bubble bath you choose or with carefully placed flowers. To keep clutter at bay, perhaps just bring in candles when you want to take a bath.

Use Plush, Oversized Towels. A simple luxury is stepping out of the bath or shower into a warm, plush oversize towel. Pamper yourself and purchase a few. White is always my color of choice as it's easy to see when you need to launder them. Bleach as needed!

A Mirror, Framed or Hung with a Beautiful Ribbon. Add a soft touch to the mirror in your bathroom. Have it framed in wood or a style that complements your décor. If you want more femininity, hang your mirror with a satin ribbon.

Upholstered Furniture. If you have a large bathroom, include a plush, upholstered armchair, chaise, or bench to add luxury and warmth.

Hang Some Art. If you have space for a small table or chest of drawers, display a bust or a small sculpture. Hang a beautiful, unique painting, but be sure to frame it with glass that is humidity-resistant so that the image is protected.

Have Robes and Slippers Ready. A plush white cotton or luxurious silk bathrobe wraps your body in warmth after you leave the comfort of the bath. Don't forget a pair of cozy slippers.

Add Soothing Music. Set your iPod to your favorite playlist or radio station on iMusic or Pandora and lose all track of time. For me, the most relaxing music is instrumental, without lyrics.

Unique Bowls, Vases, or Stools. Visit local antiques or collector's shops, keeping an eye out for special items that will enhance your décor. Once my bathroom was remodeled, I was determined to find a wooden stool to place next to my claw-foot tub to hold a glass of wine or some reading material. While in Portland, Oregon, one weekend, I stopped at a collector's shop that specialized in Asian furniture and discovered a worn and rustic three-legged stool. I was glad I held out until I found this perfect piece; it was exactly what I was looking for, and it fit perfectly.

Bring in Plants or Flowers (an Orchid, a Bud Vase, Bamboo, etc.). Bringing in a touch of Mother Nature provides a balance of the clean and the natural. After all, when we step into a spa, we want to be brought back to our center; we want to find calm and eliminate all that is unnatural and not sitting well with our minds and bodies.

Be Creative in an Inspiring Office Space

As I imagined how I wanted my home office to look, I reflected back on the film *Something's Gotta Give*, in which Diane Keaton's character, a writer, ecstatically and emotionally finishes a play in her office overlooking the Atlantic Ocean. I also remember, as a child, visiting the home office of one of my friends' parents—a cozy space with a worn, tufted leather sofa, shelves of books, and a wooden chair on wheels tucked under a small desk placed next to a south-facing window. Others may not have been drawn to it, but for me it was intoxicating—the leather, the light, the books, and just enough space to get away from the world and do some solid thinking. I thought about how such a space could help a writer or planner become inspired and creative, how it could comfort them but at the same time challenge them to be greater than they ever thought they could be.

I'll admit, that is asking a lot of a small space in one's home, but like any room within your home, it needs to provide you with comfort, and an office in particular should be welcoming and inspiring in its aesthetic.

Each person will define her space differently based on what she needs in order to produce quality work. Below I present a list that is general, but at the same time gets at the basics (the bones) of a quality office. What you do with each element is up to you.

Make Wise Color Choices. When it comes to painting or wallpapering your office, choose colors that you feel are inspiring, not depleting. After all, this room has a very focused purpose; in it, you will create a product that reflects your best artistic or managerial abilities. Some may prefer a clean, streamlined color base (white or off-white perhaps); some may prefer neutral earth tones (taupe, chocolate, beige, etc.); others may want to be a bit more creative and colorful (yellows, greens, shades of orange). Whatever you choose, remember to consider the accessories and furniture you'll bring in; you might want to keep the foundation (walls, floors, etc.) calming and add color (if any) with photos, pillows, shelving décor, etc. In any case, let what inspires you and prompts you to create be your driving force when you decide on the colors in your office.

Create a Place of Inspiration. Once you've decided on the color of the walls, decorate them and the other surfaces in your office with images and objects that create a place of inspiration. Perhaps a bamboo plant or flowers. Is music a must in your office? Why not include a quality radio or dock for your iPod? As a writer, I need seating that is comfortable, whether I'm working at the desk or plopped down on the couch with my laptop. No matter what each of us does in our office, we all need furniture that is welcoming and soothing. Finally, whether it is a collection of framed photographs, a stunning painting from a secondhand store or an art gallery, or an idea board full of images, quotes, and beauty—what you view above your desk should stimulate your creative juices to do their magic.

A Perfectly Suitable Desk. Height, leg room, total counter space, and necessary storage space—all depend on the type of work you do on a regular basis. If you are an artist, you are going to want ample counter space to lay out your materials, but if you simply need room to type, a smaller desk may work just fine. Whether or not you adhere to the rules of feng shui, place your desk in such a way that you have visual command of the room. From where you are sitting, be able to see the door or entrance to your office; in other words, do not place yourself with your back to the door. Initially this may not seem like a big deal, but this orientation guarantees a high level of energy and command of the room, especially when you welcome someone to your office for an interview or meeting.

When It Comes to Technology: Quality vs. Quantity. Less is more, and while you may not think you can afford an Apple laptop or desktop, trust me, it is worth saving up for, especially if your work depends on using a computer daily. I recently upgraded from a PC laptop that I had used for three years, during which I spent just as much if not more for servicing than I would have on purchasing an Apple. Eliminate the headaches and purchase quality when it comes to the tools you depend on.

Open Space. In order for you to unclutter your mind and produce what you have on your to-do list, your desk must be free of unnecessary stuff. Use a standing file for paperwork you need at your fingertips; keep documents you will need infrequently—for reference, taxes, etc.—in a file cabinet or drawer.

Creative Trays, Pencil Holders & Caddies. When I explore yard sales I always keep my eyes open for unique dishes that can function as holders for pencils, my current reading material, business cards, etc. Right now, my writing utensils are stored in a milk-glass goblet. Using unique elements makes your desk original and attractive, and having something beautiful on your desk is both soothing and stimulating.

A Lamp. The best lamp is one that radiates the perfect amount of light. The fun part is choosing a lamp and shade combination that matches your design aesthetic. It always amazes me how so much personality can exude from just one small piece of necessary furniture. Remember, don't feel you have to use the shade that comes with the lamp. If you adore the lamp, purchase it, then shop for a shade that matches your preferred aesthetic.

Nature. Whether you choose to display a gorgeous bouquet of fresh flowers, a bamboo plant, or a bud vase with a single flower picked from your garden, having items fashioned by Mother Nature at your fingertips is sure to inspire.

A Comfortable Chair. A chair that supports your back and is comfortable is an absolute must when you're engaged in long stretches of work.

Bookends. A big desk that has room for a short row of necessary books benefits from gorgeous bookends, which have a function but also add a nice design element. When I redecorated my office recently, I discovered Marie Antoinette bookends on Etsy and had to purchase them. They speak to the Francophile in me, as well as the history buff, and they stimulate interesting conversations when guests inquire about them.

Love Your Efficient & Beautiful Laundry Room

Laundry rooms and mud rooms, while not gathering places, are frequently visited and are very useful for keeping the rest of the home clean and its residents looking put together.

Here are a few ways to create a welcoming and calming work space as you wash and dry your clothes, and iron and delicately wash other items that need special attention. These suggestions don't break the bank, but they do impart a luxurious touch that will improve your spirits as you go about these necessary tasks.

Choose a Calming Color. Paint the walls in neutral tones, or soft blues, greens, and yellows.

Add a Bouquet of Freshly Cut Flowers. The arrangement doesn't have to be perfect—in fact, the more haphazard the better. Use your laundry room as your place to experiment with floral ideas.

Be Prepared. For stains, that is. For a stain-fighting cheat sheet that prepares you for any accident that may come your way, google "Martha Stewart Stain Removal Basics," print off the handy PDF that is provided, slip it into a plastic page protector, and post it on the inside of a cabinet door.

Pre-sorting. Use baskets or lined bins that are labeled according to types of clothes that can be washed together—whites, reds, darks, sheets, etc. This will save time and eliminate accidents.

Creative Décor. The laundry room is not typically a place your guests will visit, so have some fun with your décor. Perhaps prints or paintings that evoke a raised eyebrow or a deep belly chuckle?

Clear Canisters. Instead of having the orange Tide box on your shelf, why not place your laundry detergent in a beautiful, oversized glass canister? Use canisters for clothes pins, rags, fabric softener sheets, and other items as well. Target offers classic glass canisters in a variety of sizes at great prices.

Think Vintage. Hit the yard sales and scour the tables for antique wooden boxes, silver platters, and clear pitchers. For a minimal price, you can add creative storage and a touch of originality to your workspace.

The Kitchen: A Place to Relax, Create, Nurture

The kitchen truly is the heart of the home. It is where you are nourished, and where you can create, using your hands to feed those you love. But organizing your kitchen can be an intimidating task, especially if you didn't spend a lot of time "helping" your parents as a child. And even if your mother, father, or grandparents did introduce you to the magic that can happen in the kitchen, pulling this room together on your own can be a somewhat daunting proposition.

Full disclosure: I am obsessed with the Food Network and The Cooking Channel. On Saturday mornings, if I don't have other plans, I look forward to letting my imagination run wild while Giada blissfully saunters around her modern kitchen and Ina Garten asks the question "How easy is that?"

Thus I can attest that cooking becomes easy with practice. The most luxurious dishes can be quite simple when you have the right tools in your kitchen—though not too many—and recipes that you're comfortable with. (See chapter 11 for a few of my favorite simply luxurious recipes.)

No, I still cannot flip an omelet like Bobby Flay (I am determined to keep trying, though I keep a mop nearby just in case). But I have learned that herbs make a tremendous difference; that lemon, garlic, and shallots should always be on hand because so many recipes seem to call for them; and that cooking at home will save money and trim your waistline.

The following sections provide a list of supplies you will need in both a cook's kitchen and a baker's kitchen. People sometimes classify themselves as either a cook or a baker. However, learning to be both will ensure you are prepared no matter which recipe tempts your taste buds.

What is the difference between a cook and a baker? There are many ways to distinguish the two, but for the purposes of the two sections that follow, a cook is anyone who creates all three meals—breakfast, lunch, and dinner (but not desserts or morning pastries). Cooks are free to adjust the amount of ingredients (more salt, less lemon juice, etc.) to create the taste they prefer. On the other hand, baking pastries, breads, and desserts requires precise measurements.

The advice in the two sections below will outfit you for nearly any traditional task required of you in the kitchen. The first list, for those who call themselves cooks, contains supplies and necessary utensils for a successful cook's kitchen.

Cook's Kitchen Utensils

The short and simplified advice that follows will set you up to prepare a gourmet meal if necessary.

Good-quality Cookware. Investing in good, heavy pots and pans—such as those from All-Clad, Le Creuset, Sur la Table, and Cuisinart—will help you cook foods more evenly and speed up the cleaning process. Items to include in your set: at least two saucepans, one small and one medium-sized; a large soup pot/Dutch oven; a small skillet with a lid; a large skillet with a lid; and a tall pot for boiling pasta water.

Sharp Quality Knives. Sharp knives are safe knives. A dull knife can be dangerous because it doesn't slice where and when we want it to. We then apply more pressure and sometimes slice something we weren't intending to slice—for example, my left thumb, twice; after the second time, I bought a knife sharpener and it's never happened again. I like Smith's sharpeners, which are inexpensive yet effective. As for which brand to purchase, the Barefoot Contessa uses Wüsthof cutlery, but every chef has his or her preference. Currently, I am using and loving Wüsthof. Before you buy a knife, visit a housewares store to see if the grip is to your liking. A high-quality all-purpose knife is an investment that will last for years, so take it for a test drive.

The Fewer the Gadgets, the Better. All you really need are a food processor (which shortens lengthy prep time to seconds); a micro-plane or box grater; a simple, handheld lemon press; and a blender. When you have fewer gadgets, you have more counter space to work on and cleanup is quicker. Remember: Your goal is to create a simply luxurious kitchen, one that is high functioning, but streamlined.

Necessary Handheld Tools. The essentials to keep within reach are heatproof rubber spatulas; measuring cups for both liquid and dry ingredients; measuring spoons; tongs with rubber bottoms; a whisk; a sifter; a fine-mesh strainer; kitchen shears; wooden spoons; a colander; a large pasta fork/tong; and a basting brush.

A Beautiful Set of Ceramic Mixing Bowls. In *The French Kitchen Cookbook*, Patricia Wells recommends using only white ceramic mixing bowls. They allow the kitchen to look organized even in the midst of a mess, they can double as serving bowls and still look chic, and they match everything. Mosser Pressed Glass offers a quality nesting set that will look beautifully streamlined on your shelves.

A Few Sheet Pans (Baking Sheets). Keep at least two baking sheets (also known as half sheets) on hand for making bruschetta, roasting vegetables, and preparing simple weekday dinners. Why two? Because inevitably, one will be in the dishwasher when you need to make a quick appetizer. Be sure to line the sheet with parchment paper or aluminum foil for quick cleanup.

Aluminum Foil. You'll need foil for covering roasted or grilled pieces of meat or fish after cooking and allowing them to "rest" (reabsorb juices and flavors). I also place it on my baking sheets and ceramic baking dishes to make for easy cleanup.

Thermometers. You'll need three: an oven thermometer to make sure your oven is at the correct temperature (makes a crucial difference); an instant thermometer to test meats; and a candy thermometer to test hot oil for frying.

You'll find many more utensils at your local kitchen store or chain store, such as Sur la Table or Williams & Sonoma, but the list above keeps things simple while providing the basics for creating luxurious meals for yourself, your family, or dinner guests.

A Baker's Kitchen

Dessert lovers, why not create your own delicious treats and impress your guests? Bakers find it easy to entice people into their kitchens. Nothing is as sweet as the scent of freshly made bread, an apple pie hot out of the oven, or chocolate chip cookies warm and begging to be enjoyed. Here's my list of must-have items for the baker's kitchen:

- KitchenAid standing mixer. This is an investment, but it will last your lifetime and probably your granddaughter's as well. I recommend the tilt-head mixer instead of the bowl-lift mixer; the tilt-head makes it much easier to add ingredients.
- Hand mixer. For making whipped cream or for those small batches of cookies for which you don't need the KitchenAid mixer.
- Sifter
- Fine-mesh sieve
- Food processor (for making pie/tart/scone dough)
- Pastry frame (for rolling out pastry or bread dough with ease)
- Rolling pin
- Silpat non-stick baking mat
- Cookie sheets/half sheets
- Springform pan (for cheesecakes)
- Large and small tart pans (with removable bottoms)
- 9x9 glass/ceramic baking dish
- Icing spatulas
- Graduated mixing bowls (ceramic/glass)
- Stainless-steel ice cream scoop (for perfectly sized cookies)
- Pie dishes
- Cake pans
- Ramekins and/or flan dishes
- Bread pans
- Muffin tins (large and small)
- Measuring spoons and cups
- Double boiler
- Wooden spoons
- Whisks (large and very small)

- Cake pedestals (for a fabulous display)
- Scale (for precise baking) — optional

Cooking and baking can be very pleasurable when you have tools that make the job easy. Nothing is more frustrating than dull knives and needing to mix everything by hand.

One of the easiest forms of therapy for me is to make a meal in my kitchen. Even when it seems the day hasn't been productive and nothing has gone according to plan, when I know I can come home and create a delicious meal, and pair it with a luscious wine that is waiting to be enjoyed, I am able to breathe a bit better and relax into the evening, knowing that I accomplished at least one wonderful thing before the day's end.

Create an Outdoor Oasis

There is nothing quite like hanging your laundry on a clothesline to absorb the scent of the outdoors or stepping out your backdoor and picking fresh tomatoes off the vine or cutting fresh basil for a salad. The naturally beautiful scent of homegrown fresh basil always awakens my senses after a long, cold winter.

While most of us aren't able to create the lavish outdoor spaces we see in magazines such as *House Beautiful* or *Elle Decor*, we can still spruce up a miniature version of our own where we can dig in the dirt for some free therapy on the weekend or gather friends and family around a table to enjoy a BBQ on a cool summer evening. Or we can establish a nook in the lawn or on the porch where we can sit, relax, and watch the sun set after a busy, yet fruitful day. Here are a few ideas to help you create an outdoor oasis:

Less Is More. Lawn furniture, that is. Place two Adirondack chairs side by side on the best spot on your lawn and lounge there in the afternoon with a good book and a glass of crisp Chardonnay, or perhaps grab a nap with your feet up on a matching ottoman.

Create a Small Garden. A garden needs to be only the size of a small guest bathroom (5x7 or 5x12), and you can plant only those vegetables that will, for the most part, take care of themselves as long as they are watered regularly. The key is to enhance the soil (natural fertilizer is best). Then place your plants in the soil after the last freeze.

Build an Herb Garden Close to the Kitchen. Whether you plant herbs in the garden, give them their own separate bed, or put them all together in one large pot or on a windowsill planter, this is a wonderful way to bring the flavor of the garden into your everyday meals, and it will save you money.

Hang a Clothesline. Not only will you be saving on energy, but your sheets and clothes will smell like summer.

Find an Outdoor Table at a Local Yard Sale. Choose one that can stand the weather and fits in with the outdoor style you are going for.

Hang Pre-planted Baskets. Choose flower baskets that strike a balance with those in your ground-level beds. Then Mother Nature's beauty will be everywhere you look when you step outside.

Plant Annual Flowers That Simply Make You Smile. Choose sunflowers, pansies, begonias, or anything that strikes your fancy. Just make sure to place them where they will survive — in the right spot for the sun and shade they need.

Add a Few Perennials Every Year. Before you know it, you will have created a reliable display of beauty for spring, summer, and even fall.

Now Enjoy It. Turn the television off in the evenings and step outside, sit in your chair, and just soak in the quiet beauty.

Organizing & Simplifying Your Sanctuary — and Your Life

Having an organized home to return to each night is a tremendous boost to your mood. To keep things simple and luxurious, set up systems that keep you and those in your household organized for both regular and unexpected occurrences.

While some people may enjoy the adrenaline rush of hustling to get things done at the last minute, I consider such intensity unnecessary stress. If you will be patient and disciplined and do the necessary work ahead of time, the result — a thoroughly and beautifully organized home — will be much more satisfying.

Use a Planning System

Whether you are a techie or old school, it is important to choose a planning system that works for you. Those who enjoy technology may keep their entire daily, weekly, and monthly schedules on their smartphone calendars. Personally, I love my Franklin Covey planner, in which I can write down, cross out, and doodle at any given moment. If you're looking for an app that allows you the feeling of accomplishment that comes with crossing to-dos off your list, try Any.Do.

Whichever method you choose, have a system in which you write down your daily to-do list and upcoming appointments. This will relieve your mind from having to remember it all so that you can be in the moment. Each morning, before the day begins, I look at my agenda to see what I have in store, and each evening I look ahead to the next day and plan how I will make it all work.

Important Documents

Create a filing system to organize all your documents—your bills, invoices, insurance policies, financials, etc. Whether you have a filing cabinet or drawer in your house or a simple filing tote (which works great if you're just getting started), organize it, with folders and tabs, in alphabetical order so any document will be easily accessible when you need it.

Now that you have a place for your documents, what should you keep and for how long? Following the advice of *Consumer Reports*, I stick to the following:

Keep for a Year or Less
- Bank records (remember most banks now have online statements on file)
- Credit-card bills
- Current-year tax records
- Insurance policies
- Investment statements
- Pay stubs
- Receipts
- Monthly bill receipts (create an easily accessible file for "bills to pay"; when you pay the bill, write the date on the receipt and file it)

Keep for a Limited Time
- Household furnishings paperwork (warranties, instructions, etc.)
- Investment purchase confirmations
- Loan documents (keep in a safe-deposit box until loan is paid off)
- Savings bonds

- Vehicle records (title, registration, and receipts should be kept in a safe-deposit box; all maintenance information can be kept at home)

Keep for Seven Years
- Personal federal and state tax returns
- Necessary receipts

Never Toss
- Keep in a safe-deposit box: essential records such as birth and death certificates, marriage licenses, divorce decrees, Social Security cards, and military discharge papers
- Estate-planning documents
- Life insurance policies
- Defined benefit plan documents
- Safe-deposit inventory

Have a Hard Copy

In our ever-more-technological world, more and more people are going completely paper-free. And while this is very environmentally friendly, you should keep a hard copy of a few documents:

- Contact information—addresses, phone numbers, etc.
- Passwords and usernames
- Important documents saved on your computer

Having a backup hard copy of your most important information and documents will give you peace of mind and, depending on the circumstances, may spare you the stress of spending time and money to re-create them.

Save Time

One simple thing you can do to save yourself time and avoid running late is to designate a spot for your keys and other essentials (sunglasses, purse, coat, umbrella, etc.) you need when you step out of the house. Be on the lookout for a unique bowl or dish to place on your foyer table and always drop your keys there as you walk in the door. Or create a nifty key hook system.

Whatever system you set up, get in the habit of leaving your most important items in the same place every time so you don't waste valuable time looking for them.

Have a Toolbox Handy

This tip is absolutely mandatory for someone living on her own, but even when you are married or living with someone, I highly suggest having your own toolbox. My mother still has hers, and she doesn't have to rummage through my father's gadgets to find what she's looking for. Purchase a simple small toolbox to hold the following: screwdrivers (flat and Phillips-head), a hammer, needle-nose pliers, a wrench, nails, hooks, twine, electrician's tape, heavy-duty glue, and anything else you might need; also have your own electric drill, which may not fit into the toolbox. Having your own tools means you'll be able to take care of minor repairs around the house without depending on someone else.

Drive Happy in a Clean Car

If you commute in your own vehicle, keeping your car clean, free of clutter, and inviting to any passengers makes spending significant portions of your day with your hands attached to the wheel more enjoyable. Just for a moment, think about your car as a mode of public transportation. How do you prefer the subway, bus, or train to look when you step on board? "Clean, sanitary, and free of garbage and clutter" is my answer.

Each time you park your car in the garage, take everything with you that you brought in that morning, even if that means extra trips. Plan monthly vacuuming, exterior washes, and upholstery cleanings, if necessary; if you have children or dogs who tend to leave reminders of their presence, place a towel or seat cover over your seats to protect them. When you are traveling, keep a portable garbage sack wrapped around the back of your seat or console, and empty it regularly at rest stops.

Do It Now

One of the easiest ways to keep your home, car, and office clean (thereby eliminating the need for massive periodic cleaning sessions) is to pick up after yourself as you go about your day. Take your dishes into the kitchen and place them in the dishwasher after each snack or meal; put away the mail after it arrives (in either the recycling bin or its appropriate file); fold up the blanket after you take a nap; make the bed each morning; leave the bathroom clean after getting ready to go out—little actions like these, which take maybe two or three minutes, save you from needing to do major cleaning blitzes, and your space is always tidy and pleasant.

Make Your Closet Helpful

Often the part of my routine that slows me down in the morning (but also the one I enjoy the most) is deciding what I'm going to wear. The decision making may be difficult, but you can make it easier on yourself by organizing your closet by colors and styles (blouses, skirts, trousers, dresses, etc.). Once you know what you want to wear, you will know exactly where to find it. Just be sure that at the end of the day, you remain organized by putting items back in their proper place. The same goes for belts, scarves, jewelry, and shoes (organize by color and heel height).

De-Clutter: One Room at a Time

Whether you are just learning to become organized or have been that way your entire life, you need to address the inevitable clutter of unwanted material that inevitably accumulates, especially if you aren't living alone. No matter when you decide to clear out and organize, I highly suggest you take it one room at a time.

If you don't rush, you will clean more completely and not make hurried judgments about what should stay, what should be donated, and what should be tossed.

Once you've organized each room in your home for the first time, subsequent bouts of de-cluttering will be much easier. You'll probably find you'll be less likely to keep things you don't need — you will edit as you go. In any case, take your time. And hey, if you finish one room early and want to start on your second room for the day, go for it.

When tackling each room, take everything out of the closet, off the shelf, and out of the cupboards, and thoughtfully decide which category it should fall into — keep, donate/yard sale, or garbage. If you aren't sure, here's what I suggest. Place any items you can't make your mind up about in a box. Write the current date on the outside of the box and then store it away. After a year, when you happen upon this box and realize you haven't missed anything that's in there, without looking inside, donate it or toss it or sell it — you clearly don't need it.

CHAPTER SIX

Good Health & Radiant Beauty: Look & Feel Your Best

The body is like a piano, and happiness is like music. It is needful to have the instrument in good order.
— Henry Ward Beecher

hen you feel good, you look more radiant. And when your body is running at its optimum level and you are allowing it to do what it is capable of doing, you feel more confident and are more likely to grab what is deservedly yours.

We live in an environment that makes it all too easy to be catered to: the drive-up windows, the frozen dinners, the enticing television shows and multiple reruns of our favorites (yes, I love *Murder, She Wrote* reruns, but why not watch them while you are on the treadmill?). And then there's technology — our computers keep us in our chairs for hours at a time.

While I would never wish away the amazing changes and evolution our culture has undergone, it takes a disciplined person to know how to balance all of the conveniences we are given. After a long day, the couch may be beckoning, but instead of stretching out in front of the TV, you can actually increase your energy for the next day by going outside and walking or running for twenty or thirty minutes. Not only will you see the benefits in the next day's work, you will have a much sounder night's sleep.

As a young girl, I was active in ballet, gymnastics, softball, soccer, and basketball. I am very thankful to my parents for enrolling me in such a variety of classes, as I thoroughly enjoyed participating in them. But beyond my enjoyment, they also gave me confidence in myself and made me willing to try new things — whether athletics or anything new and exciting that presented itself.

Fitness is a regular part of my life — one I can't imagine living without. It helps me to feel better, to de-stress and unwind. Your body is meant to move, and while there are some extreme ways to get physical exercise, the simplest daily activity can have a tremendous effect.

After being a successful athlete in high school and college, then becoming a step aerobics instructor and completing two marathons, I finally found yoga in my early thirties. During my twenties I had been quite certain that in order to look slender and be fit, I had to punish my body. At one point when I was a step aerobics instructor, I was working out five to six days a week for more than two hours at a time, and while I wasn't gaining any weight, I wasn't losing much either. As the body exerts itself, it needs fuel to replenish itself, and I was enjoying the eating part.

Once I tried yoga, I began to incorporate it gradually into my weekly schedule, practicing only once a week; I was still walking quite often, as I was training for my second marathon. After completing the marathon, I attended two yoga classes a week and shortened my walks, but I tried to walk almost every day because I have two spaniels who need to strut their stuff. I also noticed I wasn't as hungry but was still able to enjoy what I love to eat in moderation (including salmon, cheese, chocolate, and wine).

After a month of following this schedule, I accomplished a milestone that I had been unsuccessfully trying to achieve all of my adult life — dropping those pesky last 10 pounds. Standing at five-eleven, I finally reached my goal weight of 144 pounds.

Six Pillars of Lasting Good Health

The cycle of maintaining your health is a beautiful thing because as you choose to improve your health, you also improve your outer beauty and your quality of life — your skin glows, your decision making becomes more concise, you become more alert, and you rid yourself of unnecessary body fat.

One of the assured ways of living a richer and more enjoyable life is to take staying healthy seriously. Our body is a machine and must be paid attention to regularly.

View getting and staying in shape as a necessary appointment in your daily schedule. Write your workout agenda in pen in your planner and refuse to let another demand take its place. Do this with conviction.

What I realized as I segued away from a heavy workout schedule and marathon training was that I had been making it more difficult than it had to be. While achieving my goal of staying fit wasn't easy—it did and still does require constant self-discipline to watch what I eat and stay active—sometimes we get in our own way. In other words, when we choose to keep it simple and keep it consistent, amazing results gradually arrive and stick around.

I now follow what I think of as the six pillars of lasting good health (from which beauty of course follows). Here are my simple, tried-and-true guidelines:

Exercise for 20 to 30 Minutes Every Day. The Institute of Medicine suggests melding your exercise regimen into your daily routine. Simply taking between 5,000 and 10,000 steps a day is a wonderful goal. No matter which type of exercise or combination of types you choose, make sure you are challenging yourself, but not hurting yourself.

Eat What You Want but in Moderation. Brian Wansink, in his book *Mindless Eating*, says that the best way to lose weight is to do so mindlessly: "Our body and our mind fight against deprivation diets that cut our daily calorie intake from 2,000 to 1,200 calories a day. But they really don't notice a 100–200 calorie difference because they're not as sensitive within this range." His advice is to make three food trade-offs (for example, if I have dessert, I can't enjoy my lavender-honey dark chocolate truffle before bed) or new food policies (for example, never eat while driving) that will reduce your intake by 100 to 200 calories per day. The result? A year later, you will have lost 10 to 20 pounds.

Quality Food in = Health and Beauty. Garbage in = you get the idea. Cigarettes introduce toxins into your body, and so do processed foods. Eat only real foods. A good way to follow this advice is to eat only those ingredients you can pronounce. Stick to the outside aisles of the grocery store — fruits, vegetables, fresh meats, and artisanal cheeses and breads. Do your best to shop at your local farm stands or farmers markets.

Stay Hydrated. Water is simple, inexpensive, and calorie free. Make water your go-to beverage.

Sleep Six to Nine Hours Each Night. In 2007 the Sleep Division at Harvard Medical School determined that sleep should be treated as a priority, rather than a luxury. Sleeping "may be an important step in preventing a number of chronic medical conditions," such as diabetes, obesity, and hypertension, and in extending life expectancy.

Challenge Yourself, yet Enjoy. I tried just about every exercise before discovering that simple and less jarring is the best way to go. Running, kick-boxing, step aerobics, swimming, Pilates, tennis, volleyball, basketball — I have done them all, whether I was teaching the class, part of the team, or on my own. And what I have discovered is that walking and yoga have left me fitter and leaner than I ever thought I could be. Yes, yoga can be tough (and I no doubt could challenge myself more in class), but I see benefits not only in my fitness, but in my mental calmness as well. Find an exercise that can strike that balance — something that is challenging, yet rewarding, and enjoyable enough that you will want to stick with it.

These six pillars to lasting good health are points that most people are aware of. However, knowing something and doing something are two entirely different things, so I'd like to share with you some thoughts, ideas, and alternatives to regularly incorporating these foundational principles into your daily life.

The Mind-Body Connection: Shape Up Your Attitudes about Being Fit

The first wealth is health.
—Ralph Waldo Emerson

Think Health, not Looks. The beauty of this idea is that the looks part is the cherry on the top. It will come, but it will take time. So in the meantime and for all time, focus on improving your body for your health.

Respect Yourself, but Be Honest. Always respect and listen to your body. As my yoga instructor repeatedly reminds us, push until you are uncomfortable, but not until you are in pain. In order to improve we must do something more, yet do it gradually, while paying attention to what our bodies are telling us. The more in tune we are with that message, the better we will be able to take care of our bodies and thus ourselves.

Immerse Yourself in Your Passion & Get Happy. I sometimes look back on the times in my life when I gained a few pounds and other times when I magically lost a few. Both correlated perfectly with my state of happiness and contentedness: happy = weight loss/maintenance; not happy = weight gain. Instead of trying to find happiness outside of yourself, seek it from within and discover your passion. The MacArthur Study on Successful Aging revealed that being immersed in activities that we love has a profoundly positive effect on our longevity and the quality of our lives. Once you find out what activities those are for you, search for a way to enjoy them as much as possible.

Read *French Women Don't Get Fat,* then *The French Twist.* After digesting Mireille Guiliano's successful experience with merely walking as exercise and Carol Cottrill's experience with a long list of exercises before finally finding walking to be quite enjoyable and beneficial, I too finally realized it was more than okay just to walk, and I've never looked back. Thank you, Mireille and Carol!

Talk Positively about Yourself. You can reach the goals you have set for yourself. Be gentle, be patient, but be determined.

Accept Compliments. You truly are enough just as you are at this very moment, so it is imperative to filter out negative or hurtful comments and to not brush aside genuine compliments.

Surround Yourself with People Who Enjoy a Balanced, Healthy Lifestyle. The people who surround us have more influence on our lives — our habits, attitudes, and overall lifestyle — than we realize. When we are supported as we pursue healthy activities, we are much more likely to stick to them.

Weight Management without Deprivation

Food is a pleasure to be enjoyed throughout our lives, but food is not why we live our lives. On the other hand, it is important that we not see food as the enemy, but rather as a key element in achieving our best lives. As long as we understand what we are putting into our bodies — putting ourselves in the driver's seat and taking back the steering wheel from the advertisers and the weight-loss books — we can eat well without feeling deprived.

While we should not routinely devour a bag of Oreos, we certainly can eat a decadent artisanal *macaron* once or twice a week and not feel guilty about it. After reading *Salt, Sugar, Fat,* by Michael Moss, I became incensed by the science that the manufacturers of processed foods use to encourage customers to never feel completely full and to continue to crave more.

Ultimately, I became more informed about what makes up the food that surrounds us on a daily basis, and I was motivated to eat only real food. The good news is that I have never eaten more delicious and satisfying meals in my life. And the better news is that my waistline is looking its best as well. Yes, it is possible to eat well without deprivation, if we choose to become properly informed.

Let me get you started on the path to becoming informed. Like me, you can experience an "aha!" moment when you realize you can enjoy chicken marsala and a side of roasted vegetables, along with a glass of cabernet sauvignon and a scrumptious chocolate mousse for dessert, and not gain weight.

Forget Diets. First of all, a diet, by definition, is simply what we eat and drink, but the American dieting industry has turned it into the bad word that it has become — one that means "deprivation." Also by definition, any diet that asks you to change your way of eating in the short term is not going to work in the long run. Ultimately, it comes down to permanently changing the way we eat. We can enjoy just about everything we want, but in moderation and as long as the foods we eat fit the guidelines of a balanced diet.

Change Your Lifestyle. Clean out the cupboards. Toss the easy-to-eat processed snacks. Throw out the soda. In *Fit to Live*, Dr. Pamela Peeke explains that stocking our cupboards and fridges with foods that promote eating well helps us make healthier eating choices throughout each day. Hungry upon arriving home from work and haven't had time to go to the store? As you open your refrigerator, why not be greeted by sliced cucumbers, artisanal cheeses, and apples?

Eliminate Processed Foods. Whether you ascribe to a vegan, paleo, vegetarian, or any other particular eating regimen, simply refuse to eat anything out of a box.

Water, Water, Water. Drinking water regularly flushes out toxins from your vital organs, provides nutrients to your cells, and prevents dehydration so that you continue to feel energized throughout the day. The Institute of Medicine recommends "adequate intakes" for women of 2.2 liters (about 9 cups) a day and for men 3 liters (about 13 cups).

Three Meals & a Snack Are Enough. If you eat proper (healthy and balanced) meals, you'll find this is true. It is all about training your mind and your body. Books to check out: *Eating Mindfully* by Susan Albers; *Naturally Thin* by Bethenny Frankel; and *French Women for all Seasons* by Mireille Guiliano

Eat Your Veggies & Don't Worry How Many. The veggie snacks that I chop up and place in a container in my fridge for snacking include bell peppers, carrots, cucumbers, and radishes. Also, broccoli, fingerling potatoes, leeks, and brussels sprouts are easy and delicious vegetable side dishes for your everyday dinners and guests; I bake them, with a splash of extra virgin olive oil, salt, and pepper, at 375 degrees for 20 minutes. There will be no need for dip; you'll discover that olive oil and seasonings provide a delicious healthy favoring.

Almonds: An Easy & Simple Snack. One of my favorite afternoon snacks is a handful of roasted, unsalted almonds, half an apple, and a few slices of parmesan cheese, along with a cup of soothing black tea.

Eat at a Table. Enjoy the conversation or just your own thoughts or something engaging to read, but respect the ritual of enjoying your food. Refuse to eat while driving, standing up, or walking down the street. Eating is a pleasure that deserves to be savored.

Eat Local Foods in Season. When you eat fresh fruits and vegetables, especially in season (the times of year when they yield their harvest naturally), you are increasing the flavor that you get to enjoy without adding extra ingredients and unnecessary sugars. Pick up pears and brussels sprouts in the fall, asparagus and rhubarb in the spring, berries and tomatoes in the summer, and turnips and mandarin oranges in the winter.

Savor Your Food in Small Portions. When you savor your food, you slow down, and when you do this, you tend to decrease the number of calories you consume. It takes approximately 20 minutes for your mind to get the message that you are full, so take your time and let the message arrive. Enjoy your company and the flavors the chef took such care to incorporate.

Make a healthy lifestyle your lifestyle. Your body and mind will thank you. Hopefully what you will notice is that staying in great shape doesn't have to be a grueling endeavor. As long as you are consistent, challenge yourself to stay active, and eat moderately, the benefits of treating your body as the beautiful temple that it is will slowly reveal themselves.

Simple Beauty Routines

Life can become a chaotic roller coaster that sometimes you can't seem to control—unless you are organized. Organization is essential when it comes to finances, household tasks, and your career. It is also important when it comes to taking care of yourself.

I have always found it useful to figure out specific routines that I need to follow in order to help me feel my best, look my best, and limit unnecessary stress. I enter these routines as appointments in my planner, and I consider them just as important as balancing my monthly budget. They are a part of the foundation that strengthens my confidence and helps me put my best face forward.

When I have a hair, facial, massage, or pedicure appointment, I schedule my next appointment before I leave the salon. That way I am working face-to-face with the receptionist. It always helps to give yourself as many scheduling options as possible.

Below are the beauty routines I follow.

Daily
Morning
- Dry brush entire body.
- Moisturize body.
- Brush teeth and floss.
- Splash face with warm water.
- Moisturize face, neck, and décolletage.
- Apply primer.
- Apply makeup.
- Spritz on a scent.

Evening
- Brush teeth and floss.
- Use facial cleanser.
- Apply toner.
- Use a moisturizer (night cream).
- Apply eye cream.
- If your feet are dry, rub them with rich moisturizer and cover with socks.

Weekly
- Exfoliate face and body. I use St. Ives apricot scrub for my face and Eminence Coconut Sugar body scrub or a simple mixture of equal parts oil olive and sugar.

- Manicure (at home).
- Facial (at home—every other month I treat myself to a spa facial).
- Deep-condition hair (Keratase or Moroccan Oil hair treatment).

Every Other Week

- Pedicure. Twice a month, I give myself one pedicure at home, and if my budget allows, I'll treat myself to a spa pedicure every so often. I usually opt for nude with a hint of pink; it looks good with every outfit and elongates the leg. I prefer two coats and a top coat.
- Airbrush tan (a seasonal choice; while you certainly can use self-tanner at home, many salons offer a professional spray tan done by an esthetician).

Monthly

- Massage (a true luxury; only if the budget allows).

Every Six Weeks

- Eyebrow and lip wax.
- Haircut and color (sometimes every 8–10 weeks if hair is long or being grown out).

Every Two Months

- Facial at spa.

Every Six Months

- Teeth cleaning.
- Makeover at beauty counter to learn about new colors and buy makeup that has run out.

Yearly

Reassess and see how your schedule is working.

CHAPTER SEVEN

Dating, Relationships & Moving On

You have to figure out what you want for yourself before you can lock anyone
else into your dreams.
— Kristine Gasbarre

ach year as the holidays approach and families gather, the norm around the table seems to be coupledom, or at least an implied pressure for everyone to be paired up in some capacity. To be fair, not all families apply the same pressure or a constant barrage of questions to anyone who either doesn't arrive with a significant other or simply states that she is single, but there are still many families who feel it is fine to let loose with all kinds of questions, some extremely personal.

In defense of all those who are owning their singleness or as inspiration for those who may still be uncomfortable with it, I want to emphasize what Kristine Gasbarre says in her book *How to Love an American Man*.

Each of us undergoes our own process of figuring out what we want out of this gift called life. The answer is not something we are given when a diploma is handed out or when we turn a certain age. Instead, it is the end point of an arduous journey that we must travel until we discover what makes us tick, what stirs our passions, and what we can't live without.

Following Your Heart While Keeping Your Sanity & Integrity

Once we figure out where we want to place our energies for our own sakes, then we can be a partner with someone and committed to a healthy relationship. It is one of life's biggest mistakes to enter into a relationship believing that the relationship will fulfill us.

We must come to the relationship already fulfilled and content, knowing which direction we want to go in life. Communicating that honestly to your partner is the first step in building a foundation for the relationship — one that is strong because it is honest and based on your discovery of who you are as an individual.

This is not to say that the relationship won't provide its own fulfillment—it absolutely will. In fact, a solid relationship will enhance the fulfillment each person has created in her independent life. But in a healthy, lasting relationship, both people must know how to fulfill themselves independently, and so they must come to the partnership knowing what it will take for it to enhance their life.

While there is no guarantee that any given relationship will go the distance, why not put the odds in your favor and ease the burden or pressure you may be feeling. Instead of thinking you must be in a relationship, discover what satisfies you, what fills you up. The reality is that when you pursue what you love, you light up without knowing it; you gain confidence, and your energy is a magnet, drawing to you people who are also fulfilled in their own lives and are seeking the same in others. In other words, being content makes us more attractive.

As I look back on my younger self, I see with ever more certainty that I often wasn't clear about where I was going and what I wanted. How could I possibly have thought I could build a lasting relationship on such a shaky foundation?

The beautiful "aha" moment—the truth that I didn't know then but do now—arrived when I became clear about what fulfills me. Now I am comfortable talking about what I want and don't want my future to look like. Now I know that having my own space isn't an affront to the relationship, but a necessity to maintain my balance. Now I know that excessive gifts won't win my heart; what will is a trustworthy and loving person who is present.

Five Things to Stop Romanticizing

> *The essence of being human is that one does not seek perfection.*
> —George Orwell

Another essential step that is vital to success in relationships is letting go of the romanticized versions of love and life that

Hollywood, our families, our churches, and our friends have conjured up and that we have bought into.

Ironically, while most people agree that perfection is impossible to achieve, romanticized visions of perfection routinely appear in advertisements, fairy tales, movies and TV shows, even religious myth. I honestly admit to being a romantic and hope to never lose that point of view, but when we buy into a romanticized version of love while remaining ignorant of reality, we tend to get into trouble.

Here are five things to stop romanticizing:

The Perfect Relationship. Unlike in math, two negatives do not make a positive. In other words, two imperfect people do not magically make a perfect relationship. Without two healthy, happy individuals, there cannot be a healthy, happy relationship. And even when two secure, independent individuals enter into a relationship, there will be hiccups along the way as they begin to understand each other. The most important thing for a relationship is for both parties to respect each other and be devoted to the relationship.

Prince Charming/Cinderella. Prince Charming doesn't exist, so stop looking for him, and you are not Cinderella, so stop trying to be perfect and just be yourself. In other words, people are flawed. And because we are flawed, we have the opportunity to learn and grow endlessly if we choose to. No matter what your relationship status is, make it a daily goal to continually become your best self, and understand that others too are on their own journey of growth. The individuals you want to seek out are those who want to learn and are trying to be their best selves, all the while enjoying the journey that is life.

The Perfect Place to Live. Any chamber of commerce worth its salt will present their city, town, or region in the most flattering light possible. But there is no one perfect place to call home. While New York City may be the dream city to live in for many, others may find it difficult and unsettling. On the flip side, a small town such as Joseph, Oregon, (population approx. 1,700) may offer stunning views of nature but be too isolating for others. There is no one ideal place to live. And the only way to know where you belong is to step outside your front door and investigate. Fly to that city you've always dreamed about, breathe the air, step into the shops, meet the people, and walk the sidewalks. Then you will know where you belong.

The American Dream. The cliché of a white picket fence that surrounds a home in the suburbs, two kids, a blithely happy mom and dad and a dog — this idealized vision still sometimes slips into our subconscious as a safe decision, one that's accepted by society. And while this scenario may genuinely bring many people happiness, assuming it will bring happiness to all is just plain wrong. Your dream should not be dictated by anyone else. It should be shaped by what you value as most important and your ability to be authentically yourself.

The Definition of Success. While the dictionary says success is "the accomplishment of an aim or purpose," parents and even friends can, knowingly or unknowingly, exert pressure on you to earn a certain amount of money, to wear certain clothes, and to pursue the American Dream — a very strict definition of success. Contrary to such rigid assumptions, success should actually be whatever you deem it to be for yourself. Depending on where you've started and how hard you've had to work to attain the goal you've had your eyes on, a success that may appear small to some may feel like a ginormous achievement to you. And if you feel successful, then you are. No outside approval is necessary.

All five of these romanticized ideals affect us in some capacity. While each might be part of our lives at some point, the key is to not fall prey to the idealized versions. In order to not make that mistake, it is imperative that we understand the truth behind the facade. Because there is a facade, whether we want to accept that or not. Hollywood idealizes the perfect relationship in chick flicks, New York City is dressed up and sterilized in our favorite sitcoms, and fashion advertisements project visions of perfection and glamour.

Once we understand that there is life after the final scene, that walking in four-inch heels for twenty blocks is insanely stupid and painful, and that no matter how fabulous you look on the outside you must have intelligent thoughts to convey as well, then by all means enjoy a light-hearted Kate Hudson movie, dive into the Big Apple and fall in love, and wear those chic new Jimmy Choos. Because life is about chasing your dreams. They really can happen . . . but always remember to do your homework first.

The Most Important Ingredients for a Healthy Relationship

Nothing can bring you peace but yourself.
— Ralph Waldo Emerson

Between the movies that reach blockbuster status (*Jerry McGuire*, anyone?) and the ideals that are subconsciously (or consciously) impressed upon us by our families and communities, it can be quite easy to accept the myth that we must be with someone to feel "complete."

However, as I have learned, and as I know many of you have learned, if we continue to seek answers, continue to wriggle out of ideas that don't sit well with us, and try to understand why they don't and what does, we will realize that each one of us is all that we need to feel happy and fulfilled. This wonderful news comes with the peace of mind of knowing that we have control over creating our own contented and joy-filled life, but it also means we no longer have excuses.

If we seek out romantic relationships to make us feel better, to answer our questions, and to make us feel accepted, then what we are doing is placing our emotional lives in the hands of our partner.

And whether that person wants this control (read co-dependence, which is not healthy) or not (they shouldn't be burdened with the responsibility of making us happy, which is unfair), when we enter into a relationship expecting something that we should be doing for ourselves, we are limiting the potential of what the relationship could have been.

So how does a modern woman complete herself?

Be at Peace with Who You Are. This doesn't mean refusing to grow, change, and improve, but it does require self-awareness. When you attain an inner peace, you are better able to steer clear of jealousy and instead become excited for others' successes. You are also better able to determine who you should welcome into your life and who will serve no positive purpose.

Embrace Your Purpose. When you embrace what you want to focus your attention on and what you'd like to leave behind as a legacy, it becomes easier to take risks as well as to walk away from supposed opportunities that do not align with your purpose. Circle back to chapter 1 and reread the section "Discover Your Purpose." Find and embrace your purpose and you'll not only be helping yourself, but you'll become a better partner in your relationships.

Live Simply & Consciously. The main premise behind living a simply luxurious life is to rid your life of anything that does not contribute to a quality way of living, and to instead focus on welcoming excellence at all times. Consciously be aware of the thoughts you allow to enter your mind, the people you surround yourself with, and the consequences and/or rewards of each decision you make.

Learn How to Be a Friend First. Reflect on the characteristics of your strongest friendships. What makes them flourish? Don't immediately look at a potential mate as a potential mate. Simply behave as you would toward a potential friend—be honest and dependable, make small gestures, and carve out time for each other. Even if there is a sexual attraction, hold off temporarily as you come to get to know the person platonically.

Enjoy Regular Alone Time. The best alone time can be soothing, rejuvenating, and empowering. Regularly find time during your week or day (even if it's just fifteen minutes) to turn off (or ignore) all technology that alerts you to messages, tweets, etc., and just breathe, savor, and relax. The more often you treat yourself to these moments of respite, the more comfortable you will be with your thoughts. It's when we really slow down that we are able to become more in tune with what we desire, need, and wish for, and also what we need to address so that we can feel even more at peace.

Contribute Positively to Others. Children are often perplexed to hear from enlightened adults that the best gifts are the ones you give to others. But now that I'm an adult myself, I've realized this idea is, without a doubt, a gem of wisdom. When we hone in on what our talents are and use them to help, assist, or bring something positive into another person's life, the feeling itself is the best gift. And if you're lucky enough to find a career that incorporates your talents and contributes to society, you're well on your way to finding the best in yourself.

Cultivating Strong Friendships & Romantic Relationships

A young mothers group, bipartisan meetings of women members of the US Congress, Lean In circles for women daring to be ambitious, any healthy relationship between two people—what do these associations have in common?

First, similar experiences and interests have brought these people together. Second, if the group or rendezvous is to be defined as successful, then it means that those involved feel their presence is noticed, welcomed, and appreciated. Most important, there is a mutual understanding of the excitement, fears, and doubts that all parties involved have experienced or will experience, which helps reduce judgment and instead establishes genuine support and understanding. Such associations promote the true connection that Dr. Brené Brown, author of *Daring Greatly: How the Courage to Be Vulnerable Transforms the Way We Live, Love, Parent and Lead*, writes and speaks about.

Making Connections

Connection is the energy that is created between people when they feel seen, heard, and valued, when they can give and receive without judgment.
— Brené Brown

Connection is about more than just physical proximity. We can feel alone while we are in a relationship with someone, in a room crowded with people, and even if we have thousands of "friends" on social media networks. So where and how do we seek authentic connections?

First and most important, we need to understand the definition of connection. Looking again at the three situations just mentioned, it is possible to feel alone when you have a partner who doesn't hear you, when what you say doesn't ring true to a crowd of people, or when none or very few of the people in your social networks would notice if you "unfriended" them.

Brené Brown explains that science has shown we are hard-wired to seek social connections, though our desired levels of connectedness may vary. Brown argues that at the core of our desire for connection is a need to know that we exist, that we are loved, needed, and valued. And when, in our minds, we don't feel seen, heard, or valued, we suffer.

What Do Faux Connections Look Like? Like fur, connections can be faux. Here's how to tell if a connection is false: It is not going to be supportive or nurturing in the long run if you have to do any of the following in order to maintain it:

- Change what you believe, value, or are passionate about.
- Be agreeable all the time, even when you don't agree.
- Date or marry someone to erase the social "stigma" of being single.
- Have a long list of "friends" on social media, but no one to call on during times of trouble, worry, or emergency.
- Listen to endless talking by one party without a sign you are appreciated.
- Give endlessly in order to please — in other words, give without question because you have been made to believe you "should" do something as the price of being accepted.

What Do Authentic Connections Look Like? On the other hand, a connection is authentic when you know the following:

- Perfection isn't required.
- You have shared similar interests and passions.
- Having a differing opinion won't exclude you from the relationship or group.
- You trust the other party or person to show up, literally and figuratively.
- You can be yourself.
- You bring value to the relationship or group with your presence.
- Both parties give and receive equally and willingly.

Everyone connects with different types of people; however, within the weave of each of these connections runs a common thread. Take some time today to examine the relationships and groups you have been the most connected to, those you have genuinely enjoyed being a part of. Think about why.

Most likely, it was because you could truly be yourself; you could "let your hair down" and feel as though you were contributing something of value. A variety of people and groups come to my mind when I think about my most successful connections: my high school sports teams, my grad school cohort, my parents, my closest friends, my niece, my pets, my students in the classroom, my mentor of more than twelve years, a romantic relationship I was too young to appreciate, and currently the readers of my blog.

How to Find Authentic Connections

Now, the how. How do we find the authentic connections that we seek?

Be Observant. While at work, pay attention to those who appear to have interests or approaches that are similar to yours or who are experts in their field. In your personal life, be curious about events and gatherings, and say yes to invitations to events that you want to learn more about or already have an interest in.

Be Curious. Be brave and willing to introduce yourself and ask questions. Listen, and be authentic in your responses. When you combine an authentic representation of yourself and a discovery of your similarities with others, sparks ignite.

Be Authentic. Don't overshare or reveal unnecessary stories about yourself in an attempt to impress or connect with someone; people easily sense desperation. On the flip side, genuine interest clearly shines through in even a casual encounter.

Be Patient. When you're getting to know new people — someone you've begun dating or members of a group you've just joined — take your time to observe who they really are; try to interact with them in a variety of scenarios and over time. First impressions are all well and good, but follow-through should seal the deal.

Keep Your Word. In other words, be honest and forthright. Do your best to match your actions with your words. People remember what you do, so make sure it's worth remembering. There will be times when you have to cancel plans, but be honest about why, and do so as much ahead of time as possible if it's a relationship you want to encourage.

Be Vulnerable. As a relationship progresses, authenticity is required if the bond is to be strengthened. And in order to be authentic, we must remove, from time to time, the masks that we put on to protect ourselves. Take a risk and invite your date to join you in your favorite pastime; in a meeting with a trusted colleague, share an idea you were afraid to bring up in front of the whole department. When you reveal yourself, you discover how deep a connection can go and whether it will last. Reveal yourself gradually, and as you do, you will draw to yourself people with whom you can create genuine connections. As an added bonus, you will become more comfortable in your own skin.

Once we understand how successful relationships work, we can focus on strengthening the ones we already are a part of and seek out new ones that might bring even more value and enjoyment to our lives. And as we live with intention, our enjoyment in what we spend time doing grows and multiples.

How to Be a Good Partner

The purpose of relationship is not to have another who might complete you, but to have another with whom you might share your completeness.
—Neale Donald Walsch

Every relationship between two people is unique. Personalities, cultures, beliefs, interests, experiences—the possibilities in all these categories make for an infinite number of types of couples. However, certain foundational elements foster healthy, lasting relationships, regardless of the people involved.

Even when a relationship doesn't work out, wonderful things may have occurred. Most relationships we enter into will end at some point, and when they do, it doesn't mean wonderful, memorable, and loving moments and actions didn't occur.

After ending a relationship a few years ago, I went through the following thought process: I may not be in a relationship at the moment, but I genuinely want to be in one again, when I finally feel I am ready and able to be a good partner in a relationship. I may be too young to know everything about how to build a good partnership, but I know what hasn't worked and what has been lacking in my past relationships.

On the other hand, I know what did work and what made my past relationships times in my life that I do not regret. And I am fortunate to be around many friends and family members who are in loving, committed relationships, and I can observe them and bombard them with questions regarding how they make it work.

However, while I have cataloged such insights, I'm also diving into my dreams and loving my single life, which is richer than any relationship has ever been for me. I'm grabbing opportunities when they present themselves, and I find I'm not afraid to take the first step and create opportunities as well.

And when the opportunity of a promising relationship presents itself, I will be more ready than I have ever been in the past to apply the lessons I've learned.

Whether you are in a relationship or want to be in one someday, here are ways to become a better partner as you both work to create a healthy, loving, respectful, and lasting collaboration:

Be Secure within Yourself. When I was in my twenties, I thought I was ready for a lasting relationship, but something was missing: I wasn't confident I had found what I was passionate about. I was still searching; I was willing to move to chase it down, and I was feeling a bit restless. I hadn't yet found an outlet for my energies that made me feel I was contributing what I had to offer to the world. At the same time, I was still creating a foundation—a career, a home, etc.—and I hadn't yet figured out how to balance it all. Once I discovered an outlet for my passions and talents and an avenue to share them so that I felt productive at the end of each day, I discovered contentment. I began to realize I could live this thing called life, and live it well, though up to that point I hadn't been sure of myself. In other words, I finally discovered what I needed to maintain my balance and feel secure within myself.

Know How to Make Yourself Happy First. Once you feel secure within yourself, you realize you no longer project expectations of what you need onto your partner. In other words, you aren't looking to that person to make you happy. After all, it isn't their job. In a healthy relationship, two secure individuals come together. While each person is able to be happy individually, they realize that two already complete people can create something even more amazing.

Eliminate Unnecessary Selfishness. Once you have discovered how to create your own happiness, you can then focus on giving to your partner. This focus needs to take place on a two-way street. Both partners should delight in the euphoria of their partner's joy. "Unnecessary selfishness" is a very subjective phrase. Often one of the partners is too selfless and gives everything—contributing too much of their time and energy, letting go of their dreams—to support their partner. A healthy balance must be struck. When both partners are conscious of and sensitive to each other's feelings, dreams, and needs, they can pretty much eliminate the wrong type of selfishness. An example of selfishness that should be curtailed is telling your partner you are "too busy" to spend time together, to take a walk together, etc. While on the surface, the statement may be true, it also reveals to your partner their place on your priority list. Strike the right balance, and make sure your priorities are in order to help maintain a healthy, respectful relationship.

Be Honest & Trustworthy. Lies and omissions rot the possibility of true intimacy with your partner. Make sure you model how you would like to be treated, and then behave in a manner (whether you are with your partner or not) that is respectful to the commitment you've made to each other and that continues to build the trust you've already created.

Be Responsible. There are going to be good and bad days. There will be days when you get upset or become moody. After the emotion has subsided, take time to determine what caused you to become upset, and take the responsibility to state and face the truth behind your emotions. If your partner's behavior made you feel left out or as though you were a third wheel, say how you feel. If you feel your efforts are being taking advantage of and your partner isn't doing their share, talk about that. Such conversations aren't necessarily easy, but they are required if you are to create a stronger bond and truly understand each other's needs. Many times misunderstandings are simply that; at other times, they can be an opportunity to appreciate the other person more fully and get a better sense of what makes your partner feel comfortable, safe, and loved.

Be Appreciative. Showing your appreciation for the little things that need to be tended to each day is a simple way to strengthen your relationship. Making dinner, taking out the garbage, calling to say when you'll be home — these and other seemingly small actions demonstrate thoughtfulness and consideration for the other person's feelings and time.

Be Able to Apologize. If at some point you were grumpy or difficult and now realize your behavior was unwarranted, apologize. Take responsibility for your actions. No one is perfect, and at times people make mistakes, reacting emotionally instead of thinking rationally. When you take responsibility and apologize sincerely, you help build trust; you'll reveal that while you will make mistakes, you don't want to hurt the other person. Then make sure not to make the same mistake twice, because that's an entirely different issue that reveals lack of respect for the relationship and the other person.

Spend Quality Time Together. When the relationship you are involved in is a priority in your life, you want to spend time together, just the two of you. Socializing with others doesn't offer moments for intimacy or bonding. Make sure you take the time to just be together — a movie, dinner at your favorite restaurant, hiking, cooking meals together, or simply staying home and enjoying time relaxing.

Have Integrity. It is said that men fall in love with their eyes and women fall in love with their ears. While this is a generalization, I do believe that women want to believe what their partners tell them. However, I don't believe this desire is exclusive to women. Most people, when they hear what they want to hear, want it to be true. The key to any healthy, lasting relationship is that the two people involved must follow through with what they say. If you tell your partner you are going to do something, make sure you follow through. If you offer your help, extend your efforts as promised.

Be a Good Listener & Observer. In order to get to know and understand your partner, pay attention. Listen well to understand who your partner is, what they like, what makes them upset, and why; also be observant of how they respond in certain situations, what makes them comfortable, what makes them smile, what makes them nervous, etc. Often you can gain great insight simply by observing their behavior.

Don't Get Lazy in Love. In time, habits are created and expectations become second-nature about how and what our partners will do. However, don't assume the behavior you've become accustomed to will always be there. If you don't exercise the muscles involved in appreciation, love, and adoration, they will wither. Let your partner know they are missed when they are away on a work trip or you are gone for business. Count your blessings, and you will be sure to have more to count.

Build Sexual Intimacy. Foster it. Talk about it. Be able to trust one another so you can be on the same page with one another and fulfill each other's needs.

Be Committed. When you have learned and come to like who your partner truly is . . . and when you realize you are with someone who has similar values, has similar goals for the future, and loves who you are (and vice versa) . . . and when you trust that both parties want to work and grow together even through the frustrating times—when these things happen for you, hold fast to this commitment. Understand that there are valleys and hills, but also trust that if you adhere to the steps laid out above, more good days and memorable moments are in your future together.

When a Relationship Ends, Learning Lessons without Getting Stuck in the Past

Sometimes we consciously or unconsciously engineer the end of a relationship when we realize that, for a variety of reasons, it isn't the best place or situation to live our best life. At other times, we are blindsided as our partner chooses to end the relationship for reasons we may not understand, at least at the time.

Either way, moving forward is crucial, but it is understandably difficult as we must adjust to a new life, perhaps a new environment, and become vulnerable again as we try to establish new and healthy relationships with friends and, when we are ready, potential partners.

How can we move forward after a relationship ends?

Sometimes we hang on to things because we are fearful of what will replace them. An oft-cited quote, attributed to various authors including C. S. Lewis and Victor Hugo, says it all: "Getting over a painful experience is much like crossing monkey bars. You have to let go at some point in order to move forward." Not knowing what you will be reaching out for or will find within your grasp is frightening.

Change can be absolutely exhilarating when we've initiated the process — applied for a new job and been accepted, said yes to a wedding proposal, or simply decided to change the style or color of our hair. On the other hand, when change is thrust upon us unexpectedly and uninvited, it is easy to become frozen by fear and anxiety; we're uncertain about what to do next, even when we know we should do something. Generally, in such situations, what we want to do initially is return to the way things were when we were content and no disruption had taken place, even when we know that isn't an option.

At some point, change will seek us without asking if we'd welcome it. In such instances, change can be like the most horrid houseguest; it's disrespectful, rude, and seems to have no clue how to fit into our lives. It seems as though it is making our lives worse instead of better.

While there are situations when change is indeed for the worse, I would argue that the majority of the time, change is an opportunity, even when we don't see it that way to begin with. What determines the beauty of the change that is thrust upon us is how we deal with it.

When change arrives uninvited — and it will — there are ways to make the most of it. We can come out ahead and even more fulfilled, exuding more strength and, in the end, thankful for the opportunity. Yes, you read that correctly—thankful that it occurred.

Why am I writing this, you may be wondering? While I will keep the details to myself, suffice it to say that at one point what I wanted and what life had in store for me were two different things. I was initially frustrated with the powers that be (the universe, God, however you think about the overarching context of our lives); however, I had enough experience to know that beautiful days lay ahead, but only if I would pick myself up, resolve to be thankful for the events that had brought me to this moment, and move forward with faith, determination, and hope.

As a young girl, I had blindly accepted the idea that happiness had to involve a partner or marriage. It wasn't until I was in my early twenties and had an engagement ring on my finger that I realized I would be no happier on the other side of the vows than I was at that moment. That was when I realized I was responsible for my own happiness. I couldn't see myself being able to chase my dreams (for example, traveling to France, which I hadn't yet done at that point) if I was playing a role I wasn't ready for.

In fact, I eventually realized I was never meant to play a role because that would mean I was following rather than being myself. Checking a box that society, Hollywood, or a religion dictates would not put me on a path toward happiness. Instead, we each hold the keys to our own happiness. It isn't until we discover these keys within us that we will be able to fully experience happiness—with or without a marriage license.

As this book goes to print, I am blissfully single, and having been in a couple of long-term relationships in the past fifteen years, I can confidently say I have never been happier with the life I have chosen than I am at this moment. Each of the relationships I exited involved enormous respect between the two parties and dissolved amicably—maybe not initially, but eventually.

As my thirties have unfolded, I am more comfortable with who I am. I have not shied away from my passions; instead I've dived in and moved forward, not always knowing what waited around the corner, but knowing I was enjoying myself along the way. Julia Child once stated, "Find something you're passionate about and stay tremendously interested in it." Well, I've done just that, and the blessings have surpassed my expectations. Should they one day include a man who is as interested in me as I am in him, fabulous! But if not, I'm doing more than just fine on my own.

What I've learned is that there are steps for successfully navigating what can be an emotional, uncertain, yet rewarding journey. Here are a few.

Understand What Is Ahead

All great changes are preceded by chaos.
—Deepak Chopra

Begin the journey understanding that the change that has occurred happened for a reason. As you move forward and make the journey from "here" to "there," understand that in order for change to happen, there will be moments of emotional anguish, obstacles that seem initially insurmountable, and moments of fear. When you accept this fact, you are well on your way to success.

Feed Your Faith, Not Your Fears

Fear, uncertainty and discomfort are your compasses toward growth.
—Anonymous

I discovered this fantastic quote on the website *Positive Provocations*. While it is easy to become frustrated when obstacles appear in our path toward the life we want to create, we must choose to feed our faith that we will overcome them, instead of feeding our fears by engaging in negative self-talk.

When you accept that in order to change, there will be difficulties, you can also choose to address such fears with faith, instead of feeding them, which will only keep you frozen. Choosing to instead nourish faith propels you forward.

Always keep in mind that an assumed impossibility is a mirage: Any obstacle is indeed possible to overcome.

Take Action

> *Nothing diminishes anxiety faster than action.*
> — Walter Anderson

Some of the most difficult times in my life have been the days immediately following an abrupt and unexpected change. For some people this may come by way of a job loss, the end of a relationship, an accident, or the death of a loved one. While it is healthy to grieve, we must not lose ourselves in grief.

Yes, allow yourself time to mourn the death of the life you thought would continue for some time, but then take action. Get busy pursuing a goal you've had but perhaps had placed on the shelf. Get busy doing your best work and chasing dreams that you now can put into action. Whatever you do, get busy. Take action. This will keep your mind busy and put it to constructive use, so that when you've given your heart time to heal, you will have produced something you are proud of.

Find a Hug

> *It doesn't matter who, when, or where . . . you can always use a hug.*
> —Hope Floats

When you choose to embrace a change that has been thrown into your lap, you are choosing growth. When you accept change, you are opening your heart, trusting that wonderful things will find you again, and bravely moving forward, even when you aren't sure exactly how it will all work out.

If you have chosen this path, you are already becoming a better version of yourself, but as I've said before, it will be difficult at times. At those times, as well as others, find a hug. Find someone who loves you and cares about you, and seek out a good hug from them. (I do love hugs from those I love; they mean the world to me!) You will need support as you progress through the change you are embarking on, but the gift of who you are becoming is worth the journey.

Setbacks Are a Part of Life

What I like most about change is that it's a synonym for "hope." If you are taking a risk, what you are really saying is, "I believe in tomorrow, and I will be part of it."
— Linda Ellerbee

Once you have determined how to move forward, the next step is knowing in which direction to proceed — in other words, ensuring that you don't repeat the same mistakes and wind up in the exact same spot again. Lessons are present in every moment of joy and every heartbreak that come our way, and it is only when we take the time to learn them that we can be confident we won't be taunted by the past.

It has been nearly thirteen years since Oprah Winfrey shared this observation with her viewers: "A lesson will keep repeating itself until it is learned. Life first will send the lesson to you in the size of a pebble; if you ignore the pebble, then life will send you a brick; if you ignore the brick, life will send you a brick wall; if you ignore the brick wall, life will send you a demolition truck." It's best to learn the lesson the first time so you are able to move on and not get stuck in a vicious cycle. Yet I know there are more lessons waiting for me, and more tests to see if I truly have learned what life has been trying to teach me.

There are many lenses to look through as we observe life. We can look at the difficulties — the struggles, challenges, and times when things aren't going as planned — as deterrents that stop us in our tracks, or we can choose to see opportunity for personal growth. Choosing the latter path isn't always easy because when we take it, those around us may not understand what we are doing. However, if we choose to live life with the goal of discovering contentment within ourselves and not of gaining outside approval, our lives become richer; we aren't wasting time looking for fair-weather cheerleaders and thus can focus on higher-level and more enjoyable ventures.

In one interpretation of Oprah's quote, we might assume that the lesson, when it's repeated, will come in a more observable and imposing state, but that is not the only way to read it. Often what is intensified is what you have to lose if you foolishly choose to not learn the lesson. Choosing to not absorb a lesson could mean a loss of opportunity at work or the faltering of a romantic relationship.

Whatever the case, choose wisely, and learn the lesson the first (or at least the second) time it presents itself so that you can move on to life's greener pastures.

This quote from motivational author and speaker Leo F. Buscaglia focuses on the upside of failure: "We seem to gain wisdom more readily through our failures than through our successes. We always think of failure as the antithesis of success, but it isn't. Success often lies just the other side of failure."

Setbacks, failures, bumps in the road, or maybe what seem like brick walls — we've all encountered them, sometimes unexpectedly, in the form of a job loss, a breakup, or finding that something we dearly wanted was out of our reach.

Whatever the scenario, a setback can stop us in our tracks and cause us to lose our confidence or question our abilities. While that initial response is natural, I recommend a more useful perspective on how to handle a situation that puts us off our game and causes us to reevaluate.

Having been thrown off course more times than I'd like to admit, I truly believe that setbacks (I prefer this term, as nothing is a failure unless we refuse to learn from it) are opportunities in disguise. And when we slip or stumble we gain a richer appreciation for the times when things go our way.

Following are nine ways to handle setbacks so they don't knock us completely off course, but instead help us build a stronger foundation from which to achieve the success we desire.

View Obstacles as Puzzles That Are Solvable with the Right Dedication. The phrase "Necessity is the mother of invention" is a stark reminder that often it takes an incessant demand and an abiding desire for our dreams to come true. In other words, not succeeding with your first attempt at the MCAT, LSAT, Praxis, or any other professional certification exam doesn't mean you won't succeed if you keep your head down and refuse to give up. Julia Child didn't find her career in cooking until she was in her forties, but she continued to seek out jobs that piqued her curiosity until finally she listened to her taste buds. Thomas Edison, the inventor of the incandescent lightbulb, made thousands (yes, thousands) of attempts until he was successful. It is dedication that is necessary, and each person's story of how they attain what they seek will be uniquely their own.

Engage in Positive Self-talk. I'm a great believer in mind over matter. We truly do become what we believe. If you wake up in the morning and drag yourself out of bed, dreading the day's events, you've already reduced the likelihood that your day will be a happy one because you are open to the negative. If, conversely, you get out of bed with a smile on your face and an expectation that whatever situations may present themselves will have success, you are more likely to find it. Life is kind of like a treasure hunt. If you're going to find the chest of gold, you first have to believe it's there.

Remain Willing to Take Risks & Accept the Outcome (Good or Bad). If you take a chance on something or someone and it doesn't pan out, chalk it up to experience. If it does, wahoo!

Experience Really Is the Best Teacher. Years of viewing, experimenting, and observing what works and what doesn't mold a coach into someone who can guide a team to success. The most essential part of the process is taking the time to evaluate what worked and why (and vice versa), so that a person can repeat a winning formula and won't make the same mistakes again. I know I would much rather be on the Duke men's basketball team, coached by Mike Krzyzewski, than on the squad of a first-time coach with no experience. As Colin Powell has said, "There are no secrets to success. It is the result of preparation, hard work, and learning from failure."

Tweak What Can Be Done Better. When you take a step back and evaluate a difficulty from an objective vantage point and with a cool head, you'll likely be able to determine techniques or approaches that have potential but need to be fine-tuned.

Eliminate What Isn't Working at All. At the same time, there will be approaches or responses that need to be eliminated altogether. We must help ourselves out and adjust the behavior and decisions that contributed to the setback.

Accept Responsibility. Not only will we gain respect, but our credibility will increase as others observe how we handle setbacks. If we move forward positively and apply what we've learned, while avoiding past mistakes, others' confidence in our ability to persevere in times of difficulty will soar.

Never Be Afraid of Failure, as There Are Benefits. According to super-successful soccer player and coach Sven Goran Eriksson, "The greatest barrier to success is the fear of failure." But this fear can actually act as a motivator to help us do our best. As a high jumper in high school and college, I was regularly fearful of each jump that exceeded 5 feet. Why? I was terrified I was going to fling my body into the standard. It was an absurd fear, since I had never done it, but I knew it was possible, as I had seen others have that dreadful collision. It wasn't until I had the opportunity to work with Dick Fosbury's famed coach Bernie Wagner at Western Oregon University that I became able to continue to jump and recorded my personal best. (Granted, this was nowhere near the heights he was used to, but it was a huge success for me.) While taking a risk that you haven't carefully evaluated is most likely not a good idea, calculated risks can have very positive effects. When we know that we can fail, we can be propelled to unforeseen heights.

Sooner Rather than Later, Get Back on That Horse! For several years, I was an equestrian rider, and my horse would sometimes throw me. It was imperative that I get right back on in order to strengthen the rapport and connection with my mount—in other words, in order for us to cultivate confidence in each other. The same can be said for setbacks. If something doesn't work, don't waste time stewing. Instead, take some time to rework your approach, learning from what didn't work the first time. Then as soon as possible, try it again.

CHAPTER EIGHT

Simple Choices & Pleasures That Make a Difference

arketers try to tell us what the "good" life looks—extravagant décor, lavish travel plans, expensive labels—but they are wrong. While such luxuries may be a treat to enjoy occasionally, it is the everyday pleasures that enrich the life we have created for ourselves and that encourage us to live more fully in the moment.

Choosing to live simply luxuriously requires us to live consciously and with common sense—in other words, with awareness of the world we live in, the community we love, and the budget we must adhere to in order to create a financially secure life today and tomorrow.

So much of attaining contentment is something we can't purchase or cultivate quickly. Rather, it is spending time with ourselves, mastering our thoughts, and living with a purpose that speaks to our intrinsic being, a purpose that will be a foundation for true joy and fulfillment.

There are many simple pleasures you can indulge in that won't break the bank and will bring a smile to your face and refreshment to your everyday routine.

Be Yourself — It Really Is That Simple

Resolve to be thyself; and know that he who finds himself loses his misery.
—Matthew Arnold

It has always been my belief that the best gift you can give yourself is the time to get to know yourself. Some may think this is an odd gift. After all, the process of getting to know oneself is not all roses and puppy dog kisses. In fact, the early stages can be full of tears, doubt, and questioning. But just as when children go through growing spurts or have their teeth straightened, the process produces an amazing result that, once completed, is generally considered more than worth the pain.

Establish Comfortable Boundaries

Once you are aware of your strengths and weaknesses, you can more easily establish the areas in which you are willing to be a bit more flexible and those on which you need to stand firm. For example, if you are someone who needs time to herself to unwind, that should be a boundary you don't waver on; if your privacy isn't something you guard stringently, you might be more flexible when it comes to uninvited guests stopping by your home. The key is to figure out what makes you comfortable and to honor that feeling.

The only reason you need to say no to anything is that it makes *you* feel uncomfortable. That is enough, and if someone tries to override you, they are not being respectful of your feelings. Very possibly a battle for control is taking place. Respect yourself enough to know what you can't wiggle on and what you can, and be strong.

Be Less Judgmental

Once you realize your talents and passions, your need to be envious or jealous of others' talents evaporates, quietly and usually quickly. It's funny how when you feel you have found your purpose, you gain empathy. You better understand the struggles of others and are more apt to understand why they are behaving as they do. Once you've found what your focus needs to be, what truly fills you up and lets you know without question that you are chasing dreams you were meant to chase, you don't begrudge anyone else their dreams, whether you agree with them or not. In fact, your appreciation of someone else's success provides a positive energy that will fuel you as you power toward your goal.

Enjoy the Comfort of Your Own Skin

When you have eliminated fear, your confidence can propel you to even more amazing heights. Think about it. When you're not sure, when you're insecure and constantly questioning, you're not taking gainful strides. Instead, you are tiptoeing. Just think of the strength and balance you are casting aside when you approach everyday tasks and larger challenges tentatively. Becoming comfortable in your own skin will get you to a place where you achieve your dreams and goals, and you'll arrive there on a more direct path — balanced, confident, and assured.

Have No Regrets

Yet another wonderful benefit of getting to know yourself is the elimination of regrets. I have come to a point where I have no regrets because, ultimately, everything I've done in the past has created the person I am today. Sure, I make mistakes and become frustrated with decisions I've made, and I know I will continue to do so. But each time it happens, I try to learn a lesson, evaluate myself and the experience, and come out on the other side with knowledge I didn't possess before.

Each bit of newfound wisdom has helped me pave a path to the life I love living today — building my blog, traveling to foreign countries, meeting extraordinary and ordinary people — all of which has taught me so much. When you know you are living the life that best suits you (that is, not anyone else's idea of what you should be doing), you are placing the responsibility squarely on your own shoulders. When you do that, you also accept that you will make mistakes. The beauty is that the mistakes don't have to become regrets. Remember: An outcome is considered a failure (or regret) only if you refuse to learn from it.

How to Get to Know Yourself

Know first who you are, then adorn yourself accordingly.
—Epictetus

Gaining self-knowledge is a continuous process because a person is continually evolving, learning new things, and living in a world that is also perpetually changing. However, knowing that the world is in a constant state of change drives home even more firmly the need for each of us to really get to know ourselves.

If you've read this far in this book, or even just read around in it a little, you probably understand that the journey of getting to know yourself is something I am quite passionate about. I highly recommend it to anyone who is seeking true contentment. At the same time, I will admit that it is not an undertaking for the faint of heart. Getting to know yourself truly takes determination, for at times it will be frustrating. However, I can honestly say, from my own experience, that it is worth all the toil, tears, and questions, because the person you end up becoming is someone you couldn't imagine *not* being.

Spend Time with Yourself

In order to become acquainted with someone or something, you must spend time focusing on and paying attention to the new person you are dating, the new task you are trying to master, or the goal you are trying to accomplish. The same is true when you are on a mission to understand yourself more thoroughly: If you truly want to get to know yourself, devote some significant time to being with yourself.

For many people, alone time is daunting. But when you are able to set aside time to listen to what you enjoy, discover what you can get lost in, and ultimately find out what makes you feel comfortable, you are doing yourself a tremendous favor. Make a date with yourself at least once a month, if not once a week. You'll become more comfortable in your own skin and will also know more about what you want.

Travel

Whether you are hopping on a plane, sailing across an ocean, or just getting in the car and heading across the state, take the time to get away. When you travel to different communities, new countries, and unfamiliar regions of the world, you expose yourself to different ways of life. Often we assume there's only one way to do something; however, the truth we uncover is that there are many paths leading to the same destination.

When you step out of the culture (the town, the state, the country, the political system, the religion) you normally live in, you expose yourself to different perspectives, new values, new worlds. And most likely during your travels you will discover something that will resonate with you, that you will want to forever keep in your life, and that ultimately reveals more about who you really are.

Try New Things

If you've never been water skiing and your friends invite you to the lake, take them up on it. If your husband takes you to the local sushi restaurant and you've never tried it, or maybe are even scared to, try it anyway. If a family member invites you to make a trip to a place you've never been, accept the invitation.

When opportunity comes knocking, don't slam the door in its face. You never know when that spark of inspiration will occur, when you will find a new interest or hobby that soon becomes a passion. Wine tasting came into my life this way more than six years ago, and now I can't imagine not taking advantage of all of the beautiful local wineries in my area.

Listen to Your Instincts

The only way to come to trust your instincts is to use them. For most women, listening to our instincts is one thing, but following them can be an entirely different proposition. Also, your instincts may not lead you in the right direction the first few times you listen to them, but give them time. Exercise them. Condition and train them as you would your physical body. Your subconscious will work for you if you let it and are willing to listen.

Journal

Journaling sometimes means recording your thoughts once a day in a systematic and serious way, but another stimulating way to keep a journal is to carry a journal in your purse or keep one on your bedside table and make a note of thoughts that pop into your head at any given moment. Whether it's an idea for your next dinner party, a quote that inspires you, or a movie you want to see, keeping such a journal is a daily, detailed reminder of what matters to you.

While a given thought may seem insignificant at the moment, upon reflection the pieces of who you are, what moves you, and what you are passionate about will form a mosaic and become clear. The next time you are at a bookstore or stationery store, browse through the many journals they offer and treat yourself to one that catches your eye. A beautiful journal will motivate you to fill it with lovely ideas and inspirations.

Conquer Your Fears

Have you always wanted to sing in public, but never thought you could? Let a friend take you out for some karaoke. Always wanted to dance like a star, but were afraid you'd trip over what you thought were two left feet? Sign up with your best friend for that dance class you saw advertised in the paper. Always wanted to cook, but were too intimidated for ask for help? Sign up for a cooking class at Sur La Table, Williams-Sonoma, or your local community college. If something continues to speak to you, whisper to you, piques your interest, but you're too fearful to try it, maybe that is exactly the thing you should be doing. Believe it or not, our fears are sometimes a treasure map to where we've always wanted to go. So respect and listen to that voice, that yearning. It may be smarter than you realize.

Test Your Strengths

Quite often it happens that a woman learns her true abilities when she is thrown a curve ball she hasn't anticipated and simply has to act and not think. For example, as I mentioned in chapter 6, I tried to get rid of ten to fifteen pounds for almost ten years, but it wasn't until three summers ago and the day of my marathon that I realized I don't need as much food as I had been thinking.

On the morning of the race, I needed fuel, but had only minimal choices on hand. I choose the one protein I had (a protein bar), grabbed a small bran muffin, and ate another protein bar during the race. It was all I needed. The quality of food one consumes is much more important than the quantity, and following that philosophy allowed me to shed ten pounds.

Sometimes we are our own worst enemy. Stop saying no, and attempt what you at one time thought you could never do. You might just surprise yourself.

Accept Yourself

Too often, we allow ourselves to be so bombarded, overwhelmed, and talked to about what we should be and look like, and how we should lead our lives, that we become convinced that we aren't enough. This couldn't be further from the truth.

The reality is that you are enough. You are amazing. And the journey of getting to know yourself will be more fruitful than you will have ever imagined once you take on the challenge. When you accept who you are, you experience the most amazing natural high — a combination of peace of mind, freedom from the influence of others, and love of life. I wholeheartedly suggest doing this for yourself.

If you remain vigilant, determined, and respectful of yourself, the outcome will be a stronger, more loving, and more contented you.

Choose Yourself

It wasn't about . . . choosing a man or choosing a bag or choosing a life. It was about, choose yourself.
— Michael Patrick King

Whether or not you are a fan of *Sex and the City*, you might want to look at an interesting article written by Meredith Bryan in May 2010's *Elle* magazine about its creator and writer Michael Patrick King.

It's true that women of all ages enjoy watching Carrie, Miranda, Charlotte, and Samantha for the fashion, relationships, and friendship, but King says these were all just "the fireworks display to get our attention." Ultimately, his message and the message that truly resonates with me is that, during a time in our culture of ambivalence and lack of boundaries and wondering which way to go, these women are choosing themselves. Whether or not you agree with their decisions, they are true to who they are, and this should be the message you, as a woman, should be grabbing onto.

Yes, the story is fictitious. Yes, if it were grunge clothing, squalid living conditions, and mundane, humdrum, routine lives, you most likely wouldn't watch, and, yes, I understand the producers want to make their money back and more. But the message, I feel, is a valid one. If *you* won't choose yourself and your dreams, who will?

First of all, no one knows your dreams better than you do. It may take some time to solidify exactly what you want as you learn from failed attempts and misdirection, but we usually don't get it right the first time. And I would argue that 99 percent of the time we don't get it right the first time because we can always learn something and improve upon whatever it is we are trying to do, whether it's in our romantic lives, our career pursuits, or our fashion choices. I for one do not want to go back to wearing what I thought was "so cool" in the eighties — perms and shoulder cutouts, anyone?

You may ask, if I am always choosing myself, aren't I being selfish? I wholeheartedly *disagree*. Choosing yourself doesn't mean acting against your good conscience; you are simply choosing the direction that will capitalize on your talents, which hopefully will benefit both you and those around you.

Not choosing yourself can actually promote more selfish desires. When you constantly accommodate other's life plans and fail to respect your own, you tend to fill the void with instant fixes—too many material items, excess food, and other unhealthy behaviors. The worst outlet may be projecting your unfulfilled dreams onto others, pushing them in the direction you desired but didn't have the courage to take. And why? Because you didn't value yourself.

Take a moment to ask, Am I choosing myself? If you are, pat yourself on the back and support others to do the same. If you're still in a quandary, look to those who will support you, no matter what path you take.

Simple & Luxurious Rituals

Humans are creatures of habit, for better or worse. Sometimes the routines we become accustomed to are mundane yet necessary, like putting the trash out on the curb every Sunday night. But there are other routines—rituals, as I like to call them—that you can incorporate into your life to add luxury to each day. While certain luxuries are grand expenditures, many other luxuries cost nothing or next to nothing, yet bring a tremendous amount of joy. Here are some ideas for incorporating simple rituals into your routine:

Beauty

Nothing reveals a woman's opinion of herself like the way she cares for her appearance. Creating beauty rituals that you attend to just before going to bed or upon awakening confers many benefits and makes you feel you are being pampered. Some examples:

- Use moisturizer over your entire body after stepping out of the bath or shower.
- Remove all makeup before getting into bed, and apply a rich facial cream to hydrate your skin (eye cream too, if you'd like).
- Before leaving the house, give yourself a spritz of your favorite scent.
- Regularly get a blissful night's sleep to restore and invigorate not only your skin, but your body and mind.

Fitness

You do not have to be as energetic as Jane Fonda or as ripped as Jillian Michaels to include the daily ritual of fitness in your life. View fitness as an opportunity to improve your life, to restore your energy so that you can do the things you want to do. One of my enjoyable morning rituals is taking a walk with my dogs. Some mornings it is a very vigorous, long walk, but on other days it is just a stroll to allow the dogs to frolic and play. Either way, it is a ritual that I try to indulge in, and it makes me feel good.

Bedtime

What do you do that flips that switch in your mind, conveying the message that you're going to start winding down and are ready to sleep? Going to bed early or late, reading a book in bed, watching your favorite comedy (even if it's a rerun—for me, *Frasier* or *Will & Grace*), sipping a bit of tea, tucking your kids in and reading to them, sitting on the porch with a cup of decaf—whatever your rituals, they communicate to your body and, more important, your mind that you are about to give them both some rest. If you don't already have such rituals, think about something that brings you pleasure that you can see yourself doing most nights before you drift off into dreamland.

Morning

If you are not a morning person, this one might be a bit more difficult to introduce into your life, but I'm a firm believer in bringing a bit of ritual to your morning routine. Whether it's stopping by your local coffee house and chatting with the barista, reading the paper while you sip your morning cup of tea, perusing your favorite blogs, looking at your daily calendar to prepare for the day ahead and making a note about when you will find some time for yourself—whatever you choose to do, make sure it's something that you look forward to and that lifts your spirits.

Weekly

Some of the best rituals are ones you don't get to enjoy every day. And because you don't indulge in them every day, they can be a bit more decadent. I know a handful of couples who reserve Friday nights for dinner at a good restaurant. What a beautiful way to end the week, no matter how rambunctious it may have been. This ritual provides a time for these couples to celebrate its culmination and reflect on successes they may have enjoyed.

Or how about a weekly trip to your favorite bookstore, a weekly gathering of good friends for brunch, coffee, or a walk, or the indulgence of purchasing a bottle of wine you've never before tried and pairing it with a decadent homemade meal? Knowing you're going to enjoy something special every week will provide a bit more motivation for you to push through your work and do your best.

Accessorize Your Work Week with Regular Pampering

A field that has rested gives a beautiful crop.
—Ovid

Stylists and fashion gurus have long advised using accessories to complete an outfit. And there's always a balance. You don't want to be without any accessories at all (shoes, handbag, watch, etc.), but you never want to wear too many pieces of jewelry, as excess always detracts from true beauty. After all, accessories are meant to accentuate what is already there.

I like to compare the work week to one's foundational wardrobe essentials. Most of us have a work week in one form or another, and we often let it take on a life of its own and take us over. Instead we can choose to make it well-balanced and fulfilling by "accessorizing" it each week with moments, activities, actions, and thoughts that improve its quality, no matter what the work gods have in store for us.

Below are a few examples of "accessories" that might spruce up your week:

- Schedule time during each day when you will catch your breath, close your eyes, or put your feet up without distraction.
- Attend a fitness class led by your favorite Pilates, yoga, or cycling instructor.
- Buy ingredients for your favorite meal and schedule a day to sit down and enjoy it with your favorite company (yourself, someone else, or a few special friends).
- Sip luxurious coffee and/or tea every afternoon. (My favorite teas, from Fortnum & Mason, Palais de Thés, and Mariage Frères, are a treat each time I enjoy a cup.)
- Schedule a pampering treatment—a blow-out, manicure, pedicure, massage, etc.
- Go out to dinner in the middle of the week, to help yourself "get over the hump," or on Friday, to celebrate the end of the work week.

- Pick up your favorite fashion, news, or cultural affairs magazine. (*Vogue* and *The New Yorker* are two I eagerly look forward to.)
- Once or twice a week, order a decadent cup of *chocolat chaud* at your favorite chocolatier, coffee shop, or patisserie.
- Sip a crisp French rosé paired with a decadent brie, Genoa salami, and water crackers.
- Wear more dresses to work.
- If you don't subscribe to a daily newspaper, pick up a copy on the day it runs your favorite weekly feature — style, food, science, etc.
- Carve out time for reading every day.
- Have brunch with someone you enjoy or want to know better.
- Before heading out the door, don't forget your lips, lashes, and concealer.
- DVR your favorite television program and watch it on your own time, without interruption.
- Read your kids a bedtime story.
- Keep up with the local entertainment or social section of your newspaper and plan an outing with your significant other, a good friend, or on your own. Attend a unique event — a book signing, concert, wine tasting, film, etc.
- Wander through a bookstore, looking at the new titles or meandering through the magazine section.
- Keep a journal, and at the end of each day write what went well and nothing else, even if it's as small as "I washed my hair." Focus on what is working. This positive record will uplift you and stimulate increased energy.

- Step outside and, while taking a walk, play your favorite podcast; give the day's stresses a break from knocking around in your mind.
- Stay inside playing classic jazz tunes while getting lost in a fantastic book.
- Meditate, even if only for five minutes.
- Bestow a few hugs and kisses on those you love.
- At some point each day, or at least once a week, read a blog post or article that makes you feel good, that inspires you, and that gives you hope and motivation.
- Indulge in dessert up to three times a week, but stick to one serving so you don't feel guilty afterward.
- And my perennial, go-to, simple luxury recommendation: On the days you do not indulge in dessert, enjoy a decadent truffle at the end of the day as a reward for eating well.

The beautiful reality of simple luxuries is that they are everywhere, waiting to be savored—from the first cup of freshly brewed coffee or tea we sip in the morning to the way we spend our last waking hour before getting some sleep: reading a wonderful book, listening to our favorite music, or catching up with our loved ones.

No matter where we find ourselves in the life we have created, the simple luxuries are there. However, they can be easy to ignore, so we must seek them out, take breaks, turn off our cell phones, and allow ourselves to indulge without feeling guilty.

Studies have revealed that working endlessly does not produce the best results. In fact, leading a balanced working life that includes a quality vacation at least once a year, breaks throughout the day, and weekend respites allows the mind to recharge and perform at its best.

I encourage you to welcome moments throughout your day and week that allow you to take a deep breath and relax, indulging in a simple luxury that slows down your heartbeat just enough that you can appreciate all the things in your life that are going well.

Revel in Solitude Often

[The wise man] is his own best friend, and takes delight in privacy, whereas the man of no virtue or ability is his own worst enemy and is afraid of solitude.
— Aristotle

Finding time to be alone is something I cherish and need on a regular basis in order to find my balance, be sure of my focus, and gain clarity for the decisions about what will be best for me in the long run.

Unfortunately, many people miss out on the priceless benefits of being comfortable with time spent alone. For a variety of reasons, being alone sometimes gets a bad rap, but I'd like to turn that around and show you that solitude — being able to be comfortable and at ease with your own company — is a sign of inner peace and the key to creating a contented life.

Often, when we quiet our surroundings, we are bombarded by thoughts — often fears — we otherwise try to silence with the hustle and bustle of our lives. But we must slow down and listen to such thoughts.

Consciously choosing to deal with your fears is the first step in controlling them. When you face your fears directly, you strip them of their power and learn to handle them. You free your gaze so you can appreciate your past, enjoy your present, and feel prepared for the future, knowing you are heading in the direction that is best for you, one that is not influenced by others' judgments, opinions, or pressures.

Here are a some specific benefits of finding time to be by yourself without interruption or distraction.

Discover Unknown Strengths & Self-confidence

Knowing how to be solitary is central to the art of loving. When we can be alone, we can be with others without using them as a means of escape.
—Bell Hooks

As with anything new, you may feel trepidation as you first attempt to spend time on your own, but once you've resolved to spend time by yourself, you will be amazed at what you can do without anyone's help.

Some of the "aha!" moments I've had—traveling successfully in a foreign country when I didn't know the language well, making flaky, buttery pie crust, painting and plastering one of my rooms, raking all the leaves in my yard (40 bags full), organizing a soiree—were things I didn't know I was capable of. I know you too will find amazing strengths you didn't know you had. It often isn't until we are placed in a real situation that requires our best efforts that we realize our true abilities. Trust yourself. I have a feeling you will be very pleasantly surprised.

When you discover your true strengths and realize how much you can do on your own, you boost your self-confidence. Once you realize you can depend on yourself, you have created a person who is healthier and more able to be a solid partner in any relationship, a person who is capable of creating a successful and dream-fulfilling life.

Understand What Makes You Tick

Establishing your boundaries in life is one of the healthiest and simplest things you can do to prevent frustration. And the only way to truly know where your boundaries are is to take time to be by yourself. What are you unwilling to compromise on because it is at the core of your values and beliefs? What can you give a little on and not feel as though you have lost a piece of yourself?

Knowing the answers to these questions is crucial to future successful relationships, whether they be with your significant other, colleagues, friends, or family. Once you know where you stand, you are positioned firmly and confidently in your truth and can't be knocked down. This knowledge comes from taking the time to listen to yourself when you have time alone, without interruptions or judgments.

Allow Yourself to Relax

Solitude is a gift. When you carve out time to just *be* in your own company, you are allowing yourself to catch your breath and relax. Without the demands of others weighing on your mind, you can do as you please. As Sarah Jessica Parker's *Sex and the City* character Carrie Bradshaw states, you can revel in your "secret single behavior." Whether you are in a relationship, have children, or are flying free, it is always a good idea to make time to be alone.

There is a difference between being alone and being lonely. As I said before, feeling lonely can occur when you're surrounded by endless numbers of people, but being able to be alone well is very empowering.

Let Yourself Be & See What Happens

One of the more memorable takeaways from *Runaway Bride*, starring Julia Roberts, concerns how the heroine likes her eggs; until she wakes up to who she really is, she likes her eggs prepared the way the man in her life likes them. It isn't until she is on her own, not in a relationship (and not jumping from one to the next without an opportunity to catch her breath and her bearings) that she realizes how she truly prefers her eggs.

Solitude allows you to not be edited by the opinions, choices, and judgments of others. When you are on your own, you don't hold back and can be completely honest with yourself, try new things, attempt new hobbies without fear of rejection or failure, and eventually become more sure and confident in what you truly desire. Every woman owes herself a chance to figure out what her passions are without outside influences weighing in.

The Gift of Reading & Continued Learning

What we become depends on what we read after all of the professors have finished with us.
— Thomas Carlyle

Reading is the most inexpensive way to travel the world, expand your mind, and consequently discover who you are and what you are passionate about.

The wonderful thing about reading is that it doesn't have to end with school. It truly is a pleasurable pursuit that stays with each of us long after the last page is turned and the book is closed.

Choose to Read & Set Yourself Free

Reading is to the mind what exercise is to the body. It is wholesome and bracing for the mind to have its faculties kept on the stretch.
— Augustus Hare

That is what makes reading so powerful. Not only are you learning about a plot that is unfolding or a history that has taken place, but you are enhancing your vocabulary, picking up subconsciously how to construct sentences, and how to be a better conversationalist. Reading is truly a multifaceted pastime.

An opportunity to be freed from our circumstances comes the moment we immerse ourselves in any given book. To be able to read is a gift—one that, I have to be honest, I sometimes take for granted. But it is without question true that, as S. I. Hayakawa said, "people who have read good literature have lived more than people who cannot or will not read."

Reading exposes you to the world, so that you are not boxed in, confined to what someone else believes. Instead you can make up your own mind, entertain multiple viewpoints, and get to the bottom of issues. Reading stimulates your curiosity—a quality that helps tremendously as we seek to live a full and contented life. To be curious is to have an innate thirst for knowledge, the peace of mind that comes from knowing that if you can't hop on a plane and visit the country of your dreams at any given moment, you can pick up a book that is set where you would someday like to find yourself. (It is very telling that I have shelves of Paris-centered books, no?)

When I read my first piece of classic literature in high school, I vividly remember saying to myself, with unedited glee, "The author is speaking about life. I can apply this to my life!" That was the moment, however elementary my thought process was then, when I fell in love with literature. Not only do books teach me about life; what keeps me coming back and picking up book after book after book is that they can teach me so much about who I am, what I can become, mistakes I should try to avoid, and, in so many cases, risks I should be willing to take.

Without question, being well-read should be viewed as just as important—if not more so—as looking good when you peek at yourself in the mirror. With intelligence comes the ability to have a quick wit and an understanding that beauty fades while intelligence remains.

The following quotation is attributed to both English essayist Joseph Addison and American philosopher Mortimer J. Adler: "Reading is a basic tool in the living of a good life." I would take the idea to another level and say that reading is a simple luxury as well.

Never Stop Learning

The highest result of education is tolerance.
—Helen Keller

On July 12, 2013, a fifteen-year-old girl, Malala Yousafzai, spoke for the first time since a horrific assassination attempt on her life orchestrated by the Taliban, which had banned young girls from attending school. Beginning at age eleven, Malala had been an advocate for Pakistani girls and their right to an education. Refusing to be silenced, she continued to go to school, and in October 2012, as she rode in a bus returning from class, her life was nearly taken.

She was shot in the left side of her face; the bullet traveled through her neck and shoulder but, miraculously, didn't strike her brain.

After multiple surgeries to repair her skull and ear, Malala has spoken at the United Nations and Harvard University and has met with Queen Elizabeth and President Obama. She continues to advocate for every child's right to an education, and in honor of her efforts, she was on the short list of nominees for the 2013 Nobel Peace Prize.

Malala's story serves as a reminder and an inspiration about the power and life-changing effects education can have on an individual's life. Sadly, as reported by ABC news, more than 32 million girls around the world are still not educated or able to attend school. Those of us who have been educated take this opportunity for granted much of the time, but a number like that—32 million girls who do not receive schooling—is a wakeup call, a reminder that we must value education as a gift that can't be taken away and as a key to unlocking the door to the future we desire.

Studies have proved that attaining an education yields a suite of important benefits, for individuals and for society as a whole. Those of us who are college graduates or in the process of attaining a degree are already aware of many of these benefits, especially those that have an impact on us personally. However, I want to also encourage the continual support of education for ourselves and for others, whether inside a classroom or in the classroom of life. Socrates was right—the more we learn, the more we realize we don't know. Education is a lifelong endeavor.

Another, more generalized gift of knowledge is that we no longer have to rely on faulty sources of belief that may have constrained us in the past and kept us from reaching our goals. When we know better, we can do better. We can move forward with confidence, assured that we are traveling in the right direction. We can stand up for ourselves and for others and speak out with confidence, like Malala.

No matter what your level of education, I urge you to never stop learning. When you don't have an answer, seek it until you find it. When you see someone who is seeking information and you can provide the correct answer or point her in the right direction, do so. I can't help but think of Pap, Huck Finn's father in Mark Twain's classic tale, who was disgusted by the fact that his son was becoming educated and might learn how to read and write, unlike himself and Huck's mother. Twain's satirical jab is the irony in Pap's approach. In order to improve his life, he should be helping his son get a leg up; instead he trips over his own perceived loss of authority.

When we are supportive of education, knowledge, and wisdom, we strengthen and help not only ourselves, but the community and world we live in. To not do so is to hurt ourselves and prevent ourselves and others from reaching their full potential.

Grab onto knowledge wherever you can find it—and it is everywhere. You don't have to be sitting in a classroom to learn something new every single day. As long as you seek it, you will find it.

Simplify with Weekly Routines

Any darn fool can make something complex; it takes a genius to make something simple.
—Albert Einstein

Monday is a day that can be either loathed or loved, depending upon what your job is or what your week looks like. In my experience, Monday comes with a hefty helping of routine. While the word *routine* can have a negative connotation of "boring" or "mundane," for me a weekly routine has a way of being comforting, and it can be that for you too if you've designed the life you desire.

As Sunday afternoon and evening roll in, I begin to settle into a groove, slowly coming out of my weekend revelry and focusing on what needs to be done. I like the security of a routine because once I have it set, I can then tweak and manipulate it to make extra events and unexpected activities work. In other words, once I know what I have to get done and how I'm going to do it, I can let go.

It may sound odd that organizing and simplifying allows for more flexibility and less rigidity, but it's true. Sometimes when we don't plan, our daily routines become overwhelming, and we aren't able to enjoy the many wonderful and pleasurable experiences that can come our way unexpectedly throughout the week.

Once you know that your kitchen is stocked with what you need to make healthy meals, that the laundry will get done, that all appointments are scheduled, gas is in the car, and your home is a welcoming abode, you can relax and enjoy yourself—without the nagging feeling that there's something you ought to be doing.

Daily Routines

By now, you know I love lists, right? Here's one for the routines I've worked out for a smooth sail through the day.

Stick to a Regular Sleep Schedule. Being well rested is an important key to maintaining high energy, managing your weight, keeping your skin beautiful, and having a clear mind. Even on the weekends, while it may sound impossible, do your best to stay within your routine. When your body is tired, it will speak to you. When you listen to it, each day will go much more smoothly, and you'll be better prepared for those unexpected moments that require you to be at your best.

Have a Breakfast Routine. It may sound dull, but during the work week, stick to simple, healthy breakfast menus. Especially if you have children, don't offer them an endless list. Stick to one or two options that will provide them the energy they need throughout the day, and run with it each day of the work week. Save the weekends for special family breakfasts with bacon, French toast, or other out-of-the-ordinary items.

Make the Bed. It takes less than five minutes, and a carefully made bed and a neat boudoir are a welcoming sight to come home to after a long day, when you have just enough energy left to turn down the sheets.

Pick Up the House Every Night. After putting the dogs and/or kids to bed, cleaning up the kitchen, and brushing your teeth, do a quick run-through of your house. Place anything left lying around — newspapers, toys, blankets, shoes, clothes, electronic devices — back where it belongs. This not only will save you time in the morning when you're looking for those things, but it keeps normal household mess from building up to a point where you would need to devote an hour or two to straightening things up. Anyway, who doesn't want to wake up to a tidy home? There is something liberating about starting the day with one or two fewer chores to do.

Leave the Bathroom Clean. Whether you are the only one using your bathroom or you share it with others, make sure you have provided a home for toothbrushes, beauty supplies, and styling tools. When you have finished your daily cleansing and beauty routine, return everything to its spot. For an extra touch of simple luxury, clean the countertops with a disposable wipe, reducing bacteria and creating an inviting environment for yourself and your family, as well as any guests who may stop by.

Get & Remain Organized. Within your home office, or in another designated spot in your home — a small desk in your bedroom or the top of a filing cabinet — *get organized* by removing all clutter and creating a filing system that is easy to follow and that you will adhere to consistently. Designate a place for everything: incoming and outgoing mail, business cards, pens, notepads, inspiration board, charging station for your technology, etc. The key to *remaining organized* is to follow the system you have created. Not only will it save you time, but it will allow your mind to be open to more ideas and a flow of imagination. Another aspect of being organized is how you travel with your electronic devices. Do you have the proper carrying cases for your laptop, iPad, etc.? Knowing that you're always able to function, regardless of where you are, and knowing where you will place these items when you return home will give you peace of mind.

Use *One* Calendar. There are dozens of options for keeping track of yourself, and it doesn't really matter whether you use a fancy computer spreadsheet or a hard-copy notebook. The most important thing is to keep it simple. Decide which one system works best with your way of doing things and then, regardless of whether other people understand it, stick to it. I used to have a Blackberry and tried to use its calendar, but then I realized I love handwriting my daily schedule, so I reverted to a Franklin planner and have never looked back, even since switching to an iPhone. Never use more than one calendar, which is a recipe for confusion. Using one calendar means you know exactly where everything is and don't have to wonder which calendar contains that necessary information you're searching for. Once you've decided on a calendar system that works for you, you're freed up to do what you do best.

A Regular Beauty Routine. There will always be special occasions when our beauty routines become a bit more elaborate, but for the regular workday, create a routine that is simple and leaves you looking and feeling your best. For example, moisturize your entire body, wash your face with a gentle cleanser (Cetaphil, for example), apply moisturizer, concealer, moisturizer with SPF, blush, a dash of eyebrow color, a simple neutral base to your eyelids, eyeliner, a bit of shadow, and smudge-proof mascara (I swear by Bobbi Brown's). Finish with some deodorant and your favorite perfume, and voila!

Weekly Routines

Follow this simple list and you'll control your chores, not vice versa.

Clean the House. Believe it or not, you can eliminate considerable work for yourself if you will simply schedule an hour or two each week to do a basic overall cleaning. This eliminates dust from piling up, dog hair from becoming a nuisance, and gunk from becoming difficult to remove. You may get comments from people who say your house isn't that dirty from week to week, so why should you give yourself more work to do? But you'll actually save a lot of time over the long haul by performing simple maintenance. So turn on your go-to television show or play your favorite tunes and get busy. My date with my house is every Friday after work so that I can enjoy the weekend in a comfortably clean home. Choose any day of the week and time of day that works for you.

Plan Your Menus. Before the week begins, take some time to assess the week ahead and determine what meals you would like to fix. Not every day of the week needs a new meal, as you can depend on your pantry and leftovers, or you may be eating out on certain occasions. Have a plan, make a list, and make a date to head to the grocery store.

Grocery Shop. In the past few months, I have begun to go grocery shopping once a week, and then make quick stops throughout the week to pick up fresh ingredients. I find that with weekly trips to the supermarket I spend less and tend to not overbuy as much as I did when I wasn't organized. Keep a grocery list in your kitchen so that when something runs out you can quickly add it and will have it handy when you next head to the store. There may be times throughout the week when you want to purchase fresh produce, bread, or meat, but for the basics (milk, eggs, yogurt, rice, canned goods, frozen foods), try to go once a week to save time and money.

Organize Your Laundry. If you have a family, you may find it necessary or just smart to wash one load a day, but if you live alone or there are just two of you, weekly laundry duty should suffice.

Regardless of how often you do laundry, have a handful of bins, baskets, and containers that are organized by color and/or fabric (darks, whites, towels, rags, lingerie, etc.). As you shift your clothes into the laundry room, immediately sort each item into its appropriate basket so that when you decide to start the washer, all you have to do is set the dial, add the detergent, and toss the clothes in.

Plan the Week

At the beginning of each week, block out fifteen minutes or half an hour to open your planner and think about the week ahead. Preparing yourself for what will be expected of you not only means you can be more productive; it also means you can be more productive with grace and ease.

A well-run life is one that is organized and well planned. It doesn't mean you are a robot doing the same thing each week. On the contrary, choosing to be organized actually allows you to avoid a rigid schedule because, as keeping up with things becomes a habit, what has to be completed is tended to and you can more fully enjoy your life.

CHAPTER NINE

Traveling the World in Style & Comfort

Travel is fatal to prejudice, bigotry and narrow-mindedness, and many of our people need it sorely on these accounts. Broad, wholesome, charitable views of men and things cannot be acquired by vegetating in one little corner of the earth all one's lifetime.
— Mark Twain

Twain bluntly and accurately describes one of the greatest benefits of seeing the world. To not understand other cultures often breeds fear, which can cause us to become dependent on a belief that a particular way of life is best. To remain in this belief, to refuse to seek out information, is detrimental to the education you can allow yourself to soak up. Ultimately, it's not a matter of declaring any one way of living as being best. Instead, we need to realize that there are many different ways of choosing to live; we need to be accepting and understanding of the diversity that so richly makes up our world.

Expand Your Mind, Travel the World

I vividly remember my first trip abroad in 2000; I was in college and traveled to France to study for the summer. The anticipation was intoxicating, and the trip across the Atlantic somewhat overwhelming. I can remember the adrenaline rush that kept me going for twenty-seven hours until I finally fell asleep, utterly exhausted, at my destination— Angers, France.

It became instantly clear to me that other cultures get along just fine going about life in a way that may seem foreign to outsiders, just as my cultural tendencies might seem foreign to someone else. I can remember conversing (or trying to converse) with students from Spain, Norway, Sweden, and Germany, and at first feeling not very self-assured; however, at the same time, I felt completely at ease because everyone else was trying to live their life as well in the best way they knew how.

That was my first extended trip abroad, and I was more than eager to fly home after the summer. But I had caught the bug, the one that now constantly encourages me to hop on a plane or a train (I love the ease of traveling in Europe) and get away from my day-to-day routine—so that I can appreciate it even more when I come home.

Often when I return from one of my adventures, I experience a "traveler's high," in which I imagine living in the place I have just visited. More often than not, I come back to earth and realize I've created a pretty wonderful life right where I am, but the traveling strengthens my appreciation of it. It also opens my mind to understand that there are many ways of living and living well, and we should not be quick to judge cultures we don't understand.

I would be willing to wager that most people, all around the world, are just trying to make it through the day, and meanwhile achieve a bit of happiness and feel loved for who they are. The variety from culture to culture is what makes this world a place of curiosity, possibility, and beauty. After all, the potential for beauty can be found in so many wonderful, exotic, unexpected places if only we choose to see it, be less judgmental, and observe without preconceived notions of what "should be."

I've heard it said that one way to have a truly happy life is to travel abroad twice a year. I think there is something to that. Whether you are traveling to relax and unwind, to spend time with family and loved ones, or simply to get away from the daily routine, being away helps you to understand and realize how wonderful your life is already or has the potential to be. The perspective you gain in your journeys expands your world and lets you welcome in more happiness.

Whether it is a trip around the world or to the other side of your state, consider trying to incorporate a few more miles in your life. You might just be surprised at the ways travel can add to your world.

Make Travel Comfortable & Simply Luxurious

How can we travel luxuriously these days, you might ask, with all the security checkpoints, body scanners, and long lines? First of all, everyone's definition of a vacation is different, but the tools required to make sure you make the most of a vacation are similar in almost any traveling scenario. Here is what I suggest.

Pinpoint Your Priorities

At this very moment, you most likely can easily imagine your ideal vacation; however, if you are traveling with others, their definition of what is ideal may differ greatly from your own. When planning travel with friends or loved ones, be sure to communicate well in order to avoid disappointment. For some people, lying around poolside drinking fruity specialty drinks fits the bill, but others may want to explore and tour a city or some beautiful countryside.

In fact, you should go through the same process even when you travel alone. First, ask yourself, What needs to happen in order for me to come back refreshed, satisfied, and exhilarated? Then get busy laying out a trip that will answer those needs.

Plan Early. While there can be some fantastic deals for those who wait until the eleventh hour, it isn't something I would suggest if you know with certainty you are going to take a vacation and have a particular destination in mind. Planning well in advance allows you to investigate the greatest number of options and to compare the prices charged for transportation, lodging, and special events. My simplest and most fundamental advice is to plan ahead, but be flexible. The Internet makes it easy to plan and make reservations as we create the trips of our dreams. As you make your plans, be sure to ask about cancellation policies, fees charged for changing reservations, etc.

Map Out an Itinerary. I highly recommend planning out what you want to see, purchasing tickets for certain events in advance, and mapping out your day-to-day excursions, keeping in mind that some events happen only on certain days (for example, le Marché aux Puces in Paris is open only on Saturday, Sunday, and Monday, and the Musée du Louvre is closed on Tuesdays). That said, once you arrive, be flexible and open as opportunities present themselves. Having a plan gives you a foundation, as opposed to arriving and not knowing what to do when.

Make Lists. People who travel frequently, regardless of the length of a trip or its destination, often make a checklist, which is a great way to eliminate the potential for worry—or even panic—when you're already on the plane or are five hours away from home. While you'll want to tweak the list a bit according to the type of vacation you are about to embark on, the necessities usually stay pretty constant—toothbrush, blow-dryer, makeup, lingerie, etc. (You'll find detailed packing lists later in this chapter). The most essential checklist is the one for the clothes you'll take, which should allow you to feel your best and exude confidence. If a bit of pre-vacation shopping is necessary, I say go forth and fill that suitcase!

Prep Your Home for Your Return

The best way to end a vacation is to come home to a clean and tidy sanctuary—all the laundry done, clean sheets on the beds, and an empty garbage can. Before walking out the door, prepare your home for your return.

- ✓ Arrange pet sitting.

- ✓ Discard anything in the fridge that won't last.

- ✓ Empty your kitchen garbage can. Arrange for regular pickup of your garbage, trash, and recycling (this may require help from a neighbor).

✓ Clean the house.

✓ Do laundry before you leave so you won't have to deal with it as soon as you return.

✓ Place a hold on your mail; if possible, have it all delivered your first day back.

✓ Schedule a house sitter or someone to care for your yard while you're away. Or ask a neighbor to keep an eye on your house; be sure to provide a way to reach you should anything out of the ordinary occur.

✓ Pay any monthly bills you can't pay online while you're away, or schedule bill payment through online banking. When you're up to date on your bill paying and thus certain of your budget, you're clear about how much money you can spend on your trip.

✓ In winter, turn down the thermostat to a level that will keep the pipes from freezing. During the summer, you can probably leave the air off, depending on where you live; in warmer climates, set the temp higher, but keep the humidity controls on.

Planning Your Packing

The only way to pack is to plan carefully in advance. Rushed, haphazard packing sets the stage for moments of "I have the perfect dress/shirt/skirt/pair of jeans . . . and it's at home in my closet" remorse.

To Carry On or Not. If you are traveling for a week or less, try to simply pack a carry-on and to take an onboard tote onto the plane; if you are flying internationally, regardless of how long, most airlines allow you to check one bag for free; check their website for their baggage guidelines. Traveling with only a carry-on means your luggage won't be lost, and it allows you to more easily change flights and get to your accommodations.

Onboard Tote. Always carry a well-stocked travel tote. Having one that suits your needs and doesn't require you to take other bags makes the traveling process much easier. Purchase a quality tote; make it an investment that will last. Think about your needs. Do you travel with a laptop, tablet, legal documents, children, pets, etc.? What will ease your mind and keep you comfortable during a flight? The list below assumes you have a carry-on piece of luggage and that your onboard tote is a second item you can place on the floor in front of you. Choose a tote that can hold the following:

- Laptop
- Tablet, iPad, or reader
- Journal
- Makeup for touch-ups (lipstick, lip gloss, mascara, concealer, etc.)
- One or two of your favorite tea sachets (a simple luxury while flying; just ask for hot water)
- Books, magazines, and newspapers not downloaded on your tablet
- Reading glasses
- Wallet
- Planner (if not on one of your electronic devices)
- Cell phone
- Ear buds
- Small hairbrush
- Sleep aids (sleep mask, Tylenol PM, scarf, etc.)
- Miscellaneous necessities: hand lotion, breath mints, Tide-to-Go, bobby pins, rubber bands, nail file, etc.

Keep the following options in mind when you're buying an onboard tote: What is the handle drop? You need to be able to put it on your shoulder comfortably; seven to eight inches is minimal, but see what feels best. Leather or a heavy cloth fabric can handle weight without stretching or ruining the bag. Choose a color that is versatile (brown, black, or a classic print). Do you want compartments? Make sure it's wide enough to hold your laptop. Will it be easy to remove items (laptop/tablets) for security checks?

Dry Cleaning. Once you decide on your wardrobe, take anything that needs to be cleaned to the dry cleaners well in advance. After you pick up your clothes, keep the plastic bags and use them as you pack to prevent wrinkles: Lay the bags between the items, then either roll or fold, and *voilà,* no wrinkles!). If you don't have dry cleaning bags, follow Diane von Fürstenberg's packing advice and roll, roll, roll to avoid wrinkles.

Travel Intangibles

I know, I know, I've suggested that you carefully take stock of your priorities and plan what you want to do on your vacation, but always keep this in mind: If you feel as though you are on a strict itinerary while on vacation, is it really a vacation? You are a well-organized, wonderful human being, but even you—yes, you—need to let it flow. Let your hair down. Once you do so, you'll open yourself to some amazing moments and stories to tell upon returning.

Take a Few Extra Days. I'm talking about breathing room. Traveling is often stressful. To compensate, schedule a couple of days to recover before returning to work. Doing so allows you to unwind and savor the moments you've just experienced. If you don't want time alone at home, plan to extend your vacation by a couple of extra days. Studies have shown that it takes about forty-eight hours for a person to become fully immersed in vacation mode. So why not extend the period of immersion?

Stay True to Your Health. Hear me out on this one. I'm not suggesting that you head to the hotel's gym and run in place for miles on the treadmill. However, I am recommending that you incorporate exercise into the events you plan. Walk as much as possible; whether in museums, on tours, or at theme parks, just walk—or bike, swim, surf, whatever brings you enjoyment. Including a bit of calorie burning in your daily activities will mean that when your life goes back to the daily routine, you won't feel guilty about your time away.

Beauty Preparation. Before you take off, make sure you tend to your beauty regimen, which may mean scheduling appointments well in advance. After all, you want to feel beautiful as well as properly packed. Here are a few preparations to consider:

- Pedicure and manicure
- Haircut and color
- Spray tan
- Necessary waxing (brows, lip, bikini)

Reading Material. If you have access to a tablet, use it when you travel. While I always prefer holding a book in my hands to using a reader, you can save so much space by buying Kindle versions (iPad has a free Kindle app) of books that it makes no sense not to use a tablet for reading on trips. I also have my magazine subscriptions on my iPad and always download the most recent issues before stepping on the plane. Download the day's current paper, too, so you can stay up on the news while up in the air.

What to Pack: Your Essential Travel Wardrobe

When making a list of what to pack, I always start with the outfit I want to change into upon arrival, then the number of outfits I will need, depending upon the length of the trip and the type of activities I will be engaged in.

Your most important goal when you pack: *Keep it simple.* Stay away from complicated wardrobe ensembles and too many accessories. Think layering; choose classic neutrals and only a few flattering colors. The specifics of your trip will shape your wardrobe packing list, but these are the essential categories; read on for more detailed suggestions.

- Sleepwear (chemise or pjs, travel robe)
- Underthings (1 pair of panties/day, 2 or 3 bras, including a strapless, if necessary)
- A simple, neutral wardrobe that allows you to mix and match: 1 or 2 dresses; pants or jeans; 1 or 2 blouses; cashmere sweater(s); jacket, blazer, and/or coat (per weather conditions); workout clothes for exercise (optional)
- Scarves and jewelry: add color with 1 or 2 scarves, necessary belts, silver and/or gold hoops/earrings
- Shoes: ballet flats; heels (if necessary); boots (optional); trainers for exercise (optional)
- Toiletries and beauty utensils — travel blow-dryer (under 1800 wattage), curling iron, straightener, etc.
- Converter and/or adapter
- Charger(s) for your phone and other devices
- Watch
- Laundry bag (small, plastic)

Make a Packing List . . . Then Edit

Bear in mind that this advice is coming from someone who loves fashion, which means I approach the packing of my suitcase with the mind-set of looking stylish first; however, I know that I have to keep versatility and functionality in mind as well.

A few weeks prior to your departure, make a list of each day and the outfits (and accessories and beauty supplies) you will need. If you will have access to a washer/dryer, keep this in mind: laundering your clothes will let you repeat certain outfits, pack fewer socks/underwear/etc., and mix and match your items. After creating the original list, go back through with a discerning eye — do you really need that third pair of heels?

Here's a basic, all-purpose list you can start with. Tailor it to fit your personal needs and the needs of each trip.

Clothing

- ✓ 4 pairs of undies
- ✓ 2 bras (one strapless)
- ✓ 3 pairs of socks
- ✓ White button-up shirt
- ✓ Short-sleeved blouse
- ✓ Nautical top
- ✓ Pair of jeans, ankle or cigarette leg
- ✓ Optional pair of pants (chinos, corduroy, etc.)
- ✓ Jacket
- ✓ Cardigan
- ✓ Camisole (for layering)
- ✓ Swimsuit
- ✓ 2 T-shirts
- ✓ Simple jersey dress
- ✓ Maxi dress (if you're hitting the beach or taking in warm weather)
- ✓ Comfy cashmere sweater
- ✓ Pajamas
- ✓ Robe (if your hotel doesn't supply one)

Footwear

- ✓ Ballet flats
- ✓ Nude pumps
- ✓ Black pumps
- ✓ Walking shoes (for strolling)
- ✓ Espadrilles
- ✓ Heels (only if necessary)
- ✓ Trainers (if you'll be exercising in a serious way)

Accessories

- ✓ Sunglasses
- ✓ Scarf
- ✓ Oversized tote
- ✓ Classic pair of earrings (gold or silver) that can go with anything
- ✓ Day handbag
- ✓ Clutch
- ✓ Watch

Stocking Your Toiletries Tote

Creating a sanctuary at home is something that evolves over time, and smart women who seek simple luxury have everything they need for optimal self-care in their home spa, a vital part of a true sanctuary. And when you travel, you don't have to forgo the tranquillity and comfort you enjoy at home. If you stock an efficient toiletries tote, no matter where the train/plane/car stops, you can always look fabulous, present your best self, and be in a genuinely pleasant mood.

First things first: You must have a toiletries tote that exudes style. And yes, Louis Vuitton makes fabulous totes at exorbitant prices, but why not seek out a vintage makeup train case? They are sturdy, unique, and have a history. Or choose something even more creative—a hat box. Simply place an organizer inside that holds all of your traveling essentials securely.

Whatever form you choose for your travel carry-on, here's a beginning list of toiletries that will ensure you have a fresh face and a calm spirit, and the ability to be ready for any occasion or situation.

- Facial cleansing pads
- Makeup necessities (tinted moisturizer, mascara, blush, concealer, and lip color)

- Lip balm (rosebud salve, Vaseline, or your choice)
- Toothbrush, toothpaste, and floss
- Deodorant
- Body lotion
- Facial moisturizer/eye lotion
- Hand bands/bobby pins/soft headband
- Shampoo/conditioner
- Razor
- Sunscreen
- Perfume
- Fingernail file/clippers
- Hairbrush
- Hair products in travel sizes (hairspray, thickening spray, mousse, etc.)
- Comb
- Small carrier for jewelry
- Cotton balls/Q-tips
- Bubble bath
- Shower cap
- Candle
- Baby powder

Optional
- Adapter and/or converter (for international travel)
- Blow-dryer
- Contact solution and holder
- Feminine toiletries and necessities
- Reading glasses
- Allergy medicine
- Antibiotic ointment
- Pain medicine
- Band-Aids

After more than a decade of traveling on my own, I have fine-tuned my tote so that now I can just grab it and go, confident that I will be able to look and feel my best. Trying to choose the right clothes is tough enough, so it is a relief to know that my tote is stocked and always ready to go. A tip for saving time and stress as you plan your next getaway: After you return home from a trip, make a list of tote items that are low and restock them well before your next adventure.

Planning an International Trip

During the summer of 2012, I traveled to London, where I enjoyed a week of the Olympics. Then I went on to Paris, a city I'd yearned to return to for more than twelve years. I quickly booked myself a return trip to Paris during the summer of 2013, and with each trip my appreciation for traveling has been heightened. Traveling abroad can be one of the most amazing experiences of your life. Making the most of it requires attention to details and careful pre-planning.

Investigate the Culture. Each culture has its own customs and expectations. Take time to read up in order to avoid the occasional faux pas or dirty look. Be mindful of expectations of dress based on one's gender. Be knowledgeable about state holidays or religious celebrations that may coincide with your visit.

Learn at Least a Little about the Language. If you don't know the language, do yourself a huge favor and take a course in the fundamentals that will teach you at least a few common conversational phrases. Knowing the basics will alleviate considerable stress as you will be better able to not only communicate with locals and vendors, but also read signs and directions. I made it through level 1 of Rosetta Stone's French online program in a couple of months, and it helped immensely.

Passport. Make sure you have a valid passport. Most US passports are good for ten years; if you need to renew yours or apply for a new one, start the process four to six months in advance. The basic fee is $110, with the possibility of additional smaller fees. If you're renewing, you will have to provide a new headshot (personnel at your local post office will take a government-accepted photo for $10 or $15) and your current address. You can print out the renewal application found on the US government website http://travel.state.gov/passport/renew/renew_833.html. If you are acquiring a US passport for the first time, visit http://travel. state.gov. In 2014, the total cost was $135. You will need to provide proof of citizenship (birth certificate or certificate of citizenship), as well as photo identification, such as a valid driver's license, certificate of naturalization, or military ID. Once all documents are accepted, you can expect to receive your passport in four to six weeks.

Money. Traveler's checks are no longer a savvy or necessary way to carry money when you travel; a major downside is that you pay high exchange-rate fees each time you cash one. Depending upon where you are traveling, using your ATM/debit card is a frugal way to avoid excessive fees, and it serves as an automatic currency exchange. In the UK and France, there are oodles of ATMs, also known as cashpoints (UK) or cash machines (France). You will be charged a fee to use ATMs in another country, and possibly one from your bank as well, so check with your bank to see how much you will be charged. My bank allotted me two free withdrawals and after that a 3 percent charge based on what I withdrew. If you do want to exchange cash or traveler's checks, visit a bank, travel agency, or post office; ascertain their exchange rate and learn about any commission fees before you request a transaction. Before leaving home, be sure to inform your bank that you will be traveling (where and when) so that your card is not blocked when the security system detects unusual patterns of spending. Also check with your bank about maximum withdrawals for ATMs. There are online ATMs and off-line ATMs — in other words, those that are associated with your bank and those that are not. Make sure the maximum withdrawal on both is suited to your needs. If not, you can petition for the maximum to be raised; it is very rare for such a request to be rejected.

Check the Exchange Rate. As you budget for your trip, find out the currency exchange rate for the country you will be visiting. You don't want to be at the ATM withdrawing 500 pounds, thinking you're withdrawing $500, only to discover you've taken out $200 more than you meant to.

Electronic Devices. The electric voltage used outside North America is twice what Americans and Canadians are used to (220–240v, compared to 110–120v). In order to use your electrical devices you will need one of two things and possibly both. An *adapter* is simply a device to change the plug type and does not convert voltage. For devices that use up to 250 watts of power (laptop, iPad, cell phone, Kindle), you will need only an adapter as most of these devices convert the voltage automatically. I purchased an adapter that can be used in most countries (except India and South Africa) from Walkabout Solution for $30, and it works wonderfully. However, since I needed to take along a travel blow-dryer and curling iron, I also needed a *converter*. Most blow-dryers use at least 1,000 watts of power (check the tag on the cord). I purchased a good converter that could handle up to 1,800 watts, also from Walkabout, for $35.

Cell Phones. Not being able to use my cell phone was one of the most liberating things when I traveled internationally, but for many people, ignoring the cell phone is not an option. If you want to use your phone, begin by checking with your provider; they can let you know if it can be used where you are going (for example, in some places Apple's iPhone 4s works, but the iPhone 4 doesn't). Then you will want to check in about the rates for calls, texts, and data usage. Another option to save money is to download the free app Viber, which allows you to make free calls and send texts and video without charge to anyone as long as they too have a Viber account. If your phone can't be used, there is always the option of Skype or email; Internet cafés and free Wi-Fi are easy to find, including in airports.

Prescriptions/Contact Lenses/Other Necessities. Make sure to refill all necessary prescriptions before your trip. Also, if you wear glasses or contacts, make sure you have backup lenses should you break your glasses or lose your contacts.

Flight and/or Trip Insurance. When purchasing your tickets, it is wise to buy flight insurance. The cost is relatively minimal ($20–$50), and having this insurance gives you some breathing room as you'll save money if you find you have to edit your trip. Trip insurance on items you are traveling with is also an option, although when flying the airlines covers your luggage should it be damaged or lost, and often your homeowners' insurance covers these items as well. While I have never bought trip insurance, you might want to look into it if you're traveling with valuable items that are irreplaceable.

While at Your Destination

The captain has skillfully landed the plane and the vacation you have long anticipated is about to begin. Knowing how to put the proper currency in your pocket, learning how to find transportation, being savvy about what to wear . . . these are a few simple but invaluable bits of knowledge that will ensure a successful getaway.

Currency Exchange

As mentioned earlier, traveler's checks have become passé; as long as you are traveling in a country with secure banking systems, you'll find ATMs (aka bank machines or cashpoints) nearly everywhere. They are an easy way to access the local currency without paying high exchange fees. Remember, your bank will most likely charge a fee for international withdrawals and potentially a percentage, depending upon how much you withdraw, so look into this before you leave.

You may wonder if you should carry any of your country's currency with you and exchange it at your destination. I usually keep a small amount of US currency in my wallet for traveling to the airport and getting back home at the end of the trip, but there is no need to take cash with the intention of exchanging it. As long as you have a debit and/or credit card and know you will have access to an ATM at your destination, you don't need to risk carrying and potentially losing cash.

Use Public Transportation

Even if you prefer to walk when you visit other countries, become acquainted with the local public transportation system. (You'll still get plenty of exercise; when I was in London I rode the Tube regularly, yet I still walked at least six miles daily.) Both the Tube (London) and the Metro (Paris) are fairly easy to navigate with time and a good map, and there are many helpful websites to assist with most questions you'll have.

In large metropolitan areas, such as London and Paris, there are many public transportation options—subway, bus, train, taxi, bikes. In smaller communities you'll often have access to a high-speed rail system for moving from town to town, as well as buses. Using bikes is a wonderful idea if you want to be your own tour guide and see more of a city or region.

When to Hail a Taxi

I highly recommend choosing the luxury of a taxi to take you to and from the airport or train to your accommodations; it is a great way to avoid stress, exhaustion, loss of time, and unnecessary frustration. When you have your luggage in tow, getting on and off subway trains can be excruciating, especially during peak hours when trains are packed and the stairs never end. The extra 30 euros I spent on a taxi when I made my last trip were more than worth it.

In Paris I used the highly recommended EcoCab taxi service to and from the airport, and I was very impressed. You can book them online prior to the day you'll be traveling, and you can pay online, which makes the trip even smoother.

Protect Your Valuables

Always be aware of where your purse or wallet or handbag is at all times. Never leave it unattended or turn your back on it. When walking, keep your purse tucked under your arm or firmly clutched so it can't be ripped out of your hands. Upon arrival, make sure you know where your passport is and where you can keep it during your stay that is assuredly safe.

Camera

To begin with, make sure the camera or device you are using to take pictures is fully charged (and pack the charger). Everyone takes pictures differently, but don't be afraid to take both posed and candid images. Including people in scenery shots makes the images more personal. Have fun with poses, and remember, capturing something on film or in pixels is a way of creating a visual journal. Be creative and don't edit yourself, so that when you look back ten years from now, you'll be able to remember precisely what you experienced on your journey.

Journal

If you're like me, you love to record the events of the day so that you can remember all you did long after your trip is done. Allow yourself time to do this each day if possible; find a quiet thirty minutes or so—at a café, in a park, or somewhere else that you enjoy—and let your pen go to town. At the time you may think there is no way you could ever forget all that has happened, but trust me, you will forget certain details, and reading about them years down the road will make you smile and appreciate your decision to keep a journal.

CHAPTER TEN

Indulging Your Inner Francophile

Perhaps you have already noticed my proclivity for all things French. And if you're assuming I'm a Francophile, you would be correct. I can't help it, I have a secret love for the French culture (okay, not so secret anymore).

The moment the wheels touch down after I come back across the Atlantic from France, I'm already getting excited about returning to Paris and counting the days until I can again indulge in a buttery, mouth-wateringly delicious *pain au chocolat* that nobody in the States seems able to make as successfully as the pastry geniuses in France. The cobbled streets; the gardens; the street markets, abundant with fresh food and artisanal wares; the cafés, with their street-facing tables and chairs; and the exquisite street style that is unique to Paris — it all just brings a smile to my face.

The French Way

Even when I'm going about my daily rounds here in the States, I try to incorporate ideas I've picked up as I've read French-inspired memoirs, cookbooks, and fiction. Here is an impressionistic array of ways to get in touch with your inner Francophile — that is, to incorporate the French lifestyle into your everyday life, regardless of where you live, your budget, or whether or not you can speak a sentence of French.

Embracing the Best in Food and Wine. Cook your own meals more often, but don't hesitate to purchase pastries, desserts, and breads from your favorite patisserie or boulangerie. . . . Enjoy a croissant with homemade jam on the weekends. . . . Cook with fresh seasonal produce (canned in winter). . . . Create a diet regimen that incorporates quality, flavorful food, but eat in moderation. . . . Drink rosé when dining in the afternoon. . . . Buy from local vendors, markets, boutiques. . . . Cook with real, not processed food. . . . Take time for lunch — a long lunch, a full meal, along with a glass of wine perhaps — and enjoy yourself. . . . Indulge in quality cheese. . . . Purchase a fresh baguette in the morning. . . . Enjoy the walk to the patisserie as you greet the day. . . . Enjoy smaller portions. . . . Eat more slowly, savor what you're eating, and breathe. . . . Drink wine, which is rich in antioxidants (of course, enjoy it in moderation). . . . Indulge in café time. If you're on your own, take along a newspaper, book, or your favorite magazine. Sip a cappuccino or cup of tea and lose track of time. . . . Begin every evening with an aperitif — nothing overly large, strong, or excessive, simply a chance to relax and settle in. . . . Eat in courses, which allow you to savor what you have in front of you, slow down your eating, and encourage your "hunger meter" to register when you are actually full. . . . Several evenings a week, enjoy a simple, yet filling meal — a small main course, a salad, and a bit of cheese, and wine, if you're so inclined. . . . Keep less food in your refrigerator and shop more often for fresh food. . . . Treat yourself to sparkling water with a meal every once in a while.

Making Fashion Personal. Create a signature style that flatters your figure and lifestyle and stick to it. . . . Build a capsule wardrobe for each season. . . . Buy fewer clothes, but higher-quality items. . . . Wear more dresses; they are comfortable and chic. . . . Ignore fashion trends. . . . Luxurious lingerie is a necessity — invest in it without guilt. Wear more of it. . . . Purchase quality ballet flats for every occasion. . . . Indulge in classic wardrobe choices that are interchangeable. . . . If an item doesn't pair with at least two other items in your closet (creating two separate outfits), don't purchase it. . . . Always look presentable. . . . Create a quality wardrobe (fewer items, but more that last and work with many other items) and a simple beauty regimen. . . . Knowing you look beautiful will positively affect your mood, which always makes for a better day, no matter what is in store. . . . Bring on the blazers! Choose classic colors to begin with and create more outfits with the clothes you already have. . . . Love the Breton (nautical)

top, with black or navy stripes. . . . Wear knee-high boots
(preferably flats or wedges, but heels are okay as well) for winter
and maintain a chic, effortless style.

Building a Style & Taking Care of Yourself. Embrace
your femininity. . . . Be sincere. Eliminate fake niceties. . . . Be well-
mannered. . . . Discover your signature scent. . . . Find time to
treasure hunt—visit flea markets, consignment boutiques, and yard
sales. . . . Delay gratification. Faster isn't always better. . . . Expand
your cultural creative awareness. Stay abreast of the arts—new
museum exhibits, films, books, lectures, recitals, plays, etc. . . .
Invest in quality skin-care products. . . . Wear less makeup and
show off your glowing skin. . . . Have regular facials. . . . Regularly
(every six to eight weeks) visit a hair stylist/colorist you trust. . .
. Maintain a simple style. . . . Don't wash your hair every day. Use
dry shampoo and invest in a quality blow-out from time to time. . . .
Enjoy the finer things—the luxurious things—in life. . . . Buy less,
so you can purchase quality items and experiences. . . . Establish
daily, weekly, and monthly rituals that bring pleasure into your life.
. . . A physical workout shouldn't be a torture. Incorporate physical
fitness into your daily routine. Walk more, drive less.

How to Find Your *Je ne Sais Quoi*

The French phrase *Je ne sais quoi*, which means "I don't know what,"
refers to a certain special, indefinable quality that draws us to
someone or something. It's a phrase that often comes to me when I
try to describe the intoxication I have with all things French—
especially the ability of French women to exude style, confidence,
and an air of mystery.

I recently took a college course titled Know Thyself, and I've
gradually found increasing ease and a growing sense of inner calm
as I come to understand what knowing oneself is all about. I've

come to realize that the only person we will ever have the opportunity to truly understand is ourselves. Yet ironically, in today's world we are so busy trying to figure out what everyone else wants, desires, and expects that we often forget to examine exactly who we are. It should be the other way around!

Take fifteen minutes a day over the next week or so to think about yourself. At the same time, focus on three qualities — originality, simplicity, and courage — that are often possessed by women of whom we say, "She has a certain *je ne sais quoi.*"

Originality

Allow yourself moments of solitude. Keep certain things to yourself. Be impossible to define by anyone but yourself. How? Never stop growing, learning, and searching for new knowledge about yourself and the world. Follow your own path even if no one seems to understand why. Don't be agreeable if you don't agree.

Ignore stereotypes; by their very definition they are inaccurate and a coward's crutch. Continue to learn. Listen to what continues to call to you. Indulge in conversation with those who intrigue you.

Simplicity

Choose your friends wisely, then nurture, nurture, nurture. Become observant of all that goes on around you. Some of my most enjoyable experiences have been when I have chosen to be a wallflower and have simply taken in my surroundings — the people, the weather, the behavior, how an event is playing out. So much can be learned by observation.

Speak when you have something to say. Don't simply speak to fill the silence. Silence isn't necessarily a bad thing. Choose your words wisely, as they have great power; they can welcome or isolate, console or harm, inform or manipulate, encourage or terrify. What legacy do you want to leave behind?

Meditate. Slow down. Be still. Focus on your breathing. Clear your mind.

Turn routines into rituals to be enjoyed. Grocery shopping? Choose a favorite time of day, find a wonderful market, and take your time — examining the fruit, reading the wine labels, gazing across the cheese display. Oh, and pick up a lovely bouquet of flowers as an exclamation point to punctuate a wonderful outing.

Appreciate your unique beauty. Channel your inner Diana Vreeland. Dress for the occasion. Practice self-discipline. Appear to live effortlessly. Part of what makes someone attractive is the mystery. How does she do it? Such a question works much like a magnet.

Courage

Take the time to understand the rules, then break them when necessary. Don't be afraid to make a mistake. Be willing to take risks. Choose battles that pair up with what you value most. Wisdom comes with experience; in order to gain it, a woman must be willing to spread her wings.

Always choose quality over quantity — in clothing, relationships, décor, thoughts, and other areas in life. Turn off the technology and just go where the moment takes you.

Travel wherever your curiosity pulls you. Read biographies and autobiographies of people who capture your attention.

Embrace your femininity. This doesn't mean you have to dress head-to-toe in pink (unless you want to); it does mean you should be authentically who you are. Femininity doesn't mean all women should act alike, but it does mean we shouldn't shun our innate unique talents. No stereotyping — every woman is uniquely her own individual.

Strive to be respected, not liked. Remember Willy Loman in *Death of a Salesman*? Ignore the outside world's opinion. Pay it no mind. You will intrigue them all the more.

Keep a record of your thoughts. And then review what appears regularly. Listen. Act. Remember . . . you have but this one and only life. How will you design it? Most important, when you find that certain something within your own life that makes your ordinary routine sing, giving you pleasure that you could have never have imagined, revel in it, luxuriate in it, and then build upon it so that it remains within your life.

Scarves, Stripes & Style

Channeling my inner French style involves feeling a bit more confident, much more sensual, and all the more certain that I know how to pull together chic, timeless style. Always choose stylish over sexy. Choosing to be sexy is objectifying one's outer self, while choosing to be stylish is a reflection of inner self-respect.

Why Not . . . Wear a Scarf?

Wear a classic sheath dress and simply throw a scarf over your shoulders for a simple, yet luxuriously fabulous look. And speaking of French scarves and style, at the top of the list of the purchases I'd recommend is a piece of art on a scarf from Hermès. It's an investment, but you'll know you have added to your signature style.

Whether the calendar says it's fall, spring, winter, or summer, a scarf is always a tasteful and wise choice to add to your wardrobe. While I've always loved scarves, I must admit it wasn't until a recent trip to Paris that I came to feel less intimidated by them. Yes, you read that correctly. Intimidated.

Why would anyone be intimidated by a small piece of fabric? Well, on the surface it seemed to me that it was the scarf, but when I dug a little deeper, I realized I was reacting to the confidence with which French women wear their signature accessory. Of course, women across the globe wear scarves, but very rarely as I was growing up did I observe women wearing scarves in the manner depicted in French books, magazines, or movies. That stylishness intimidated me, as in: Would I ever be able to carry it off?

It took some time, but I finally have completely embraced the option of wearing a scarf, and I hope you will too, if you don't already. The key is to realize there is no "right" way to tie a scarf. In fact, there are so many options that it boggles my mind still. Better yet, because there are endless colors, prints, and fabrics, the type of scarf you choose to wear ultimately comes down to your signature style. As long as you wear it confidently and purposefully, you will avoid the moment of doubt I spoke of in chapter 1. I felt insecure wearing a scarf in high school because I was insecure; it had nothing to do with the accessory.

Incorporate scarves into your daily wardrobe. Own them as you would pairs of shoes. You can never have too many, and remember, the right scarf to complete your outfit is the one you feel most confident wearing.

A Simple Accessory. Always invest in quality accessories. Purchase a piece of jewelry or a scarf or a belt not because it's a trend or the "it" item but because it will last and it speaks to your sense of style. Jewelry can provide a wonderful finishing touch for an outfit, but the beauty of a scarf is that it can take center stage and eliminate the need for additional accessories. Not sure which necklace or earrings to wear? Choose neither and wear a beautiful silk scarf. Not sure which type of scarf to buy? My rule of thumb for simplifying the decision-making process is to wear a print scarf with a solid ensemble and a solid scarf with a beautiful print blouse or dress. Keep it simple, and choose colors or prints that go with your most flattering colors and complement your capsule wardrobe pieces.

A Layer of Warmth. In the summer, wandering around Paris and London in the evening or early in the morning, I found myself needing just a little extra warmth, but not necessarily a jacket. A wool blend or silk blend scarf is perfect in the summer; in the winter, a cozy wool or cashmere scarf is ideal paired with a heavy coat. When you travel, always carry a scarf in your onboard tote to stay comfortable on air-conditioned planes.

A Touch of Color. My capsule wardrobe's colors stick to a simple palette — neutrals and accents of navy. A beautiful print silk scarf adds that necessary pop or finishing touch that can change up an outfit just enough to make it special.

Create a Signature Style. There are endless ways to wear scarves — the slip knot, wrap and tie, double wrap with French knot, and the simple wrap, just to get you started. Continue playing with the scarves you have, and settle on a few ways that work best for your wardrobe, personality, and lifestyle. Hermès offers a free app — Silk Knots — that shows the endless ways to tie a scarf.

Why Not . . . Wear Stripes?

When it comes to coordinating my spring and summer wardrobe, nautical stripes (aka Breton stripes) will always be one of my favorite options. While nautical tops are a classic choice that is always on trend (see the box in chapter 4), they were ubiquitous on the spring 2013 runways. Designers played with color, bright bold combinations, and creative variations that went way beyond the classic Coco Chanel striped top and had fun with their interpretations of a popular choice of women of all ages.

Here are a handful of ways to incorporate stripes into your spring and summer wardrobes.

A Classic Choice. Paired with dark denim jeans or white cropped trousers, or worn under a classic jacket or trench, a striped top is always in style. Boatneck is my favorite neckline, but always choose the most flattering style for your body type. If you're traveling and not sure what to wear, choose stripes and you'll look chic, timeless, and sophisticated.

Dress Up or Down. For work, for day, or even for a delightful date night, stripes can be dressed up or down. Think black-and-white stripes and a black knee-length skirt, paired with nude or statement heels—ooh-la-la, indeed, without breaking a sweat.

Mix Vertical & Horizontal. Get creative and play with vertical and horizontal stripes. Looking to add a few inches to your frame? Remember: Vertical stripes elongate. When choosing stripes for pants, wear them vertically from top to bottom. The illusion is quite powerful, and as long as it is tailored so that it silhouettes and doesn't hug your frame, you will radiate confidence and a touch of mystery. On the other hand, stripes can act as a bit of camouflage, but make sure that horizontal stripes don't become a second skin; keep them loose, not tight. Choose tops that are properly fitted and have a little give so they move with your body; otherwise, the camouflaging won't be able to work its magic. The beauty of having a few striped items in your wardrobe is that they never go out of style. Invest in quality fabrics and craftsmanship; striped tops and trousers can be worn from year to year without any worry about their trendiness. Add a classic solid coat and simple accessories, and the classic pattern makes a fabulous statement.

If you are just beginning to stock your closet with stripes, start with a classic navy-and-white or black-and-white Breton long- or three-quarter-sleeve top. For great prices and assured quality, try these three online shops that offer many different styles and colors: the Original Breton Shirt Co., Chance, and Petit Bateau.

See, Eat, Sleep & Enjoy: Experiencing Paris

The national characteristics ... the restless metaphysical curiosity, the tenderness for good living, and the passionate individualism. ... This is the invisible constant in a place with which the ordinary tourist can get in touch just by sitting quite quietly over a glass of wine in a Paris bistro.
—Lawrence Durrell

The dream of Paris — streets imbued with beauty, food, and love — dances in the minds of those who will travel for the first time to the City of Light. Such a dream, while containing aspects of the truth, is a romanticized version that Hollywood and advertisers have created. The sky is bluer, the love deeper, and the food (well, it's true about the food, I must say). We're told that a magical tingle will unquestionably occur when we step on the terra firma of Paris.

The reality is that without preparation, without knowledge, without flexibility, patience, and a willingness to be present and open-minded, a trip to Paris can result in what the Japanese have called the Paris Syndrome. The Japanese embassy in Paris handles ten or twelve cases each year in which starry-eyed Japanese tourists fall into a state of shock; disappointed when their expectations aren't met, they must be transported home, accompanied by a nurse. Of course, that's a small number considering that in 2012 more than 29 million people visited Paris, but I'm willing to wager that many more than a dozen people each year experience a certain level of shock when their expectations don't measure up to reality.

Why does this happen? Is Paris not as grand as it has been presented? I would argue that it is far grander than one can imagine, but again, visitors must prepare before arriving at Charles de Gaulle Airport.

I can remember in 2000 arriving in Paris with next to no grasp of the French language. I immediately wanted to be whisked back to the States and was too intimidated to dine in French cafés and bistros, let alone attempt the Metro. When I returned in 2012, my experience was far different, as I came with basic conversational language skills and an idea of what I wanted to see, but still far too little preparation.

Which brings me to my 2013 trip, in which I became totally enamored of the city. Why? How was I able to cure a small nibble by the Paris syndrome bug? Let me explain what I have discovered and give you some additional insights from expats who've lived in the city.

Language Skills

Today, compared to fourteen years ago, far more shopkeepers, locals, and Parisians of the younger generation are able and willing to speak English with those who stutter with their attempts at French. That, of course, is very nice for visitors, but it is still very helpful to know how to read basic directions and converse in a simple conversational manner ("thank you," "how much," "where," "which way," etc.).

Either take a French class with your local Alliance Française (most major cities have a chapter), purchase Rosetta Stone (it's what I did, as I live in a rural area), or hire a tutor (an option especially in college towns). Begin as soon as possible.

Pack Adapters & Converters

On my first trip to France, I was unaware and did not bring either an adapter or a converter, which meant I had to air-dry my hair. However, I learned my lesson, and I now travel with an adapter from Walkabout Solution and a converter for my hair dryer.

Become Friends with the Metro

Based on horror stories I'd heard, I was fearful of going "underground." And when your French is far from superb, that fear can keep you from making the attempt.

What I've discovered is that the Metro is actually a very easy place to navigate if you know even very little French; you just need to match up words and colors and follow arrows. Also, I find it a calm respite after walking along the busy streets during the hot summer weather in Paris.

Acquiring a Metro map is a must; also, download the free Visit Paris by Metro app (it can be used offline). Keep your bag tucked close, be aware of your surroundings, and you'll be fine.

Purchase 10 billets (tickets) or a one-, three-, or five-day Metro pass so all you have to do is slip your ticket into the turnstile and be on your way. The ticket stations are inside the station just as you descend the stairs, and they accept credit cards.

Later in the chapter, I've included more extended suggestions for success with the Paris Metro.

Create an Itinerary, but Be Flexible

Coming [to Paris] has been a wonderful experience, surprising in many respects, one of them being to find how much of an American I am.
—Augustus Saint-Gaudens

Make a list of places you want to visit and then look up the days and hours they are open. Each museum, shop, boulangerie, etc. keeps unique hours. For example, the Louvre is closed on Tuesdays, a favorite boulangerie of mine is closed Saturday and Sunday, and on Mondays some businesses are closed. Do your homework.

Plan for Jet Lag Fatigue & Frustration

We forget we are not infallible. If, like me, you don't live on the US East Coast, you'll travel many hours to get to Paris, and when you arrive and it's midday, for some reason you think you'll be fine. It's a good idea to remain awake and go to bed on Paris time; if you do, accept that your emotions, your energy, and your perceptions may be a bit skewed. It takes me about two days to get into a regular rhythm, but the key is to not let your mind take the upper hand. If nothing else, such travel is a wonderful reminder of how valuable and necessary sleep is for the mind to function at its optimal level.

What to Skip

A final reminder. Whenever you are in Paris at twilight in the early summer, return to the Seine and watch the evening sky close slowly on a last strand of daylight fading quietly, like a sigh.
—Kate Simon

The best part of the day for enjoying the city in the summer, without encountering tourists, is in the morning; knowing this will allow you to see the beauty of the city without as much editing. If I'm going to skip any part of the day and choose to take a nap or work at my rented apartment, it will be the afternoon. The hottest part of the day is usually between 3 and 5 p.m., so this schedule also helps you avoid sunburn and heat exhaustion. Once you've rested up, heading out for a lovely evening is absolutely divine.

Sign Up for a Day Tour

The whole of Paris is a vast university of Art, Literature and Music . . . it is worth anyone's while to dally here for years. Paris is a seminar, a post-graduate course in everything.
—James Thurber

If you don't know the city well, the best way to connect with people is to take a tour, which will provide context, ideas, directions, and a tour guide who speaks your language and can answer questions. If you love food, I highly recommend Paris by Mouth, which offers tours that focus on your preferred foods. (Visit my blog's "French-Inspired Living" page for a list of recommendation for tours, accommodations, sites, taxis, and books.)

Be Open & Present

A walk about Paris will provide lessons in history, beauty, and in the point of Life.
—Thomas Jefferson

While you should come to Paris with an itinerary, as the day moves along, allow it to take you where it will. If you are an avid photographer, allow your camera and events that catch your eye to dictate your plans. Allow meals to continue as long as the conversation warrants. If you are tired, return to your room and take a nap. If you are full of energy, take the Metro to another destination you've been curious about. Inspiration is everywhere, if you will only choose to look. Let go of your expectations and absorb all that you are seeing, hearing, and feeling.

Eliminate Stress

Certain aspects of travel are stressful. For me, the biggest worries are, when I arrive, finding the apartment I've rented with all my luggage in tow, and when it's time to depart, getting to the airport on time.

Because I know that these are two stresses I have, I've chosen to eliminate them as best as I can. Scheduling a taxi that will wait for you at the gate when you arrive (with your name on a sign) and that will pick you up at your hotel or rental to take you to the airport is money well spent. I have used EcoCab with great success, for arrivals especially. I suggest you purchase flight delay insurance as well.

Pinpoint what stresses you out the most when you travel — being disoriented about directions, not knowing the language, losing sleep, etc. — and do what you can to eliminate those pressure points.

Let Go of Expectations (Yours & Those of the Folks You've Left Behind)

People wonder why so many writers come to live in Paris. I've been living ten years in Paris and the answer seems simple to me: because it's the best place to pick ideas. Just like Italy, Spain . . . or Iran are the best places to pick saffron. If you want to pick opium poppies you go to Burma or South-East Asia. And if you want to pick novel ideas, you go to Paris.
— Roman Payne

I know several people who, when they learn I'm going to Paris, give unsolicited advice, which I always listen to. After all, you never know when they are going to suggest something that exactly matches what you're interested in, and I've visited and loved many places recommended by people who have traveled to this wonderful destination.

On the other hand, while Paris is full of sites to see, it's also a city to just exist in. What I mean is that because the way of life in France is something I am drawn to, I love simply going about a daily routine the Parisian culture is known for—fresh baguettes or other bread in the morning, shopping the local, fresh markets throughout the week, dining at length with wine and exquisite fare in the afternoon and evening, and just wandering around, allowing inspiration to hit me.

Do what you love on your next trip to Paris, and let the world's expectations fall by the wayside. You'll return from your travels far more content.

While we all have expectations of Paris, don't expect to fall in love any more readily than you would on any other given day in any other city. The trip will be what you make it, so when things don't go as planned, relax, take a deep breath, perhaps get some sleep, and start fresh in the morning (or evening) with a destination in mind and be malleable.

Mastering the Metro & the RER

The Paris Metro, which moves more than 6 million Parisians and tourists to and from their destinations each day, is one of the most efficient mass transportation systems in the world. And with a few simple pieces of information, it can be easily and safely navigated, even by someone who has never ridden a subway. The RER (Reseau Express Regional, or Regional Express Network) is a rapid transit system that connects at several points with the Paris Metro. Here are some tips to help you get around using these two systems:

Simple Things to Know. Every building in Paris is less than 500 meters from a train station. Know the end point of the line. Push the button on the train door to get off or get on (on most lines). The stops along each line are on display in each subway car. Follow the *Sortie* (exit) signs to get out of the station.

Pack a Metro Map. Carry a map of the Metro. A first glance at the map can be perplexing, but it is actually quite simple. There are 15 lines and 368 stops on the Metro. Follow arrows, colors, and line numbers (Metro) or letters (RER). Each line is labeled with the number/letter, color, and end destination of the line. The Metro will help you move about Paris more quickly. The RER is an express train line that connects the heart of Paris with the outlying suburbs. The Metro and the RER are intertwined. I was initially anxious about using them, but the moment I stepped into the Metro, I saw I had no reason to worry. It is as easy as connecting the dots and playing a matching game. Simply know the number of the line you need and the corresponding color; then make sure you know the end destination on that line (you'll follow that station's name on signs in the tunnels to get to the proper train).

Buy Billets (Tickets) Online or in the Station. Nearly all metro stations have an unmanned booth where you can buy tickets. As with an ATM machine, you simply follow the screen's instructions to purchase your tickets. You can set the screen to communicate in various languages. Credit cards are accepted. You can also purchase Metro tickets online.

To Save Money, Purchase a Paris Visite Pass or Book of Billets. Depending upon how long you are visiting Paris, there are two popular options to help you save money on transportation; each can be purchased at each metro stop. The first is a Paris Visite pass (good for the Metro, buses, and all public transport systems) for one, two, three, or five days; make sure you purchase the pass in the morning, not the evening, as the day you purchase it will count as one day. When purchasing the Paris Visite pass, you need to say which zones you want to travel in; if you want to mainly stay in the heart of the city, choose through zone 3, but if you wish, for example, to travel to Versailles, your purchase will need to include zone 5. The second option is to purchase a book of billets (tickets, in this case discounted as you are buying them in bulk) that you can use whenever you hop on the Metro.

Download Helpful Metro Apps. If you are traveling with a smartphone, download the Visit Paris by Metro app; once it's downloaded, you can use it offline. It is in English and provides line-by-line directions for getting to your preferred destination and lets you know which attractions are nearby. I use this app constantly on my trips to Paris and find it very helpful. If you know French and want additional information about public transport in France and neighboring countries, another app to download is SNCF. Food blogger and chef David Lebovitz swears by this app, and as he's an expat who lives in the City of Light, I trust his expertise.

Be Aware of Pickpockets. Paris is a fairly safe city to visit, as it thrives on tourism and needs to ensure tourists feel safe; however, as in many large urban centers, there are pickpockets. Not too long ago, the Musée de Louvre closed its doors when its workers went on strike, indignant about the lack of security against pickpockets. A guide from *Haven in Paris* gave me a short course in how pickpockets work and how to protect yourself. We were traveling on the Metro, and he pointed out a pair as they worked the train. It was both amazing and a bit scary. Here's what I learned:

- Pickpockets generally work in pairs.
- They are usually short in stature and appear to be harmless; often they are children, but not always. They dress and behave in a way that allows them to blend in.

- The best environment for a pickpocket is a tight crowd with lots of jostling, so you'll think nothing of that nudge on your hip.
- They will often create a distraction or will notice that you are focusing your attention on something else (perhaps your phone).
- They usually carry a bag across their body or have a pocket in front where they can quickly place the things they pilfer.
- Women: Carry your bag under your arm and close to your body, and keep your bags closed/zipped.
- Men: Move your wallet and phone from a back to a front pocket.
- Don't wear flashy or expensive labels. In other words, don't make yourself a target.
- Dress like a Parisian rather than a tourist. In other words, no shorts, flip-flops, or destination T-shirts/sweatshirts. Appear confident and be alert.

Use the Metro as a Respite from the Busy, Bustling Streets. Once you gain a basic understand of the public transit system — that is, once you have the Metro at your fingertips to get you where you want to go — your trip becomes much more enjoyable. Trust me, you will still do a lot of walking. So feel free to eat that *pain au chocolat,* because you will work it off as you poke into neighborhood boutiques or make your way through your favorite museum. I often find the Metro to be a cool respite when the weather is warm, and my feet appreciate the break.

The Metro can be daunting at first, especially if you're traveling alone or if, like me, you grew up on the West Coast, where underground transportation doesn't exist. But as long as you're armed with knowledge, the Metro will be a wonderful aid as you create a memorable trip.

CHAPTER ELEVEN

Entertaining, Holidays & Other Celebrations

Organizing a celebration for any occasion can put a lot of strain on the hostess who has graciously decided to open up her home, and then there are the holidays, which are a whole other matter.

Through many trials as a young hostess, I have learned that it is easy to set the bar so high that you do not enjoy yourself. When I was in my early twenties, I tried to learn how to cook a turkey. My mother, attached to my ear through the cordless phone, talked me through the process (she was in Oregon and I was in California at the time). A few years later I jumped at the chance to host Thanksgiving for our entire family in my new home in Oregon. While the bird was mouth-watering, my house didn't perform very well (a broken microwave, followed by a plumbing situation). Needless to say, that was not pleasurable; my house was not up to the challenge, and I was overwhelmed and, frankly, ecstatic when that particular holiday came to an end.

With each subsequent social event that I put on, I made adjustments (and properly prepared my kitchen and home as well), and I soon found that the gatherings I most enjoyed were either small intimate dinner parties or large festive gatherings to celebrate a specific occasion, at which I served only drinks and a few appetizers.

Throughout my progression to hosting competence — starting with several early fiascos and moving gradually to success and at last a fine-tuned approach — I've discovered that it's all about knowing your strengths and limitations as a hostess. These are different for everyone, but the key is to not put yourself on the bottom of the priority list. Ultimately, the intention is to organize a gathering that your guests and you yourself both enjoy. Throughout the planning and execution of each event, it is very important to make sure both you and your guests are satisfied.

How to Host & Enjoy a Dinner Party

There is nothing I look forward to more after a busy day or week than a beautiful dining room table, beloved friends, captivating conversation, and delicious food. So many luxuries coming together make for a wonderful opportunity for catching up and unwinding.

Earlier in my life, when I would hear the term "entertaining guests" I envisioned days of preparation, then a house full of people, and then a demolished house to clean up afterward. To me, that did not sound like a simple task—nor did it sound like fun. I've tried big parties, tweaking them each time to better create the best possible environment, and I have come to believe that for me two sayings remain true—less is more, and quality over quantity. For me, a dinner party is the ideal party.

A few selected menus and recipes follow later in the chapter, but first let's consider how to prepare yourself and your home for a successful dinner party. With just the right number of guests, a can't-miss menu of recipes that are sure to impress, and a before and after routine that will leave you feeling invigorated and looking forward to the next occasion, here is the simply luxurious approach to entertaining, during the holidays and really for any other occasion or celebration. Then bring on the food, the friends, and the unforgettable conversation.

The Perfect Number

A memorable dinner party is one that allows your guests to be relaxed and involved in engaging conversation. Whether you will sit down for dinner around a table or invite guests to mingle with small plates of food from a buffet, try to keep the number of your guests to between six and ten. With this number the conversation will tend to occur naturally, and no one should be left out.

Plan Ahead

A few days before — possibly a week or more — and depending on whether you are sending out invitations, sit down and plan exactly what you would like to serve and how much prep time you will need so that you aren't rushed but will be able to relax and enjoy the evening. Also plan the beauty maintenance you'll attend to in order to make sure you look and feel your best. Nothing will ease your mind more than knowing everything is under control prior to the day of the event.

A Prepared Bar

Have your bar prepared, whether you will serve one alcoholic drink and one specialty nonalcoholic drink or will give your guests an array of choices. Make sure that the moment they walk in the door you can supply them with a beverage while the appetizers are still in the oven. Just having something in their hand gives people something to do and generally helps them relax a bit.

The Music List

No matter what song list you play or what CDs and records you pull out, make sure the tunes you select set the tone you envision for your party. Sometimes the background music should be just that — in the background — but sometimes it can serve as a wonderful conversation starter. I tend to gravitate toward classic crooners — Frank Sinatra, Ella Fitzgerald, Louis Armstrong, and a little classic jazz: Miles Davis as well as contemporary artists within the same genre — Diana Krall, Jon Batiste, and Trombone Shorty. During the holidays, Bette Midler's *Cool Yule* would most likely be my CD of choice, paired with the traditional artistry of Nat King Cole, Andy Williams, and Charlie Brown's Christmas soundtrack — jazzy, festive, and fun. Be sure to keep the volume in check, and make sure you won't have to keep checking your player.

Winning Recipes

When planning your menu, stick to recipes you have tried in the past and have had success with. Also, be sure to include a few that can be made in advance, so you aren't stuck in the kitchen cooking while your guests are enjoying themselves. After all, they want your company, so make sure you are able to enjoy the gathering. Another thing to think about is the bookending of the menu—the appetizers and the dessert. The first thing your guests will taste is your carefully planned hors d'oeuvre, so make sure it is a showstopper that leaves them in awe, curious about the rest of the evening, and with their appetites whetted for the dinner itself.

Buy the Dessert or at Least One Course

Just as you began on a high note, be sure to end on an unforgettable one. Serve a dessert that eliminates instantaneously the memory of any so-so dishes you might have served during your dinner. Either make it the day before, or, if you've made everything else yourself, reward yourself and your guests with a decadent treat from your favorite bakery, delicatessen, or patisserie. There should be absolutely no guilt involved in buying dessert, and you've also eliminated a bit of stress because you've saved yourself some prep time.

Set the Table the Night Before

There are many ways to dress a table for a dinner party. First, provide a low centerpiece—a bouquet of seasonal flowers, a cluster of candles, or a bowl of fruit—which can be a nice conversation starter.

For your dishes, I tend to follow the thinking of a lady who continually inspires me with her cooking and approach to entertaining: Ina Garten always counsels that less is more and suggests you stick with the classics, letting the food and the conversation define the occasion. Simple white dishes and fancifully textured white dishes can be used, mixed and matched; it really is up to you, but the fact that they are all white in and of itself creates a strikingly simple theme.

Add white votives in clear glass holders, a beautiful monochromatic bouquet of flowers that is low so people can see above the blooms easily, and you have a very inviting, simple, and luxurious tablescape.

Choose either traditional or stemless wine glasses (20-ounce glasses work well for both white and red). Stemless glasses are nice in more casual settings or to increase functionality as they can also serve as water goblets.

Place utensils alongside each plate (forks on the left, knife and spoon on the right), or integrate them with cloth napkins on top of the plate.

Winsome Combinations

To assign or not to assign? Places at the table, that is. There is no hard-and-fast rule. The situation and the people you've invited should determine whether assigned seats are desirable. When you want to take a bit of control, here are a few things to try: Separate couples; try to seat each guest next to another person she is already comfortable with and one new person you think she'd enjoy meeting; seat the big talkers, the life-of-the-party people, toward the center of the table (not at the ends) because most likely they will be able to keep the topics flowing all night; and try to seat yourself someplace other than at the head so you can also help create conversation.

Showtime

Some people shy away from dinner parties, feeling they can be exhausting, but if you can create a system that works for you, you will create memories that your guests will remember for years to come.

I prefer to leave the cleaning up until after the guests have left. While guests may offer to help tidy up, politely decline; a dinner party is for them to enjoy, not to work. After all, you wouldn't want to be expected to clean up after yourself when you're invited to a dinner party elsewhere. When you leave the cleanup for later, you allow the conversation to continue.

Whether you serve dessert and after-dinner drinks at the table or invite your guests to move to another room is up to you. One benefit of moving to another room is that you encourage a shift in conversation and convey to your guests that you are enjoying their company and wish them to continue to enjoy the evening at your home.

When the last guest has left, sit down, on your own or with your partner, and enjoy a glass of something warm or otherwise enjoyable as you savor the lovely evening you've just given your guests. I have had tremendous failures, and I look back and ask, Why did I do that? But I've also had great successes. With each new party, I throw out what doesn't work or tweak it to make it work better, and I continue what has succeeded, in a constant process of putting on better dinner parties as time goes on.

Simple & Luxurious Menus & Recipes

As a young girl, I was given the opportunity to cook and bake, and I came to love tinkering in the kitchen. It was akin to learning a new language. Once I understood what blanching, basting, julienning, and so many other words meant, and once I had the necessary utensils (see chapter 5), I could follow the instructions and produce something I could enjoy myself as well as be happy to share with my guests.

The act of cooking can become intimidating if you've never had someone show you the ropes or walk you through a handful of recipes. Today, with the Food Network and the Cooking Channel, it is easier than ever to learn to prepare successful meals that are sure to impress.

One of the many benefits of knowing how to cook is that you can reduce the eating out portion of your budget. And when you do afford yourself the luxury of eating out, you have an enhanced appreciation of what it means to prepare a well-cooked meal.

I have gathered together here a few recipes that I enjoy often and have found to be simple, yet at the same time absolutely delicious. Since each recipe is most often a small piece of an entire meal you will serve, I have organized them into the occasions on which you might want to serve them. You will of course rearrange them as you like, to fit your tastes and the mood you are trying to create.

For many more great dishes, see the "Recipes" section on the blog—www.thesimplyluxuriouslife.com/recipes/.

A Gathering of Friends for a Cheese Tasting

The holidays offer a wonderful opportunity to serve a cheese platter at a gathering of friends, family, or colleagues. However, cheeses can and should be served year-round. There are endless varieties to please nearly every palette, and assembling the platter is as simple as can be.

Recently, I decided to learn how to create a cheese platter featuring different cheeses, foods to pair the cheeses with, and how to present them so that the flavors can be experienced and enjoyed to their fullest potential. What I discovered is that the preparation is just as much fun as the actual event. Why? Because there is taste testing involved!

Let's get started so you too can create your own cheese platter for that soiree you've been thinking about planning.

Choose the Cheeses. When making your shopping list, try to pick up four different types of cheeses in the following categories:

- Aged
- Soft
- Firm
- Blue

Another idea is to choose cheeses based on the type of milk that is used to make them—for example, cow, sheep, or goat—or perhaps cheeses from a certain region, state, or country.

How much cheese will you need? Buy one or two ounces per person.

Taste Test. A couple of years ago I discovered in the neighboring town of Walla Walla, Washington, a gourmet grocer—Salumiere Cesario—that has its own cheese room, a place that appealed to me the way Santa's workshop would appeal to a child. The room is kept at a crisp 55 degrees Fahrenheit, and the humidity is strictly controlled. Customers can step inside and taste any of the cheeses to determine exactly what to serve their guests or enjoy for themselves. Cheeses are shipped in from both nearby (Oregon, Washington, California) and afar—there are Parmigiano Reggiano rounds from Italy, Gouda from Holland, and Manchego from Spain, to name just a few. Do some research to find fine cheese purveyors in your town or somewhere nearby.

Food Pairings. There are many different options for pairing your cheeses. Start with the basics: Pick up either a French baguette, a loaf of artisan bread, or specialty crackers. If any of your guests avoid gluten, many delicious crackers are gluten-free and scrumptious. Make sure your bread and/or crackers don't compete in flavor with the cheeses. In other words, choose a classic baguette or plain artisan bread and natural crackers, but nothing with excessive flavor (exception: olive bread). After all, your bread/crackers are simply the vehicle to bring the cheese to your taste buds.

Other items to pair with your cheeses:

- Jarred condiments: chutneys, artichoke hearts, olives, honey, jams
- Sweet and salty items: toasted and salted nuts, cured meats (prosciutto, salami), dried apricots, cornichons
- Fruits: dates, figs, apples, pears, grapes (choose a subtle fruit that won't compete with the flavors of the cheese)

If you are serving your cheese platter before dinner, pair the cheeses with such savory elements as olives, chutney, prosciutto, nuts, etc. After dinner (as an alternative to dessert), pair them with sweeter elements: jams, honey, dried fruit, even toasted nuts.

Setting Up the Platter. Find a nice cheese board of wood, slate, ceramic, or marble. Use multiple boards if you want to place individual cheeses around the house in order to encourage guests to mingle.

- Label the cheeses. Use either chalk or cheese labels or flags to satisfy your guests' curiosity and let them know what they will be tasting. If there's room, include adjectives to describe the flavor.
- Provide a separate cheese knife for each type of cheese, and a sharp cheese knife for the hard cheeses.
- Include four to six different cheeses.
- Don't crowd the cheeses; you don't want a guest's wrist pressing into another cheese as she cuts a slice of the one she wants.
- Separate the strong cheeses.
- Place food pairing items in dishes or bowls around the platter or, if the platter is large enough, between the cheeses.

- Artfully place freshly picked sprigs of rosemary or thyme as decoration.
- Provide small plates and napkins, as well as toothpicks or forks.

Set up the cheeses about an hour before guests arrive. Cold mutes the flavor of cheeses, so serve them at room temperature for their full flavor to be enjoyed.

Serving Wine. When cheese is on the menu, wine is always my beverage of choice. I could write an entire chapter on food and wine pairings (perhaps in my next book!), but for now I'll keep it simple: When you're serving cheese, choose wines you love. As always, keep the whites and rosés chilled and the reds at room temperature.

My preference is to select local wines or wines from vintages and wineries I trust, and to choose wines that will complement the cheeses, not compete with them.

When in doubt, stop by your local wine shop and ask the employees what they prefer; most will be happy to describe their favorite wines, or those that would seem to suit your purpose. If you have time, spend an afternoon tasting wines you might serve; after all, the preparation should be part of the fun for the hostess.

With the endless options to choose from, you are likely to find at least one cheese to please everyone. I shared a cheese platter with my family this past Thanksgiving, and many of my guests were pleasantly surprised; cheeses they thought they wouldn't like often turned out to be their favorite selection on the platter.

If nothing else, a creative cheese platter provokes wonderful conversation with people you either know well or are just getting to know, and isn't that the reason for bringing people together, after all?

A Dinner for Two

Menu

- ○ Bruschetta with mozzarella, tomato, and basil
- ○ Chicken piccata
- ○ Broccoli with garlic and soy sauce
- ○ Chocolate cake

Bruschetta with Mozzarella, Tomato & Basil

- ▪ French baguette, sliced on the bias
- ▪ Tomatoes of your choice, sliced and diced
- ▪ Fresh mozzarella, sliced
- ▪ Extra-virgin olive oil (basil infused if possible)
- ▪ Balsamic vinegar
- ▪ Basil leaves (julienned)

Preheat oven to 400 degrees. Slice baguette, placing slices on a baking sheet. Drizzle olive oil over each slice. Place a slice of mozzarella on each. Place baking sheet in the oven and watch carefully for 2–4 minutes. Remove when cheese has melted and is slightly bubbly and baguette is toasted. Place one tablespoon of diced tomatoes on top on the cheese, followed by a pinch of basil and a drizzle of balsamic vinegar.

Chicken Piccata
(adapted from a Giada de Laurentiis recipe)

- ▪ 4 skinless and boneless chicken tenders (or 2 chicken breasts butterflied and cut in half)
- ▪ Sea salt and freshly ground black pepper
- ▪ All-purpose flour, for dredging
- ▪ 6 tablespoons unsalted butter

- 5 tablespoons extra-virgin olive oil
- 1/3 cup fresh lemon juice
- 1/2 cup chicken stock
- 1/4 cup brined capers, rinsed
- 1/3 cup fresh parsley, chopped

Tenderize chicken. Season chicken with salt and pepper. Dredge chicken in flour and shake off excess.

In a large skillet over medium-high heat, melt 2 tablespoons butter with 3 tablespoons olive oil. When the butter and oil start to sizzle, add 2 pieces of chicken and cook for 3 minutes. When the chicken is browned, flip and cook the other side for 3 minutes.

Remove and transfer to a plate. Melt 2 more tablespoons butter and add another 2 tablespoons olive oil. When the butter and oil start to sizzle, add the other 2 pieces of chicken and brown both sides in the same manner. Remove the pan from the heat, and add the chicken to the plate.

Into the pan add the lemon juice, stock, and capers. Return to stove and bring to a boil, scraping up brown bits from the pan for extra flavor. Check for seasoning. Return all the chicken to the pan and simmer for 5 minutes. (If you are serving it with rice or risotto, instead place it in the pan with the rice/risotto to absorb even more flavor.) Remove chicken to the platter. Add the remaining 2 tablespoons of butter to the sauce and whisk vigorously.

Pour the sauce over the chicken and garnish with parsley.

Keep in Mind
- Do not forget to tenderize the chicken, using a kitchen mallet and wax paper. When tenderizing is complete, the chicken breast should be about 1/4 of an inch thick. This makes the dish.
- If you will serve the chicken with rice pilaf or risotto, feel free to let it finish cooking in the rice, as it will absorb even more flavor.

- You can substitute almost any other type of meat for the chicken.

Broccoli with Garlic & Soy Sauce
(adapted from a Barefoot Contessa recipe)

- 1 head garlic, peeled (about 16 cloves)
- 1 cup good olive oil
- 1 teaspoon crushed red pepper flakes
- 1 teaspoon kosher salt
- 4 stalks broccoli, cut into florets (8 cups of florets)
- 2 tablespoons soy sauce

Put the garlic cloves and oil in a small, heavy-bottomed saucepan. Bring to a boil and cook uncovered over low heat for 10–15 minutes, until the garlic is browned and tender. Turn off the heat and add the red pepper flakes and 1/2 teaspoon salt. Immediately pour into a heat-proof container to stop the cooking. Allow to cool to room temperature.

Blanch the broccoli florets in a large pot of boiling salted water for 2–3 minutes, until crisp-tender. Drain well and immerse immediately into a large bowl of ice water until broccoli is cooled. This process stops the cooking and sets the bright green color. Drain well.

In a large bowl, toss the broccoli with 1/2 teaspoon salt, 1/4 cup of the oil used to cook the garlic, the soy sauce, and 8 or more cloves of cooked garlic. Taste for seasoning, and serve cold or at room temperature.

Chocolate & Almond Cake
(an adaptation of Julia Child's Reine de Saba; serves 6–8)

Kitchen supplies you'll need
- ✓ Round cake pan, 8 inches in diameter and 1 1/2 inches deep
- ✓ 3-quart mixing bowl
- ✓ Wooden spoon or electric beater or KitchenAid mixer
- ✓ Rubber spatula
- ✓ Cake rack

For the cake
- 4 ounces or squares semisweet chocolate, melted (I use Ghirardelli's semi-sweet chocolate chips)
- 2 tablespoons rum or coffee (I use rum, but coffee would taste lovely as well)
- 1/4 pound (1 stick) softened butter
- 2/3 cup granulated sugar to mix with butter
- 3 egg yolks
- 3 egg whites
- Pinch of salt
- 1 tablespoon granulated sugar to beat with egg whites
- 1/3 cup pulverized almonds
- 1/4 teaspoon almond extract
- 1/2 cup cake flour, scooped and leveled, turned into a sifter
- Chocolate-butter frosting (simple recipe follows)

Preheat oven to 350 degrees.

Butter and flour the cake pan. Set the chocolate and rum or coffee in a small pan, cover, and place (off heat) in a larger pan of almost simmering water; let melt while you proceed with the recipe. Measure out the rest of the ingredients.

Cream the butter and 2/3 cup of sugar together for several minutes until they form a pale yellow, fluffy mixture. Beat in the egg yolks until well blended.

Using an electric hand-mixer, beat the egg whites and salt in a separate bowl until soft peaks are formed; sprinkle in 1 tablespoon sugar and beat until stiff peaks are formed. If an electric hand-mixer is not available, pick up a whisk; it will take a bit longer, but you'll get a nice workout in the process.

With a rubber spatula, blend the melted chocolate into the butter and sugar mixture, then stir in the almonds and the almond extract. Immediately stir in one-fourth of the beaten egg whites to lighten the batter. Delicately fold in a third of the remaining whites and when partially blended, sift in one-third of the flour and continue folding. Alternate rapidly with more egg whites and more flour until all egg whites and flour are incorporated.

Turn the batter into the cake pan, pushing the batter up to its rim with a rubber spatula. Bake in middle level of preheated oven for about 25 minutes. Cake is done when it has puffed, and 2 1/2–3 inches around the circumference are set so that a needle plunged into that area comes out clean; the center should move slightly if the pan is shaken and a needle comes out oily. While most cakes would require a clean needle (or toothpick) and no movement, this recipe is different. The movement (just in the center) indicates that the cake will still be moist. But don't worry, it will set and be absolutely delicious.

Allow cake to cool in the pan for 10 minutes. Run a knife around the edge of the pan, and reverse cake on the rack. Allow it to cool for an hour or two; it must be thoroughly cold if it is to be iced.

The flavor of the cake is rich, decadent, and satiating. So much flavor, so little flour. Who knew?

Butter-Cream Frosting
(for an 8-inch cake)

Kitchen supplies you'll need
- ✓ Small covered pan
- ✓ Larger pan of almost simmering water
- ✓ Wooden spoon
- ✓ Bowl with tray of ice cubes and water to cover them

✓ Small flexible-blade metal spatula or table knife

For the frosting
- 2 ounces (2 squares) semisweet baking chocolate
- 2 tablespoons rum or coffee
- 5–6 tablespoons unsalted butter

Place the chocolate and rum or coffee in the small pan, cover, and set in the larger pan of almost simmering water. Remove pans from heat and let chocolate melt for 5 minutes or so, until perfectly smooth. Lift chocolate pan out of the hot water, and beat in the butter a tablespoon at a time. Then beat over the ice and water until chocolate mixture has cooled to spreading consistency. At once spread it over the cake with a spatula or knife.

To serve
Press a design of sliced roasted almonds over the icing. They add the perfect crunch.

Dinner Party for Four to Six People

Menu
- o   Fontina tart
- o   Chicken marsala
- o   Mushroom risotto
- o   Oven-roasted vegetables
- o   Meyer lemon tart

Fontina Tart
(adapted from Julia Child's recipe; serves 4–6)

For the pastry
- 2/3 cup flour
- 1 tablespoon sugar
- 1/8 teaspoon salt

- 5 tablespoons chilled unsalted butter
- 3–4 tablespoons of chilled water

For the filling

- 2/3 cups heavy cream
- 1 egg
- 1/2 cup Worcestershire sauce
- 5 or 6 drops of hot sauce
- 1/2 teaspoon salt
- 1/2 teaspoon pepper
- 6–8 ounces of fontina cheese (1/4-inch cubes)

Preheat oven to 425 degrees.

To make the tart shell: Mix flour, sugar, salt together. Cut in butter until it resembles corn meal (my time-saver trick is to use a food processor; in less than 2 minutes your dough is evenly mixed and ready to be rolled out). Add the water. Roll out the dough on a floured cutting board. Roll it as thin as possible, keeping it even. Place dough in the pan of your choice, then set aside.

Using one tart pan: Prepare your tart pan (try to use one with a removable bottom) and place dough gently inside, letting the dough go above the edges about 1/2 inch. Neatly pinch the edge around the entire tart.

Using muffin tins (this recipe makes 12 tartlets): Cut out circles and place in each muffin container so that the dough comes halfway up the sides.

To make the filling: Combine the heavy cream, egg, Worcestershire sauce, hot sauce, salt, and pepper. Whisk until all ingredients are mixed together.

Place the cubes of fontina on the bottom of the prepared crust (one layer only). Pour the heavy cream mixture over the top of the cheese until it is just about to brim over the crust, but not quite. Place in the oven — 30 minutes for one 9-inch tart pan, or 20 minutes for tartlets. Remove when cheese mixture is barely golden brown. Allow to cool for 5–15 minutes.

Keep in Mind
- Use whatever cheese you like.
- Make sure the butter is chilled, and don't be stingy with it, as it is what makes the crust flaky.
- Be sure to roll the dough out as thin as you can manage. Again, this creates a more flaky crust.

Chicken Marsala
(serves 4–6)

- 1/4 cup all-purpose flour (for dredging)
- 1/2 teaspoon salt
- 1/4 teaspoon ground black pepper
- 1/2 teaspoon dried oregano
- 4 skinless, boneless chicken breast halves, tenderized to 1/4-inch thickness
- 4 tablespoons butter
- 4 tablespoons olive oil
- 1 cup sliced mushrooms
- 1/2 cup marsala wine
- 1/4 cup cooking sherry

In a shallow bowl, mix together the flour, salt, pepper, and oregano. Coat chicken pieces in flour mixture. In a large skillet, melt butter in oil over medium heat. Place chicken in the pan, and lightly brown. Turn over chicken pieces and add mushrooms. Pour in wine and sherry. Cover skillet; simmer chicken 10 minutes, turning once.

Keep in Mind

- Tenderizing is the key, so get your meat mallet out and gently pound away (great for relieving a bit of stress as well).
- Have fun with the mushrooms you choose.
- The sauce that is created is not to be wasted. Be sure to drizzle it over each of the chicken breasts as you serve your guests.
- You can find marsala wine in your local supermarket.

Mushroom Risotto
(adapted from a Barefoot Contessa recipe; serves 4–6)

- 1/2 pound fresh porcini or cremini mushrooms
- 1–2 ounces of your favorite mushroom (shiitake and chanterelle are a couple of my favorites)
- 6 cups chicken stock, preferably homemade
- 6 tablespoons (3/4 stick) unsalted butter
- 2 ounces pancetta, diced
- 1/2 cup chopped shallots (3 shallots)
- 1 1/2 cups Arborio rice
- 1/2 cup dry white wine
- 1 teaspoon kosher salt
- 1/2 teaspoon freshly ground black pepper
- 2/3 cup freshly grated Parmigiano Reggiano, plus extra for serving

Wash all mushrooms. Slice thickly and set aside.

In a small saucepan, heat the chicken stock and bring to a simmer.

In a heavy-bottomed pot or Dutch oven, melt the butter and sauté the pancetta and shallots over medium-low heat for 5 minutes. Add the mushrooms and sauté for another 5 minutes. Add the rice and stir to coat the grains with butter. Add the wine and cook for 2 minutes. Add 2 full ladles of the chicken stock mixture to the rice plus the saffron, salt, and pepper. Stir and simmer over low heat until the stock is absorbed, 5 to 10 minutes. Continue to add the stock mixture, 2 ladles at a time, stirring every few minutes. Each time, cook until the mixture seems a little dry before adding more of the stock mixture.

Continue until the rice is cooked through, but still al dente, about 25–30 minutes total. When done, the risotto should be thick and creamy and not at all dry. Turn off the heat, stir in the Parmigiano Reggiano cheese. Serve hot in bowls with extra cheese. Risotto is best when served immediately, although I also enjoy it as a leftover.

Oven-Roasted Vegetables

(serves 4–6)

- 1 bunch of asparagus*
- 1 pound fingerling potatoes
- French string beans
- Good olive oil
- Kosher salt and freshly ground black pepper

* Any vegetable works well, alone or mixed with other types.

Prepare the vegetables: Slice the fingerling potatoes in half lengthwise, snap the asparagus at their natural breaking point, keeping the top two-thirds, and trim the string beans.

Place in a roasting pan, and drizzle with 2–3 tablespoons of olive oil, 1 teaspoon salt, and 1/2 teaspoon pepper. Toss with your hands to coat the vegetables. Place in oven at 425 degrees for 35–40 minutes, tossing once during this time. Combine the vegetables in a large serving bowl and sprinkle with salt and pepper. Serve hot.

Keep in Mind

- You can use any vegetables you desire (broccoli, fennel bulbs, brussels sprouts, etc.)
- I place a layer of tinfoil in my roasting pan to allow for easy cleanup.
- The roasted fingerling potatoes make the perfect steak fries.

Meyer Lemon Tart

(serves 4–6)

For the shell

- 1 stick (1/2 cup) butter, cut into 1/4-inch cubes and frozen for hour or more
- 1 1/4 cup all-purpose flour
- 1/2 tablespoon sugar
- 1/2 teaspoon salt
- 2–4 teaspoons ice water
- 2 cups pine nuts or beans or coffee beans for baking the tart shell (pie weights)

For the curd

- 1/2 lemon juice (approximately 3 1/2 small Meyer lemons or 4 regular lemons)
- 2 tablespoons lemon zest
- 4 egg yolks
- 2 whole eggs
- 1 cup sugar
- Pinch of salt
- 1 stick (1/2 cup) butter, cut into 1/2-inch cubes

To make the pastry dough: Mix together flour, sugar, and salt on your work surface. Blend in most of the butter (reserve 6 or so little cubes in the freezer) with your fingertips or a pastry blender just until most of mixture resembles coarse meal with some roughly pea-size butter lumps.

Gradually drizzle 2 tablespoons of ice water over the mixture while gently mixing with a fork. Squeeze a small handful of dough; if it doesn't hold together, add more ice water a tablespoon at a time, stirring until just incorporated, then test again. Do not overwork the dough or the pastry will be tough. Turn out the dough onto a lightly floured surface and divide into 8 portions. With the heel of your hand, smear each portion once or twice in a forward motion to help distribute the fat. Gather the dough together, with a pastry scraper if you have one, and press into a ball. Wrap disk in plastic wrap and chill until firm, at least 1 hour.

To make the lemon curd: While the dough is chilling, bring a medium/large saucepan (or double boiler) of water to a simmer. Suspend a heatproof bowl over this, making sure the water does not touch the bottom of the bowl. Combine lemon juice and zest, egg yolks, eggs, and sugar in the bowl. Stir constantly with a heatproof rubber spatula, until the mixture is thick enough to coat the spatula (7–10 minutes). Heat should be medium to medium-high.

Remove from heat, add cubes of butter. To guarantee a very fine finish, pour the curd through a fine-mesh strainer, removing any large pieces of zest, etc. Place cellophane over the bowl to make sure the top doesn't harden while cooling, and refrigerate.

To make the tart: Preheat oven to 350 degrees. Line the bottom of a 10-inch tart pan with a circular piece of parchment paper and butter the sides.

When you are ready to roll out the dough, make sure your countertop (or rolling surface) is very clean, and flour lightly. Flour the rolling pin as well, and reserve a handful of flour. Roll out the ball as thinly and evenly as possible. Spread three of the cold butter cubes onto one half. Fold the dough in half, and roll out again, keeping the shape as circular and even in thickness as possible, making a 13-inch circle. Fit the dough into the prepped tart pan: Press the dough against the side of the pan, leaving 1/4 inch above the sides.

Line the inside of the shell with foil and fill with pie weights or dried beans. Bake for 15 minutes or until the sides are set. Remove foil and weights. Bake for 25 minutes, or until golden.

Remove the tart and turn up the oven temperature to 475°. Fill the tart shell with the lemon curd, smoothing the top. Bake for approximately 3–5 minutes, or until the top is gently golden-brown.

Cool thoroughly, about half an hour, before serving.

Keep in Mind

- Use a tart pan with a removable bottom so that you have a beautiful final presentation without having to worry about taking it out of the pan.
- Using the fine-meshed strainer makes an amazing difference in the finish of the dish. It looks much more professional and smooth.
- Stir constantly during the 7–10 minutes you are waiting for the curd to thicken so that it doesn't burn.

Again, see the recipes section on the blog for a large selection of other dishes I love.

How to Continually Enjoy the Holidays: Simplify, Simplify, Simplify

Whether you observe Hanukkah, Christmas, Kwanzaa, Easter, or any other holiday, such occasions can mean special gatherings of family and friends who may not have seen each other in a while. We all look for ways to make the most of this time, and for me, the key is simplicity.

Simplifying the holidays will create a season of fulfillment, laughter, beautiful memories, and the ability to continue to smile after all is said and done. Here are a few ways to successfully pare down, but also thoroughly enjoy any of the holidays you celebrate.

Through a Child's Eyes

Christmas, cookies and milk for Santa, stockings, and sleigh rides in the snow. As a child I can vividly remember the excitement I felt as December 25 drew near. This feeling is something to cherish as we grow older, but as adults, we can best use it in a different context.

Christmas should be about the children, and believe it or not, most children don't require expensive gifts to be happy. Think back to when you were a child and the gifts or moments you remember. Keeping this in mind, try to make Christmas something the children will remember, and have the adults be the providers, not the receivers. The children's joy should be gift enough for the grown-ups.

Give Fewer Gifts, Make More Memories

To entirely get away from giving gifts is very difficult for most of us, but I have discovered that the most memorable gifts are experiences, not things. The moments and memories you create when you give loved ones tickets to fly to their favorite city, a place in a special cooking class, or tickets to the concert of their dreams will be something they will cherish much longer than a tangible item in a box. If it is a gift for your significant other, why not plan a weekend away—book a flight, hotel room, and dinner at an exclusive restaurant. That is something a necktie can't top.

Less Is More

The holiday season brings with it multitudes of opportunities to celebrate with family, friends, coworkers, and those who live in your community. But if you're not careful, you can quickly overbook yourself and run yourself ragged. To make your holiday season one you will always remember, take the time to prioritize those events, activities, and traditions you truly want to include. Don't feel guilty when you politely say no to parties and other events that really don't interest you.

A Simple Holiday Party

Every once in a while, and especially during holiday seasons, you may want to throw your own party. But if you'd rather not throw a dinner party, you may not be sure how to make it original and, most important, enjoyable. In order to simplify but ensure a fantastic affair, stick to one specialty cocktail drink instead of stocking an entire bar. Not only will you cut down on the need to bolster your mixed drink know-how; your budget will breathe a sigh of relief as well.

A similar idea is to limit the type of food you will prepare and serve. Why not have a dessert party, a cheese and wine party, or a tapas party? Doing this keeps the menu simple—you feature your best three to five dishes. And don't be hesitant to make half and buy half; after all, your guests want to have a good time, and if the host is relaxed and enjoying herself, the company will too.

Creative Wrapping

In an effort to stay eco-friendly and at the same time wrap beautiful presents for those on your list, head to your local craft store and pick out silk ribbons of all different widths and colors. Wrap your gifts in newspaper, old maps, or brown paper bags (inside facing out) and tie one of the beautiful ribbons around the gift. The effect will be retro and classic without wasting more paper than you already had in your house, and the ribbons can be used year after year.

Keep It Personal

When it comes to sending out holiday cards, nothing is more memorable than reading a dear friend's handwritten and personalized words. Realizing that someone took the time to convey their thoughts on paper and include more than just "Happy Holidays" is a priceless gift in its own right. A typed two-page letter can feel like bragging; if you want to share the details of your life with everyone, you can send a group e-mail or post on Facebook.

Keeping it personal during the holidays takes thought, time, and consideration—each very valuable and more memorable than a mass-produced report on doings in your household. While you may be able to send out a much smaller number of personalized cards, those who receive a handwritten message will cherish it.

Shift Your Focus

Now that I'm an adult, I cherish the holidays for the feeling they create within me and around me. The gifts, especially when they are material things, don't bring the exhilaration they once did.

This time of year should revolve around another spirit of giving: helping others who are less fortunate and building up those around us. Doing this doesn't have to come by way of giving things; it can be accomplished by bestowing one's time, energy, or ideas. When we create positive memories and moments for others and with others, society as a whole shines a bit brighter, our spirits are lifted, and we believe in the impossible a little bit more. During the holiday season, focus on those you can help in whatever way you can.

Houseguests: Making Sure Both Parties Have a Good Time

In this section, I'll share some tips for being a houseguest or hosting one (or more).

When You're the Guest

Being welcomed into someone's home is one of the greatest gifts, and it's important that you not take the generosity of your host for granted. There are a few rules of etiquette to follow when you stay in someone else's home. Following them will guarantee a good rapport with your host, and, who knows, you may be invited to stay again!

Plan Ahead. Well before you'll make your trip, ask politely if you can stay at your host's home on the dates you have in mind. Once you have been welcomed as a guest, be sure to write down the exact times of arrival you discussed in order to avoid mix-ups. *An important note:* If you catch a cold or contract any other contagious illness, have the courtesy to cancel your plans; it's completely unfair to arrive for a stay at someone's home with an illness they might catch. If you must make the trip, book a hotel room.

Arrive on Time & Don't Overstay Your Welcome. On the day of your arrival, make sure you arrive on time out of respect for your host's schedule. Most hosts want time to prepare their home for a visit, so if your flight arrives early, call ahead before showing up.

As wonderful as it is to be welcomed into someone's home, always keep in mind that this is their sanctuary, their place to unwind, and nobody wants to be uncomfortable in their home. My aunt always said, "Houseguests are like fish; they begin to stink after three days," and that old adage has some validity, no matter how much your hosts adore you. Even though the visit may be going well, be sure to leave on a high note. Don't overstay your welcome.

Respect Your Host's Schedule & Share Yours. Keep in mind that your hosts will have a schedule of their own to follow, so let them know when you will be coming and going.

Bring a Thank-you Gift. Have a gift in hand when you arrive. Bring something you are certain your host will appreciate and enjoy—wine, a beautiful candle, or something special that will convey your gratitude.

Abide by the House Rules. Once you've arrived, your goal should be to make sure your host is comfortable while you are in her home. If her house rules are that young couples should sleep in separate beds, then respectfully oblige. Everyone has different values, but if you are stepping over the threshold into someone's home, you must defer to her expectations. And if you are uncomfortable with them, there are always plenty of beds in local hotels or motels.

Your Host Isn't Responsible for Entertaining You. Sometimes when you are the guest, you'll spend time with your hosts; perhaps that is precisely why you are there. But if your hosts are opening their home to you without this expectation, understand that you are responsible for entertaining yourself. Unless your host invites you to join her for a particular event or outing, have plans that you are ready to dive into. Even if she offers to have you join the activities she'll be involved in during your stay, it is always good to have some time apart from your host, especially when you have asked to stay and she has offered to have you out of kindness. Even the most willing host will appreciate a break. A good guest, one who will be welcomed back, is conscious and respectful; the goal is a memorable experience for all involved and a strengthened relationship, not one that is worn thin.

Offer to Help. Offer to help cook dinner if your host is feeding you, or offer to walk the dog if that is something you would be comfortable doing. A wonderful gesture I know almost any cook will appreciate is an offer to clean up the kitchen after the meal, or at least get all the dishes into the dishwasher. If you're there for an extended visit and will be eating breakfast, lunch, and/or dinner in your host's home, offer to pay for or shop for groceries. If you are staying for an extended period, you might offer money to help with the utilities bill. And always do your own laundry.

Be Presentable. Pack a set of presentable pajamas (top and bottom) that will make everyone comfortable, even in the early morning while you are sipping coffee. Also, take a moment to brush through your hair and do any other personal tidying up before saying good morning. Make your bed every day as you would at your own home. And even if you've been given your own room, but especially if you are sleeping on someone's couch, each morning be sure to neaten your living space — tucking, folding, and putting away anything that otherwise wouldn't be there. Your host will appreciate your attention to something so simple, as it is a way to show respect and gratitude.

Limit Internet/Phone Usage. If you don't have your own access to the Internet and Wi-Fi isn't available, or if you will be using your host's computer, be very brief; keep in mind that other members of the household will want to go about their daily routines and spend time on the Internet as well. And be aware of when and how often you are on the phone.

Strip the Bed & Gather Any Towels Used. Prior to leaving, when you are packing up and saying your good-byes, take a few minutes to strip your bed, placing the sheets into one of the pillowcases and adding any towels and washcloths that you have used (as long as they are dry).

Send a Prompt Thank-you Note. Send a thank-you note to your host as soon as you arrive home. While you probably offered a verbal thank-you as you departed, a formal letter expresses sincere gratitude and thoughtfulness.

Being a good houseguest requires a conscious effort to put yourself in your hosts' shoes and treat them the way you would want to be treated if someone was staying at your home. The goal is to create a memorable experience for everyone; the host will try to make this happens, and so too should the guest.

When You're the Host

Guests come in all forms: a family member who has traveled a great distance, a friend who needs a place to crash when they're in town for a wedding, a reunion of girlfriends from college. Here are some quick tips about how to be a good hostess—one who looks out for the welfare of her guests as well as her own.

Clean Common Areas. A welcoming home is a clean home, and the best way to let your guests know you are looking forward to their visit is to take the time to clean your home and certainly all the rooms they may spend time in.

Prepare Your Guest Quarters. When guests aren't at your home, you can easily close the door to the guest room and pay them no mind, but once you know you will have company, take time to fluff the pillows, dust the dressers and windowsills, and, if possible, provide easy access to outlets for charging electronic devices. Make up your guest beds with freshly laundered sheets, and provide clean towels and washcloths for each person. If you don't have a spare room, make the sleeping accommodations as comfortable as possible; make up the couch or pullout with clean linens. Supply pillows and blankets as necessary. It's nice to consider a few other details—an empty dresser drawer or two for them to keep their clothes neat and out of the way, closet space with hangers, an alarm clock, bedside reading material. If you can, provide a chair or bench for an additional place to sit other than the bed. As a finishing touch, add a small bouquet of flowers. Nothing is so welcoming when a guest first arrives as the sight of a beautiful bouquet specially placed for them.

Provide Your Wi-Fi Username & Password. Create a simple card with the codes for Internet access in your home.

Get Advance Knowledge (Allergies, Dietary Needs, etc.). When you're making plans with your guests and thinking about the food you'll cook or buy for them, ask whether they have any allergies or dietary restrictions.

Create a Toiletry Supply Basket. A simple comfort that you can provide your guests with little expense is a selection of toiletry items — toothpaste, floss, cotton balls, shampoo, etc. — in case they've forgotten something. Purchase travel sizes and place them in a small basket or container in the guest bathroom. If your guests will share your bathroom, place the basket stocked with amenities in their guest room.

Create a Detailed Info Sheet for Your Home Entertainment Devices. While most people are comfortable using the TVs, DVRs, and disc players in their own homes, yours will probably be set up differently, with particular combinations and sequences that make the entertainment happen. Prepare a simple "cheat sheet" that your guests can follow for when you're not there to assist them.

Communicate Your Schedule. Before your guests arrive, find out how long they will be staying; not being clear about this at the outset can be a recipe for anxiety and hard feelings. When your guests are close friends and family, you'll probably spend most of your time with them. However, you may have guests who don't require all your attention. No matter which category your guests fall into, you may have appointments or other obligations while they're staying with you. Be sure to let your guests know when you have such plans, and set them up with keys, garage door code, etc. so they can come and go as they please; also tell them how you can be reached should they need you.

Offer a Tour of Supplies & Food. Depending upon how long your guests are staying, make them feel welcome by showing them food they can help themselves to and where the dishes and silverware are, as well as anything else they might need that you are willing to share during their stay.

Provide Simple, Thoughtful Touches. Pick up fresh flowers and place them throughout your home, as well as in your guest rooms. Create a simple welcoming basket of chocolate, bottled water, and a pad of paper and pen. I was once on the receiving end of a very nice gesture: When I turned in the night before I was to wake up early for a long flight to Europe (my hosts wouldn't be waking up with me), I found a glass of chilled water on my nightstand with a note of best wishes. It was a sweet idea and a lovely way to say "bon voyage."

Welcoming people into your home is a grand gesture of trust and generosity. As someone who is very private, I am quite selective about those I allow into my sanctuary, and when I do have guests, I want to make sure they feel comfortable and appreciated. Adding simple touches to a guest room and making sure you have clear communication will help create a memorable and enjoyable visit for both hostess and guests.

CHAPTER TWELVE

The Most Important Lesson

To give up on style is to give up on life.
— Maggie Smith's character, in
Downton Abbey, season 3

Nature — the stunning countryside — is said to have inspired Beethoven's Symphony No. 6. The works of other great writers, such as Plutarch and Geoffrey Chaucer, have been credited as inspiration for William Shakespeare. Top American designers like Tory Burch and Diane von Fürstenberg have drawn upon their travels for inspiration when creating their newest collections.

Revealing our own individual style doesn't occur only when we decide which clothes we'll don each day. Our style shows also in our décor, our words, the food we prepare, the routines we keep, the trips we take, our mannerisms, and our life's journey. To choose to live with style is to choose to live an authentic life that is true to our hopes, dreams, talents, and curiosities, and to the experiences our life presents.

And when we exhibit our signature style we create inspiration that is magical, that allows our true gifts to be exercised and revealed, helping us to live our best life.

Be Your Own Curator

To blindly and ignorantly go along living a life that everyone expects you to live because it is what *they* understand, when you either haven't investigated what you want or are choosing to suppress what calls your name, is to allow someone else to be the designer of your life. You, and only you, are the person who knows how to design the life that will best enhance your innate talents, tap into your deepest passions, and satisfy your curiosities.

Instead, live in a way that is styled by you. Beginning when you wake up in the morning and start your day and continuing throughout your waking hours, style your thoughts and actions according to what motivates you to live your best life.

Perhaps you're like Beethoven and your creativity blossoms when leaving the city behind. Or perhaps visiting new destinations and locales fuels your soul and affects the meals you prepare when you return. Or maybe your insatiable love for reading and learning opens your eyes to places and ideas that speak to you—influences that perhaps you would have never experienced had you not opened that book or listened to that podcast.

The gift of living a life of independence and freedom is that we are able to be the curators of our very own life. We are able to say yes or no. We are able to take a chance or appreciate and cultivate what is working well. Most important, we are responsible for our own contentment. If your life doesn't sit well with you, begin seeking inspiration until you determine how you want to style the life you want to live. As Alan Cohen puts it, "Everything will line up perfectly when knowing and living the truth becomes more important than looking good."

Living with style doesn't mean the masses will applaud, but it will mean you will sleep soundly at night, and that is the best gift. If you hear applause, fabulous; if not, so what. Your heart knows when you're the curator of your life or when someone else is. If you remain silent and find yourself out of sync with the responses of other people, take note: You may be following instead of curating. On the flip side, when time passes in a flash and you lose yourself in the moment—intoxicated by life, not spirits—then most likely you have found your niche.

The beautiful gift of our one and only life is that the choices we make every single day determine our contentment. Choose wisely.

Let Go of Others' Expectations

To be nobody-but-yourself—in a world which is doing its best night and day, to make you everybody else—means to fight the hardest battle which any human being can fight; and never stop fighting.
—E. E. Cummings

The world—with all its intriguing people, adventures, and destinations—will always offer something more, something we haven't done, or something we hope to someday see, try, or become. However, a life well lived is one of refusal.

What? Didn't I just say that the world offers us endless options, choices, and life journeys? Yes, and that is why when we discover the path that works for our contentment, our passions, and our purpose, it becomes much easier to not be distracted by what won't fulfill us. The key is to get to know ourselves.

At first glance, a comfortable, fulfilling life may appear to require large amounts of money, but the more I inquire, observe, and experience, the more I realize that people who are genuinely living comfortably and financially secure lives are those people who say no without hesitation when something doesn't align with their life's trajectory. They are people who don't purchase everything they can, but who instead spend some of their money on what they need and tuck away the rest in a stellar investment fund or savings account.

Examples from earlier in this book: adhering to a capsule wardrobe instead of purchasing the new trends and latest accessories every season, and taking one grand vacation every year and simply going on day or weekend trips to nearby destinations the rest of the time.

I felt a great sense of satisfaction and rightness when I finally came up with the slogan I had been trying to put into words to say what living a simply luxurious life is all about. With some help from those who knew me long before the blog began, I arrived at the slogan "Refined living on an everyday income." Based on my personal experience and observations of others with both little and ginormous sums of money, those who appear to be swimming in greenbacks can feel just as strapped and stressed as someone making $30,000 a year if they continually expand their lifestyle to live the way they think they should live.

Simply because someone has more money does not mean she lives a more contented life. While there is a minimum one needs to live comfortably, there is a maximum (recent studies have pinpointed $75,000). Once you reach that point, earning more does not make you any happier. Ultimately, it comes down to how we handle the money we have earned.

After all, when we know who we are, what we need, and what we can do without, we are better able to say "no thank you" to offers, temptations, and societal expectations that don't line up with our priorities and way of living.

As E.E. Cummings reminds us in the quote reprinted above, living life on our own terms—the terms with which we are most comfortable—is a constant battle of saying no, turning away from temptations, and keeping our hard-earned money in our pocketbook when we don't need to be spending it (even though retailers would love to have us think otherwise).

The clearer you become about the direction you want to take your life and the goals you want to achieve, the easier it becomes to know whether you should say yes or no. Based on my experience, when you're uncertain of your direction, even the slightest breeze can empty your pockets, slow down your progress, or alter your direction entirely.

One of the most satisfying benefits of solidifying where you want to go is that saying no to what you don't need becomes quite easy, which leaves more of your energy to be put toward what will propel you more quickly and easily to your goals.

With patience, perseverance, and diligent focus, you can have a contented and fulfilling life, no matter what your income.

Own Your Uniqueness

People who have a "problem" (like Julia Child being 6 feet 2 inches), it either kills them or they become defiant in the face of it. And that's what her [Julia's] personality led her to. She just said, "The hell with it!" It's a lesson. Sometimes

we want to arrange things—I wish I had this, I wish I looked like this, I wish I'd
got into this school. You know, we think that there is a formula, and actually
the formula for happiness and success is just actually . . . be yourself in the most
vivid possible way you can because then you don't have to pretend. That is the
freedom [Julia Child] enjoyed in her life and that is inspirational to me.
— Meryl Streep, on playing Julia Child in *Julie & Julia*

There are books, there are gurus, there are "experts" on the formula
for attaining personal success and happiness. You may have sought
out any one of these mediums. I most certainly have, but I must say
Meryl Streep is on to something.

While many of us are fortunate enough to live in a world where
the possibilities seem endless and we can shape and mold our lives
into what we desire with a little hard work (or perhaps a lot of hard
work), we sometimes become overwhelmed with all the media and
propaganda that is thrown at us, telling us what we should be doing,
instead of looking inward to ourselves.

Often, to avoid all the confusion about the best way to achieve
success for ourselves, we choose to follow someone else's path to
success. After all, if it worked for them, why wouldn't work for us?
While sometimes this may be a good approach, if we want to shine,
more often than not we will be required to go about the quest in a
new and original way. And that is where many people flounder.

The other difficult part in choosing to let your own light shine —
whether it is your innate ability to pull an outfit together that
instantly looks stunning, having observation skills like a detective,
or the ability to charm the socks off just about anyone — is that you
often will meet resistance from those around you who have decided
to follow a predetermined path made not by them, but by society,
the culture, or someone else in their life. The truth may be that,
subconsciously, they wish they had the strength and the courage to
follow the light inside of them that has been dimmed for so long.

On the other hand, those people who are also eagerly chasing
their unique path, based on their natural uniqueness, will applaud;

they will encourage; they will not present obstacles. Others may respond the way they do when you choose to "let your freak flag fly" because of who they are, not because of who you are. Do not see the discouraging behavior of others as a reflection of you, because it isn't.

Think about your skills, the quirks of your character, and the unique qualities that have always been yours from childhood. Maybe people laughed, maybe people were in disbelief, hopefully many were impressed. But no matter how those around you responded, use it to your advantage. Be yourself. Be confident in knowing that this "gift" of your character and your personality truly is just that — a gift — and make the most of it.

The Quilt of Your Life

You have to choose your combinations carefully. The right choices will enhance your quilt. The wrong choices will dull the colors, hide their original beauty. There are no rules you can follow. You have to go by instinct, and you have to be brave.
— Whitney Otto, *How to Make an American Quilt*

Every day, we step out into the world with the intention to create a better life for ourselves and to contribute to the world. How each of us does this, however, is unique. How much easier would it be if we could just follow in someone else's footsteps or have our course laid out in a connect-the-dots instruction manual — voilà, the perfect life would be laid out in front of us! The trouble is, it wouldn't be *our* definition of perfect; it wouldn't be perfect for us.

There have been so many times when I just wanted to look up to somebody, to pattern my life after someone I admired so I wouldn't have to worry about making mistakes, being made a fool of, or being laughed at. But what I've come to realize, as I remind myself to snap out of it, is that I wouldn't want to follow someone else, I don't want to *be* somebody else.

The word I want to bring your attention to is the word *follow*.

It is always easier to follow than to lead or venture out on your own, but no one by the name of Amelia Earhart, Nelle Harper Lee, Nelson Mandela, Oprah Winfrey, Meryl Streep, Will Smith, Bill Gates, or Audrey Hepburn ever wished to be just like someone else. If they had, we wouldn't recognize them as people of talent, courage, style, and innovation.

Our lives are similar to assembling a quilt. A quilter considers many pieces, but doesn't—usually can't—include them all in the final product. Sometimes you will know immediately when someone or something (a job, a home, a town) doesn't quite fit in your quilt, and sometimes it will take time for this piece to stick out like a sore thumb and for you to see that it is not something that will strengthen the final product and, therefore, must be removed. Granted, it will take courage to remove it if it has been there for a while, but the extraction must happen.

It is up to the quilter to continually adjust, search, and demand that the particular pieces be found that will result in a quilt of the highest quality. You are the only person who can build your quilt. The good news is that you have the talent, and although there will be times when you are discouraged, you will find what you are looking for if you will rely on the most important person in your life—yourself.

Why Not . . . Create a Simply Luxurious Life?

A 2013 article in the *New York Times Magazine* placed the topic of life expectancy in the spotlight. While the average life expectancy at birth currently in the United States is 79, the number is deceiving, and the statistic itself for the past few centuries has been misunderstood as well. Why? It's an average, one that takes into account child mortality rates and every socioeconomic situation that can drastically change or skew the number.

For example, in Sweden the average life expectancy in 1800 was 32. This seems drastically low, but in reality, if one survived childbirth and early childhood, one could expect to live well beyond this number; it was the high child mortality rate that brought the number down.

What the article revealed was that the length of one's life is acutely determined by the quality of one's life. In other words, good and necessary health care, the reduction of stress, food and beverage intake, financial means of support, regular exercise, and strong, healthy relationships create a life of peace, security, and physical good health. They are what ultimately determine the number and the quality of the years in our life expectancy.

As I pored over this article, I couldn't help but ask the question, *What does a quality life look like?* This is what I came up with:

Safeguard Your Good Health

While we can't change our genetic coding, we can control what we eat, how much we move, our thoughts, and the environment we live in. We can also proactively schedule regular well-patient visits with a primary physician to catch any abnormality that may show up in screenings.

Be Secure, Financially & Physically

When we know we have money in the bank and a sound roof over our heads, our minds are able to relax. And when we reduce our stress, we help our bodies stay in optimum health. Unnecessary and excessive stress reduces the body's ability to take care of itself, and when our body can't take care of itself, it is less able to fight off viruses and diseases.

Regularly Use Your Innate Talents

Knowing you are contributing positively to society and tapping into your passions and natural talents are among the most rewarding and enriching things you can do to create a life of quality and fulfillment. If you have found the profession, hobby, or life's work that melds these two worlds of talent and societal need, you know the extreme joy they can provide. If you haven't yet found your passion or an avenue in which it fits, keep searching. Eventually, you will find your niche. The time you have spent seeking out the right path will be rewarded.

Live Authentically

When you are able to be yourself—to not hide who you are and what you wish to contribute—a burden is lifted that reduces unnecessary stress you may be carrying. Seek out people who accept you for who you are, and do your best to steer clear of those who laugh at, berate, or tease you for being different from what they understand or accept. They don't deserve the gift that is you.

Be Involved in Loving, Respectful Relationships

It's not the *number* of friends and loved ones in your life but rather the *quality* of the relationships you have with those you invite into your inner circle that creates a fulfilling life. Having in your life people whom you can trust and lean on in times of trial, and who enjoy the beauty that life presents each and every day, is something you must consciously create. There will be many people who will want to be your friend, lover, or confidante. Take the time to see if they are worthy of what they seek. Your patience and diligence will save you much unnecessary heartbreak and pain.

Cherish Your Rights, Freedoms & Protections

People who live in a country, community, and family that afford them a voice might take these situations for granted. At first thought, it may seem that having the freedom to speak and live according to who you are is unrelated to creating a quality life. But it's actually quite the contrary. Being able to speak up when you've been wronged, knowing that justice can be served, knowing that the life you've created can't be demolished for unjust reasons — in other words, having rights that protect you and your ambitions to build a wonderful life — these are blessings we must all cherish and work to protect.

Contribute Positively to Others

The time, assistance, compassion, and thoughtfulness we offer others ultimately are some of the best gifts we give ourselves, for when we do these things we are helping to improve our communities, no matter how small the initial gesture may seem. As Duane Elgin put it, "Simplicity of living, if deliberately chosen, implies a compassionate approach to life. It means that we are choosing to live our daily lives with some degree of conscious appreciation of the condition of the rest of the world." When we hone in on what our talents are and use them to help, assist, or bring something positive into another person's life, the feeling itself is the best gift. And if you're lucky enough to find a career that incorporates your talents and contributes to society, you're well on your way to finding the best in yourself.

Get Adequate Rest & Rejuvenation

Even if you have all of the other items on this list covered, if you are not able to slow down every once in a while and rest, your health and your ability to appreciate and enjoy the life you're working so hard to create will be diminished.

Take Time to Be Still & Savor the Present Moment

If you are never able to slow down, you open yourself to the possibility of making bad decisions that may cause unnecessary stress. But when you can savor the moment, you can be clear about what you truly need and what is only a craving that will soon pass. When you can find time to rest and recharge and are able to regularly be still and simply bask in the beauty that is the life you've created, you have a fruitful way to remind yourself that you have an amazing life.

Seek Opportunities to Learn & Grow

A life of simple luxury—that is, a life of quality—involves continual growth. When we choose to perpetually be someone who learns, we can never be truly "old." As we learn, we shed both our selves from yesterday and our ignorance of the past. We move forward in a life that is in tune with our values, one that is lived with great appreciation and satisfaction. A simply luxurious life.

Acknowledgments

I am continually humbled and forever thankful to everyone who has stopped by my blog, *The Simply Luxurious Life*, over the past five years. Many readers who found me early in my blogging journey have continued to stop by, which is the kindest gesture of all: the giving of their time. To those readers who serendipitously found me at any point along the way and now hold this book in their hands, thank you for your interest, support, curiosity, and desire to live the life of your dreams, curated to your own tastes. I can't properly express what the writing of the blog has meant to me, but I do know that without my readers, this book wouldn't exist. Thank you.

Without question, this book wouldn't have come to fruition without two women who believed in the potential of my book when I was beginning to have my doubts: the author of *The French Twist*, Carol Cottrill, and my editor, Patricia Fogarty. Thank you, Carol, for one of the most lovely, inspiring, and sincere conversations I've ever had; I won't soon forget it, and it led me to my editor. Patricia Fogarty deserves a world of gratitude for working with me as I navigated my writing and editing of the book around my full-time teaching schedule. I am grateful to have had the opportunity to work with her patience, careful attention, and resolute professionalism as I finally put my dreams into hard copy.

I am immensely thankful for my dear friend, Anne Stephens, who volunteered her time to read drafts of the manuscript and provided invaluable constructive feedback and guidance, as well as ardent support.

To successful author and lifestyle blogger Jennifer L. Scott, who was my distant mentor and inspiration for self-publishing, thank you for your assured guidance and confidence in the journey I was about to begin. And an important thank you to Mary

Rosenblum for sharing her indispensable advice and detailed guidance on how to navigate and successfully produce a self-published book.

To the artist behind the illustrations, Inslee Haynes. You have brought my words to life, and with each illustration you have turned my ideas into a stylish vision and surpassed my expectations. Thank you for creating these images of simply luxurious women, without which this book would not be complete.

To my brother and his family, and to all my friends and extended family who weren't sure what a blog was initially but have come to be very supportive of *TSLL* and all the unexpected journeys and projects it has inspired . . . a heartfelt thank you.

To my parents, thank you for your unwavering support and for instilling the perpetual question that seems to now always pop up in the forefront of my mind as I chase my dreams: Why not? You are always ready with a helping hand, Dad with your talent with woodwork and a willingness to lend me your financial wisdom and Mom with your paintbrush and green thumb. I am so thankful for the creativity and work ethic you have nurtured in me since I was a child.

ABOUT THE AUTHOR

photo credit: Ali Walker

Shannon Ables is an educator and the founder and editor of the lifestyle blog *The Simply Luxurious Life*, which she founded in 2009. A secondary teacher of English and social sciences for more than 12 years, she is also a professed Francophile who travels to France during the summer breaks, satisfying her wanderlust and cravings for *pain au chocolat*. She currently resides in her Normandy-style home in Oregon, with her two dogs, Oscar and Norman.

Continue to be inspired to live your simply luxurious life by visiting the blog—at www.thesimplyluxuriouslife.com—and listening to Shannon's regular podcast, *The Simple Sophisticate*, on iTunes.

13551179R10186

Printed in Great Britain
by Amazon.co.uk, Ltd.,
Marston Gate.